War Memory, Nationalism and Education in Postwar Japan, 1945–2007

The controversy over official state-approved history textbooks in Japan, which omit or play down many episodes of Japan's occupation of neighboring countries during the Asia-Pacific War (1931–1945), and which have been challenged by critics who favor more critical, peace-and-justice perspectives, goes to the heart of Japan's sense of itself as a nation. The degree to which Japan is willing to confront its past is not just about history, but also about how Japan defines itself at present, and going forward.

This book examines the history textbook controversy in Japan. It sets the controversy in the context of debates about war memory and education, and in relation to evolving politics both within Japan, and in Japan's relations with its neighbors and former colonies and countries it invaded. It discusses in particular the struggles of Ienaga Saburo, who has made crucial contributions, including through three epic lawsuits, in challenging the official government position.

Yoshiko Nozaki earned her Ph.D. at the University of Wisconsin at Madison, and currently teaches at the University at Buffalo (State University of New York). Her co-edited book, *Struggles over Difference: Curriculum, Texts, and Pedagogy in the Asia-Pacific* (SUNY Press), won the American Educational Research Association Division B Curriculum Studies Outstanding Book Award.

Routledge Contemporary Japan Series

War Memory, Nationalism, and Education in Postwar Japan, 1945–2007

The Japanese history textbook controversy and Ienaga Saburo's court challenges

Yoshiko Nozaki

Routledge
Taylor & Francis Group

LONDON AND NEW YORK

First published 2008
by Routledge
2 Park Square, Milton Park, Abingdon, Oxon, OX14 4RN

Simultaneously published in the USA and Canada
by Routledge
270 Madison Ave, New York NY 10016

Routledge is an imprint of the Taylor & Francis Group, an informa business

Transferred to Digital Printing 2009

© 2008 Yoshiko Nozaki

Typeset in Times New Roman by
Taylor & Francis Books

British Library Cataloguing in Publication Data
A catalogue record for this book is available from the British Library

Library of Congress Cataloging in Publication Data
Nozaki, Yoshiko, 1956-
War memory, nationalism and education in post-war Japan, 1945–2007:
the Japanese history textbook controversy and Ienaga Saburo's court
challenges/Yoshiko Nozaki.
p. cm.
Includes bibliographical references and index.
ISBN 978-0-415-37147-6 (cloth : alk. paper) – ISBN 978-0-203-09876-9
(ebook) 1. Japan–History–Textbooks. 2. Ienaga, Saburo, 1913–2002.
3. Japan–History–Study and teaching. 4. Education and state–Japan.
5. Textbooks–Censorship–Japan. I. Title.
DS834.96.N69 2008
940.53'52071–dc22
2007038800

ISBN10: 0-415-37147-3 (hbk)
ISBN10: 0-415-54644-3 (pbk)
ISBN10: 0-203-09876-5 (ebk)

ISBN13: 978-0-415-37147-6 (hbk)
ISBN13: 978-0-415-54644-7 (pbk)
ISBN13: 978-0-203-09876-9 (ebk)

To Hiro

Contents

Foreword

Ienaga Saburō (1913–2002) was one of twentieth-century Japan's outstanding historians. He not only wrote history; he also *made* history. He did so by suing the Japanese government over its censorship of his textbooks. Ienaga's three suits became the focus of a major and sustained anti-establishment movement in late twentieth-century Japan. They exposed the role of government "certification" in the production of Japan's textbooks. They focused attention on the inadequacies of the government's preferred "history." And they mobilized tens of thousands of Japanese—historians, teachers, ordinary citizens—in defense of an alternative vision of Japan's past. Ultimately, the Japanese Supreme Court, which is notoriously deferential to authority, found in favor of the government and against Ienaga on the constitutionality of Ministry of Education "certification" of textbooks but sided with Ienaga on several important issues of historical presentation. In a telegram to console Ienaga just before one court judgment (ironically, it was the Sugimoto judgment of 1970, most favorable of all to Ienaga), Ienaga's famous colleague Maruyama Masao predicted ultimate victory for Ienaga "in the court of history." That larger verdict is not yet in, but despite the setbacks and uncertainties of the decade since Ienaga's last suit ended in 1997, it is too early to despair.

The U.S. public has paid little attention to how U.S. textbooks are produced. Here national authorities play little role. Commercial considerations rule. There are a few big textbook companies. A few major states—most notably, Texas—play an outsized role, with right-wing, "Christian" vigilantes guarding the ideological gates as tenaciously as the Japanese right-wingers with whom Ienaga and his movement contended and contend. Our education struggles have involved teacher salaries, testing, busing, charter schools. Imagine what might have been! We might have had courtroom discussion of the nature of historical truth and public debate over textbook depictions of Hiroshima, Vietnam, environmental degradation, and the growth of governmental power.

Yoshiko Nozaki participated in the Ienaga movement as a volunteer in its international campaign. She is also a trained and conscientious historian. This committed yet scrupulous treatment of Ienaga's suits, the factors that influenced them, their effects, and the ongoing struggle is both inspiring and sobering. It offers food for thought to all of us, no matter what our nationality, who engage in the continuing contest over history and education.

Richard H. Minear
University of Massachusetts Amherst

Introduction

"Who controls the past," ran the Party slogan, "controls the future: who controls the present controls the past." And yet the past, though of its nature alterable, never had been altered. Whatever was true now was true from everlasting to everlasting. .. All that was needed was an unending series of victories over your own memory.

George Orwell, *Nineteen Eighty-Four*

This volume is about postwar Japanese social and political struggles over nation and education, war memory and school textbooks, with a focus on historian Ienaga Saburo's court challenges. More than six decades after Japan's surrender in 1945 in the Asia-Pacific War (1931–1945)[1] and the dismantling of its colonial empire, issues of war and war memory continue to reverberate, not only in Japan, but also regionally and globally, above all across Asia and in Asian diasporic communities throughout the United States and Europe.[2] Insofar as *all* histories are in part *contemporary* histories (indeed, they also chart the imagined future), the controversy over Japan's war memories and history textbooks takes us to the epicenter of ongoing Japanese political—and cultural and intellectual—struggles over the meanings of national belonging and education at domestic as well as international fronts.

Postwar Japan is fertile ground for understanding the ways in which issues of war memory and education unfold in a given society and the major part societal forces play in constructing and implementing meanings of the national past. For decades, against relentless government pressure, a significant number of Japanese scholars, educators, and citizens have sought to reflect on, conduct research on, and teach about the Asia-Pacific War from critical—and often cosmopolitan—peace-and-justice perspectives. They have challenged—or at least put up a good fight to challenge—the dominant, normative right-wing nationalist interpretations of the war.[3] Today, however, far from being resolved, the issues, at times growing in intensity, remain controversial, inextricably bound up with the nation's identity and consciousness. For the Japanese—and for people across Asia and throughout the world, for that matter—memories of war appear not only politically explosive but also culturally and psychologically complex.

The Japanese textbook controversy has had a number of issues specific to Japanese contexts—such as the state's de facto censorship of textbooks, both in its direct and indirect forms, Ienaga Saburo's court challenges to it, and extremely repetitive debates over particular events (e.g., the Nanjing Massacre and the Battle of Okinawa) and the use of particular terms (e.g., "aggression"). However, controversies of a similar nature have erupted in many nation-states, particularly in those facing state formation and nation-building after a war or military conflict. Thus an in-depth study of the Japanese case and the situated, contextual knowledge, both empirical and theoretical, gained from it offer revealing points of comparison and interpretation that illuminate contemporary global issues of war and peace, historical memory, and education.

Critics argue that history is always a site of social and political struggles, as its meaning is open to contestation.[4] It seems that, in a democratic society, history textbooks more often than not constitute a major battleground where antagonistic societal forces enter and contend for their interpretations of history, resulting in public controversies. The struggles over history textbooks can be very intense, and sometimes carried out over many years, involving a variety of actors from different sectors across the whole spectrum of a given society. Though his novel is about the revision of history in a totalitarian society, George Orwell's insight expressed in *Nineteen Eighty-Four*, "Who controls the past ... controls the future" (see the opening quote above), is relevant to what, precisely, is at stake in history textbook controversies in democratic societies.

However, democracy may require that the dominant power bloc ensure "an unending series of victories over your own memory" through more complex and subtle processes than those of the Orwellian kind; or it may only allow the hegemonic forces to win partial, limited, temporal, and incomplete victories because of the oppositional and alternative forces countering them. The Japanese history textbook controversy provides us with an interesting historical case, as the nation has moved—at least in its pronouncements—from a totalitarian regime to a democratic society (and, indeed, a capitalist one, which may add another dimension to the conflicts).

In this volume, I bring to light the complex, multi-layered battles fought over the issues of war memory and school textbooks from 1945 to 2007, locating them in the larger social, cultural, political, and educational transformations inside Japan, as well as in the context of major changes in international relations, of which the Cold War, the Korean, Vietnam, and Gulf Wars, and the changing/unchanging nature of U.S.-Japanese relations are among the landmark events. Key questions here include: How have these moments of national and international changes and conflicts pressed the nation to re-examine the nature of civil society, state power, and national priorities? How have right-wing nationalism, the dominant power bloc, and the state worked together to wield power over schools and textbooks to influence people's national identity? How have Japan's oppositional and alternative forces—so called "progressive" forces—fought against the hegemonic power(s)?[5]

The History Textbook Controversy as Multiple Games of Truth

Remembering a past war, or wars, is a particularly salient way of defining a nation and constructing national narratives and identities.[6] Research on and teaching about the conduct of wars—involving not only accounts of heroism but also narratives of war atrocities and crimes against humanity, particularly those committed by one's own nation—invariably invite contentious and ambivalent feelings and responses. The phenomenon is not unique to Japan. Public reluctance to critically examine the issues of war memory is, for example, at the center of the controversies in the United States surrounding the atomic bombing of Hiroshima and Nagasaki, including the 1995 Smithsonian controversy over a planned exhibit of the Enola Gay and the museum's presentation about the Japanese victims,[7] and the debates in Germany touched off by Daniel Goldhagen's *Hitler's Willing Executioners.*[8]

These instances indicate that struggles for counter-memories of war(s) against their dominant interpretations have taken place rather ubiquitously across the world, suggesting the possibility of, and, indeed, the need for, creating theoretical relays between these struggles, so that they can link to each other to form a network.[9] In this volume, I attempt to forge such theoretical relays in terms of three relatively autonomous fields of inquiry, or "games of truth" as Foucault calls them[10]—education, history, and the court of law. As I discuss in this volume, the Japanese societal forces that have fought the history textbook struggles for decades have come to play these games of truth simultaneously. The relative autonomy of each game of truth means that each game involves a series of questions specific to the game.

First, the controversy has been a *textbook* controversy, a struggle over education and its content (curriculum) generally, and the state-sanctioned, official knowledge taught in schools in particular.[11] The most fundamental questions concerning education in a democratic nation inevitably focus on whose knowledge—or interpretation of historical events, for example—ought to be presented to students, who ought to decide it, and the processes by which the decision should be made. Answers to these questions are inevitably political, since, as Richard Shaull states in the preface for *Pedagogy of the Oppressed*, "There is no such thing as a *neutral* educational process."[12] This does not mean that we substitute politics for teaching knowledge, but rather that curriculum policies and practices cannot be disentangled from their political effects and consequences. In other words, in a democratic society, citizens, not to mention teachers, students, and parents, need to be included in the curriculum decision-making processes in some way(s) and play an appropriate role—and so does the modern state. It is often the case that tensions arise between different groups, or between the citizens and the state. The Japanese case highlights these tensions that exist between any modern state and its citizens with regard to official knowledge.

Second, the Japanese controversy has been a controversy over *history*, and it illuminates the complexity of the game of truth in history, which begins with a question of what is historical fact, or truth. One might think this problem pertains to historical scholarship, where historians attempt to find out what *really happened*. However, what counts as historical truth (or knowledge) depends on the principles and rules of procedures that human beings, including historians, create, agree upon (or often agree to disagree upon), and implement (to a varied degree). Furthermore, the paradigm of historical inquiry shifts over the years—and, in fact, finding (or creating) a different way to produce truth may work for people whose perspectives were previously marginalized. In this sense, the game of truth in history is above all a matter of social order and power: "Ways of distinguishing true and false" are, as Michel Foucault argues, connected to "ways of governing oneself and others."[13] Historical knowledge as truth taught in schools often encourages younger generations to acquire the most prevalent ways of distinguishing true and false. Scholarship alone cannot completely settle the issue of historical truth. Establishing historical facts concerning controversial events—for example, the Nanjing Massacre and "mass suicides" in the Battle of Okinawa—often requires a paradigm shift in distinguishing true and false in the study of history and beyond, which is a challenge to the existing regime of truth and the social order it sustains.

Third, Ienaga Saburo's court challenges took the Japanese history textbook controversy into the game of truth in court, which was a very unique attempt, to say the least.[14] What kinds of role(s) can we expect the court of law in a democratic society to play in relation to a history and/or textbook controversy like the Japanese one? Ienaga in essence asked for justice, by invoking "rights to restrain government power";[15] however, the courts were (and are) part of the state apparatus. Thus there is an inherent tension within the judicial system. It is, therefore, interesting to examine the ways in which the postwar Japanese courts' judges, the majority of whom have been conservative, dealt with this tension in terms of procedures as well as rulings. Is there any groundbreaking decision made by the Japanese courts in relation to the questions of official knowledge and historical truth, and, if so, what have been the impacts of such decision(s) upon the larger struggles over national narrative and identity? In addition, since the game of truth in the court of law involved technical matters, procedures, and rules of argumentation different from those in the fields of education and history, the strategies adopted by Ienaga and his legal team and the consequences of such strategic choices deserve a close examination.

Ienaga Saburo and His Textbook Lawsuits

Historian Ienaga Saburo (1913–2002) and his work, particularly his critical contributions to shaping Japanese interpretations of the war, as well as his three-decades-long court challenges to the state's de facto censorship of textbooks, were at the center of the Japanese history textbook controversy for decades. Although aware of Ienaga's lawsuits—the so-called textbook lawsuits—for years, western scholarship has offered little comprehensive assessment of his court battles or of his work in general. Who was Ienaga before he filed the lawsuits? Why and how did he take the government to court? What impacts did his legal battles have on various social, educational, and political controversies over the issues of war and war memory?

Ienaga was for a long time at the center of opposition to right-wing nationalist historiography and the state's control over the content of textbooks. Ienaga's journey as a historian and public intellectual has, however, attracted less attention outside Japan. Serious misconceptions have also intruded,[16] so setting the record straight seems a necessary project. In the 1960s, Ienaga was one of several leading Japanese intellectuals who recognized the dual aspects of the Japanese war experience in which the Japanese were both aggressors and victims. To counter the censorship imposed by the Ministry of Education on the textbook he authored, *Shin Nihonshi* (New Japanese History), Ienaga filed the first lawsuit in 1965, and the second in 1967. The first and second lawsuits soon came to examine a broad range of issues related to education, from ancient history to postwar Japanese social, security/military, and educational policies, as Ienaga disputed all the items in his textbook that the state had ordered him to revise. While the second lawsuit was thrown out of court in 1986, the first continued until 1993.

Ienaga filed the third lawsuit in 1984, more sharply focusing on the issues of war memory and education. For example, on the subject of the Nanjing Massacre, one witness for Ienaga was the journalist Honda Katsuichi, who in the early 1970s had shaken the nation with his newspaper reports on Chinese war victims, including survivors of the Nanjing Massacre. Another topic was a series on the tragic events that took place at the Battle of Okinawa, the events remembered as the *gyokusai* or *shudan jiketsu* (what Norma Field has called "compulsory mass suicides"[17]), in which many Okinawans killed each other under pressure from Japanese troops during the final days of the Battle of Okinawa. The courtroom debates in Ienaga's third lawsuit raise core questions concerning history and education: What is historical fact? How do we verify it? Whose knowledge ought to be taught in schools, and who should determine it? The court decisions, including that of the Supreme Court in 1997, reached no clear-cut answers to these questions, which would require a critical and nuanced assessment.

It is important to note that the nexus of power and knowledge has been apparent in the controversy. For example, Ienaga's legal challenge to the state's screening of textbooks began with the question of official knowledge—who determines whose knowledge is to be taught in the schools of a democratic nation. However, it went well beyond that first question to ask what counts as historical truth and how to deal with questions of ambiguity in history and the construction of national narratives. These debates in the courts permitted the oppositional and alternative forces to make the ways the state exercised its power visible and challenge the existing norms of social relations, assumed or practiced, between the state and its citizens. However, the same debates perhaps made it difficult for Ienaga and his legal team to win a total victory because there were no simple answers to the questions of official knowledge and historical truth. In any case, the ongoing conflict over war memory and education perhaps make it necessary to recast the role of intellectuals—from the politically disinterested to the socially responsible, by (re)examining Ienaga's work historically—not only his profound influence on Japanese thoughts about peace, justice, and democracy but also the conflicts, contradictions, and incompleteness latent in the multiple games of truth he, along with his supporters, played in Japan's postwar struggles over Japan's war memories and education.

Chapters

Chapter 1 concerns the larger structural changes in Japanese education that followed Japan's defeat in the Asia-Pacific War. In particular, it discusses reforms of Japanese education that took place in the period of the Allied occupation (1945–1952), the counter-reforms by conservative forces during the 1950s and 1960s, and their impact upon school textbooks. Much of the focus of Chapter 2 is on Ienaga Saburo, as an individual within a context, and his first and second lawsuits, which challenged both the idea and the process of state textbook screening. Chapter 3 looks at postwar Japanese cultural struggles over the representation of history of the Asia-Pacific War. In particular, it directs attention to the beginnings of the controversy surrounding the representation of the Nanjing Massacre and the murder of Okinawan civilians by Japanese forces in the Battle of Okinawa. The chapter also examines the changes in textbook descriptions of war-related events in the 1970s.

Chapter 4 examines the well-reported Japanese textbook controversy that took place in the early 1980s. It describes changes in Japan's intra- and inter-national relations and politics, the textbook controversy, and Ienaga's decision to file the third textbook lawsuit. Chapter 5 analyzes the courtroom debate between Ienaga and the state concerning view(s) of history and historical facts, a debate in which there were a number of contradictions, twists, and turns. Chapter 6 discusses the course of events and court decisions in Ienaga's three textbook lawsuits from the late 1980s to its final conclusion in 1997. Chapter 7 looks at the continuing history textbook controversy in the 1990s, including the emergence of a new meaning for the term "comfort women" and the political, cultural, and educational struggles that followed in general, and the right-wing nationalist revival in particular. In the epilogue, I discuss the significance of Ienaga's court challenges and examine its implications for the continuing oppositional and alternative struggles for "truth in textbooks" to draw some conclusions from the never-ending play of Japanese politics over history and history education.

Herbert M. Kliebard states that curriculum theory concerns the question of "what we ought to teach," and that it is a normative theory that "is not, essentially, verifiable through empirical evidence."[18] The present research on the Japanese history textbook controversy, as an empirical inquiry into multiple games of truth, may not offer a direct answer to that question either. It informs us, however, about the ways social, political, and educational struggles can be fought on the terrain of war memories with a particular set of ideas and perspectives as well as the conflictive processes through which people can act—though within the limits of social and historical conditions—to bring both counter-memories of war and peace-and-justice perspectives into the knowledge taught to younger generations.

Acknowledgments

I am indebted to many people for their encouragement, support, and intellectual influence. First, I would like to thank Ienaga Saburo for his life-long struggle over history and education, without whose struggle much of this volume could not have existed. As I studied him, while overwhelmed by the quality and quantity of his work, I always felt close to him, in part because my original training in Japanese history was in the same tradition as his was. I would also like to thank the many people who supported Ienaga for more than three decades. My spouse and I were very fortunate to have had an opportunity to join the line to organize an international letter campaign in the mid 1990s.

I would like to express my sincere thanks to those who guided me in my undergraduate and graduate education and provided me with the foundations to be a scholar: Amino Yoshihiko, Miki Seiichiro, Hayakawa Sohachi, Herbert M. Kliebard, Michael W. Apple, Mary Haywood Metz, and John Fiske. They were uncompromising, and always gave me the best academic advice. This volume bears the imprint of their scholarship and perspectives.

I would also like to express my appreciation to Arai Junji, Eri Fujieda, Goshima Atasuko, Hayakawa Misao, Hayashi Hiroshi, Laura Hein, Ikeda Hiroshi, Kimijima Kazuhiko, Kogure Shuzo, Nakamura Kikuji, Shimamoto Hiroki, Yuki Tanaka, Tawara Yoshifumi, Totsuka Etsuo, Yue-him Tam, Yamazumi Masami, and Watanabe Ayako for their support and help at various stages of my research. Sylvan Esh, Amy Ferry, Rachel Fix, Susan Yepez, Ruth Hein, Dory Lightfoot, and Judith Perkins offered invaluable editorial assistance with excellent comments and suggestions. Special thanks (with a lot of respect) are due to Mark Selden, Richard Minear, and Allan Luke for their continuous encouragement, intellectual inspiration, and interest in my work, and to Peter Sowden and Jason Mitchell of Routledge for their patience and kind assistance. In addition, I would like to thank my colleagues here at the University at Buffalo (SUNY) generally, and Greg Dimitriadis, Bruce Johnstone, Rose Ylimaki, and Lois Weis in particular.

This research was supported by a number of institutions: The 1998–1999 Deans Club Graduate Student Research Award from the School of Education, University of Wisconsin-Madison; the 2001–2002 National Academy of Education/Spencer Postdoctoral Fellowship from the National Academy of

Education; a Research Grant for Untenured Faculty from the Graduate School of Education, University at Buffalo (SUNY) in 2003–2004; a Baldy Center Research Project grant from the Baldy Center for Law & Social Policy, University at Buffalo (SUNY); the 2006–2007 Dr. McGann Drescher Award from the Dr. McGann Drescher Leave Program, State of New York and United University Professions; and Individual Development Awards from the United University Professions in 2002–2003, 2004–2005, and 2005–2006. I am grateful for their financial assistance and interest in my research.

Dorothy Heldt, Gary and Lanette Price, Bob and Eppie Gruling, and my extended host families also encouraged me to pursue graduate study in the United States. My parents Nozaki Takeji and Kazumi and in-laws Hatano Giyoo and Kyoko gave me consistent support for my academic career. Unfortunately, I lost both Takeji and Giyoo in the past several years, and Dorothy passed away recently. Coping with the losses was more difficult than I had ever thought—I still mourn, but finally I began to understand that they will live in my memory forever. Above all, I would like to thank my spouse Hiro Inokuchi for his encouragement, love, and assistance through these years of research and writing. His support made much of the work on this volume not only possible but also enjoyable.

A note on Japanese names: Throughout the text, for the names of Japanese persons, I have followed the Japanese convention in which the family name or surname precedes the given or personal name (thus, for example, Prime Minister Nakasone's full name is Nakasone Yasuhiro). Of necessity, however, this rule is reversed in two situations: where Japanese living outside the country have chosen to follow the opposite (Western) order and in identifying the authors of publications in English.

1 Japan's defeat and educational reforms

The struggle over the Japanese national narrative and identity in the early postwar years, 1945–1965

New questions will be heard:

"What are the modes of existence of this discourse?"
"Where does it come from; how is it circulated; who controls it?"
"What placements are determined for possible subjects?"
"Who can fulfill these diverse functions of the subject?"

Behind all these questions we would hear little more than the murmur of indifference:

"What matter who's speaking?"

Michel Foucault, "What Is An Author?"

On August 15, 1945, the day Emperor Hirohito announced the acceptance of the Potsdam Declaration to his subjects, the Suzuki cabinet resigned en masse. Ota Kozo, the outgoing Education Minister, presented his final instruction to the schools on that day. His message was that Japan's defeat had been brought on by the people's insufficient dedication to the emperor, along with their failure to bring into full play the spirit nurtured by their imperial education. Hereafter, he concluded, students and teachers ought to devote themselves wholly to their duties as imperial subjects, and to the maintenance of the *kokutai*.[1] In referring to *kokutai*, Ota had in mind the emperor, who in presurrender doctrine was the essence of the nation and embodied the national identity. Ota, like many other officials who had promoted ultranationalistic and emperor-centered education in the service of war, persisted in his determination to secure the imperial state even while accepting military defeat.[2] In this and other related ways, much of the imperial system, which had committed all sorts of atrocities, remained intact at the beginning of postwar Japan.

A modern nation-state governs its people in part by creating and disseminating narratives. One important site of such efforts is the school textbook, especially history and social studies textbooks. After all, education is one of the most effective ways to promote a national narrative (official history) and to make and remake certain identities into the national identity.[3] The state, whether or not it is directly involved in textbook production and circulation, can readily reinforce dominant ideologies. In response, alternative and oppositional forces develop their own counter-narratives and identities. For the meanings attached to a given identity—in this case the national identity—are "an unstable and 'de-centered' complex of social meanings constantly being transformed by political struggle."[4]

The ongoing battles over educational content in postwar Japan constitute one of the crucial fronts in a long-running struggle over the identity of the nation. To be sure, struggles over the national narrative existed in Japan before and even during World War II, when official narratives such as the Imperial Rescript on Education and other "fine militarist stories" played a crucial role in Japanese identity formation.[5] The state's strict and often violent oppression made it difficult or impossible for counter-narratives (e.g., the proletarian educational movement) to redirect the nation's course.

In the postwar era, Japan professes to have become a "democratic" nation, and asserts that its educational systems have changed accordingly. As Education Minister Ota's final instruction makes clear, however, the powers that had committed all manner of wartime atrocities were still intact at the formation of the "new" Japan. Those powers retained all the structures developed in the preceding years, including the "common sense" that represented Japanese people as imperial subjects. While a series of "educational reforms" were implemented under the supervision of the occupation forces to meet the requirements of the new "democratic" era, the effectiveness of such reforms was limited by the specific conditions that existed at a fundamental level.

Worse, because U.S. policy shifted from a pro-democracy emphasis to a primarily anti-communist focus, Japan's conservative and right-wing nationalist forces, which formed a power bloc in the 1950s, quickly succeeded in seizing control over the state. Their successes included the (ultra)nationalist recapturing of the Ministry of Education (*Monbusho*; hereafter MOE), through which, by the end of 1950s, the right wing was able to "reverse" many aspects of the postwar educational reforms. This move was significant, because it enabled right-wing groups to partially impose nationalist narratives on the schools, especially in the area of history textbook content.

In this context, how did the processes of educational reforms take place at the beginning of the occupation period (1945-early 1950s) and how did the counter-reforms take place in the following years during the period of conservative and nationalist restoration (early 1950s–1965)? How did these reforms affect the actual content of history textbooks written during these two periods? The treatments of World War II-related events in the textbooks are of particular interest here, since the descriptions and meanings of these events would become a center of the textbook controversy in years to come.

Blacking-out Textbooks

The Japanese government's postwar textbook policy began with a process referred to as blacking-out (*suminuri*) textbooks. At the end of August 1945, while considering how to maintain the kokutai, the MOE instructed the schools to exercise discretion in using the existing textbooks when reopening in September. On September 20, the MOE directed the schools to have teachers delete the militaristic content from textbooks and other educational materials.[6] In all likelihood, however, the MOE's actual intention was more to conceal, than to negate, militarism in education, as some officials, looking back on the event years later, referred to its purpose as trying to make a favorable impression and to keep militarist content from the eyes of the occupation force.[7]

In any case, the textbook blacking-out did not aim at eliminating the emperor-centered education programs. While the MOE listed several general criteria for content removal, it did not specify the exact items to be removed, except those contained in the second-semester Japanese-language textbooks for elementary schools. Moreover, the items specified were mainly war-related descriptions, and many stories concerning adoration of the emperors remained, as well as the use of Kimigayo, a song wishing for the prosperity of imperial sovereignty.[8] Finally, the MOE also recommended the introduction of educational content concerning the kokutai and the moral establishment, as the blacking-out would result in a shortage of materials. This provision implied the use of the Imperial Rescript on Education.[9]

In October 1945, the Supreme Command for the Allied Powers (hereafter known as SCAP) began to issue directives concerning education, in which curriculum content and textbooks were central issues. For example, on October 22 SCAP ordered the elimination of militarist and ultranationalist ideologies from schooling, and ordered that the teachers who had implemented extremely militaristic and ultranationalistic education be purged.[10] On December 15 it ordered the abolition of any government propagation of *shinto*, including a ban on the use of some state-authored texts and teaching materials such as *Kokutai no Hongi* (The True Meaning of the Kokutai) and *Shinmin no Michi* (The Path of the Imperial Subject). In its informal pronouncements, SCAP made it clear that Japanese history textbooks would have to be rewritten. Finally, on December 31, it ordered that teaching of morals (*shushin*), Japanese history, and geography be suspended and that textbooks and teacher's guides in these subject areas be withdrawn.

While SCAP's orders were issued in Tokyo, notification of the MOE's instructions concerning textbook content removal eventually reached the local schools, and teachers began to have students black out—in some cases, cut out or paste over—parts of the textbooks. Because the MOE's instructions lacked specifics, local officials and schools needed to develop their own lists of items to be removed from the textbooks in all subject areas. In some prefectures, it was the prefecture that developed and sent the list; in others, the school officials and teachers developed the list. These locally developed lists included far more items for removal than the instructions given by the MOE. In any case, no two blacked-out textbooks emerged from the process exactly alike, indicating that each classroom teacher took some liberty in determining which items were to be removed. In a sense, though to a limited extent, a different construction of national narrative took place in each classroom.

By the middle of November, the MOE completed a list of the items to be removed from all textbooks in use in all schools, and in February 1946, it sent a second notice to the local schools. However, the notice contained only items for elementary Japanese and math textbooks. It thus failed to provide schools with a complete set of instructions for carrying out the task.[11] The MOE allowed the schools to use the blacked-out textbooks until July 31, 1946. In April (the beginning of the 1946 school year), it published and distributed "stopgap" textbooks in the subject areas permitted to be taught by the occupation forces. These textbooks were in short supply, which provoked criticism from both teachers and parents.[12]

Renewed Interest in History Teaching and the Last State-authored History Textbooks

SCAP's December 31 order referring to the development of new history textbooks encouraged some Japanese historians, including Ienaga Saburo, to articulate new national narratives. Soon after the order, Ienaga and others began to address the issues of Japan's history education, textbook writing, and publishing in the postwar era. For example, Ienaga, who was a historian and a former teacher at a high school and a teacher training school (*shihan gakko*), wrote an article on this topic in which he essentially argued for a history education based on historical scholarship, an education that would teach verified—*kagakuteki* (scientific) to use his word—facts. As he stated:

> How do we search for the correct knowledge of Japanese history that should be the content of the correct teaching of the national history? I believe there is no other way but to seek it through the right kind of research on national history (*kokushigaku*). It has often been said that history as a specialized discipline and the teaching of history are different. Some critics have even argued the two to be completely separate, but I have always disagreed with this view. In my view, the correct teaching of history has to be based on historical scholarship to the utmost.[13]

Ienaga also drafted his own history textbook in early 1946, at the request of the Fuzanbo, a commercial press (this project preceded Ienaga's involvement in writing a state-authored textbook, discussed below). His book *Shin Nihonshi* (New Japanese History) reflected his view that education should convey democratic values and the desire for peace. In 1947, the Fuzanbo published the text as a book for a general audience, because the Japanese government at that point appeared not to allow non-governmental school textbooks.[14] (It was after the state began to certify history textbooks for secondary schools through its textbook screening system that the text was eventually published as a school textbook. The lawsuits Ienaga later filed were for the revised versions of this book.)

Meanwhile, the MOE, pressed by SCAP, began preliminary arrangements for writing new history textbooks sometime in the fall of 1945. Toyoda Takeshi, historian and one of the compilers from the MOE's Textbook Bureau, was in charge.[15] In December, the MOE officially formed a committee of ten prominent historians to develop elementary and secondary school history textbook(s), and Toyoda, in consultation with the committee (and some historians outside the committee), began to draft a history textbook for elementary schools. From the beginning there had been a conflict between SCAP and the MOE. While SCAP thought it necessary to write entirely new history textbooks, the MOE insisted that it was sufficient to simply eliminate the militaristic content from already existing textbooks. Toyoda's draft began with accounts of Japanese history in terms of some archaeological findings, which pleased the Civil Information and Education Section (hereafter CIE) of SCAP. But the text also included the mythology on Japan's divine origin and epic imperial figures at great length—an element that the CIE could not overlook. The project was canceled in May 1946, just after the account of the ancient period had been completed.[16] SCAP suggested that the MOE begin a new project with historians who were not affiliated with the Textbook Bureau.[17]

The MOE launched a new project to develop three textbooks—for elementary, secondary, and teacher training schools[18]—each dividing Japanese history into four periods: the Kodai and Heian period (ancient-1192), the years from the Kamakura to Momoyma period (1192–1600), the Tokugawa period (1600–1868), and the Meiji era and thereafter (1868-present).[19] The site of this project was the refectory of the Historiographical Institute at Tokyo Imperial University, and the MOE commissioned eleven historians for the project, with each member selecting and organizing the textbook content for his or her assigned sections.[20] All eleven, however, followed three common principles: (1) prohibition of propaganda of any kind; (2) prohibition of militarism, ultranationalism, or propagation of shintoism; and (3) inclusion of accomplishments of ordinary people in the areas of economy, invention, scholarship, and art, with mention of the successive emperors' achievements if appropriate.[21]

Ienaga was asked to write about the ancient period for the elementary school textbook, later entitled *Kuni no Ayumi* (The Course of the Nation).[22] He used Toyoda's draft as a basis because he faced severe time restrictions— the manuscript had to be finished in about one month's time. But he revised Toyoda's text in some significant ways. For example, although he followed

Toyoda's example to begin the text with a description of stone-age civilization and archeological findings, he deleted much of the (remaining) mythology Toyoda had included, and he proceeded objectively to describe the formation of Japan as a state.[23]

CIE had its Japanese employees examine the manuscript daily, and, according to Ienaga, even though CIE did order them to remove some language (e.g., evaluative modifiers and adjectives), it never asked the authors to include specific descriptions prior to their writing, except for requesting that a reference to Japan's building of a democratic nation under the occupation be included in the last section and that a chronological table be attached to the text.[24] On balance, Ienaga, who believed in the separation of history and mythology, thought the CIE oversight was less oppressive than the censorship he had experienced during the war. Ienaga felt other authors shared his feeling, and indeed Okubo Toshiaki, one of Ienaga's co-authors who wrote the modern/contemporary section of *Kuni no Ayumi*, later stated that the content was left entirely up to the authors.[25] Other authors might have felt differently about the CIE's role, however, as Okada Akio, another co-author who was assigned to the Edo period and who edited the entire text with others in the end, later stated somewhat critically that the CIE had the phrase "ravag[ing] in Nanjing" (a line referring to the Nanjing Massacre) inserted in the section describing the Japanese invasion of China, from Shanghai to Nanjing in particular, in 1937.[26]

Kuni no Ayumi, published in September 1946, was the first postwar state-authored history textbook. It was also the first state-authored book to disclose the names of the actual authors. The MOE published two other textbooks: *Nihon no Rekishi* (History of Japan, published in 1946), for secondary schools, and *Nihon Rekishi* (Japanese History, published in 1947), for teacher training schools. These first three books were also to become the last state-authored history textbooks in the course of postwar education reforms.

The War-related Materials in the Three Last State-authored History Textbooks

To write the first (and last) postwar state-authored history textbooks was to develop a new national narrative. The authors were, however, constrained by SCAP's policies as well as by the larger political, social, and cultural conditions of the period. With respect to the material on World War II, the name of the war was changed from *Daitoa Senso* (The Great East Asian War), the term created by the Japanese government and used in wartime textbooks, to *Taiheiyo Senso* (The Pacific War). The change reflected SCAP's prohibition of the official use of the former term and its promotion of the latter. Beginning in December 1945, SCAP had all major newspapers, as well as *the Nippon Hoso Kyokai* (NHK, a public broadcasting company), run a series of articles and radio programs concerning the war. Those articles and programs were written or produced by the CIE as part of the re-education effort for the Japanese. The articles and programs used the term Taiheyo Senso, which quickly spread among the Japanese.[27]

To change the name of the war in the textbooks was much easier than addressing the far more complicated question of war responsibility. The latter task was not only more immediately political, but also required profoundly critical perspectives and self-reflective insights. Time did not allow the authors of the last state-authored textbooks to think the question through; even if they had been given the necessary time, however, it seems somewhat doubtful that they could have adequately addressed the question. (Subsequent history shows that it took years for Japanese intellectuals and historians, including Ienaga, to develop the critical perspectives and knowledge necessary to address the question.) At the time, the information on the war (and Japanese war crimes) was limited; the evidence produced in the Tokyo war tribunal sessions was sometimes the only source available to the authors.

In addition, the Tokyo war tribunal, which was the main instrument for uncovering Japanese war crimes and dealing with the question of war responsibility, did not fully accomplish its mission. The tribunal court began on May 3, 1946, and SCAP and Japan's ruling forces found themselves, coincidentally or not, in agreement over the issue of Emperor Hirohito's war responsibility. SCAP was inclined to use the authority of the emperor to implement occupation policies and reforms. The Japanese ruling classes—especially those close to the Imperial Court—actively helped indict Japan's top wartime military leaders (mostly from the Japanese Army). Their intent was to shift the war responsibility onto the leaders and so avoid the prosecution of the emperor. (This framework also allowed ordinary Japanese citizens to avoid questions concerning their personal and collective war responsibility—though there were, of course, some individuals who were deeply concerned about the questions.)

The process of the Tokyo war tribunal increasingly reflected U.S. interests, particularly as signs of the impending Cold War surfaced. For example, the military officers and personnel involved in the experiments of Unit 731, Japan's bio-warfare unit, were granted immunity from prosecution in exchange for providing the United States with the information they had accumulated from their experiments. Also, the verdict of the Tokyo war tribunal (handed down in November 1948) for the most part disregarded Japan's responsibility for the war in Asia. The tribunal's findings about Japan's war crimes were extremely limited and involved only a small number of indicted leaders (in addition, the United States decided to cancel the second and third round of prosecution of A-class war criminal suspects).[28] Besides, the tribunal faced difficult legal issues concerning the punishment of individual high-ranking officials for war crimes committed by the state.[29] The decision, for example, acknowledged the death of more than 200,000 civilians and prisoners-of-war in Nanjing and its outskirts within six weeks after the Japanese Army occupied the city in 1937 (an event known as the

Nanjing Massacre), and it sentenced the commanding officer of the operation, General Matsui Iwane, to death. The Tokyo war tribunal, however, did not necessarily deal with all the questions concerning the atrocity.

Another problem was that the tribunal did not regard some Japanese war atrocities as war crimes. The existence of a large number of women enslaved, forced to prostitute, exploited, and abused by the Japanese system of military comfort women (*ianfu*), for example, had been known. In fact, at the end of the war, the Allied Forces (mainly the U.S. forces) took many comfort women—mostly Korean women—in custody as POWs (as they belonged to the Japanese military). While aware through interviews that many of the women had been forced to work in the comfort facilities, the Allied forces did not consider the matter as a war crime that required prosecution of the Japanese involved. They did not feel obligated to conduct further investigations (except in two cases—one involving Dutch women in Indonesia and the other concerning Guam female residents). Nor did the tribunal court.[30]

Whether the process of the tribunal directly influenced the authors of the last state-authored history textbooks is largely a matter of conjecture. The textbooks indicate that the authors wrote about the war from an anti-militarism perspective, as they described Japan's highhanded, aggressive military operations in China from 1931 onward. All three textbooks included some descriptions of the Nanjing Massacre of 1937 in the context of Japan's power diplomacy and ever-extending battle lines. This contrasts with the wartime state-authored elementary school history textbook (published in 1943) that had described the event as one of the heroic moments of Japan's war with China. In its words: "[H]ighly loyal, strongly brave imperial officers and soldiers ... captured the capital of Nanjing on December 13th and flew the Rising-Sun flag from the top of the fortress."[31] Contrary to this old description, *Kuni no Ayumi,* in its section of modern and contemporary history (written by Ienaga's co-author Okubo) referred to the event as follows: "[Our army] ravaged Nanjing, the capital of the Republic of China ... ."[32] The line was brief but clear in signifying that the event was now seen as one of Japan's wartime wrongdoings.

Both *Nihon no Rekishi*, the textbook for secondary schools, and *Nihon Rekishi*, the textbook for teacher training schools, used the term "aggression" (*shinryaku*) to describe the nature of Japan's war against China. *Nihon no Rekishi* pointed out Japan's "arrogance" in waging the "war ... without declaration" and included the line "Our army committed atrocities when capturing Nanjing, which ... led the Republic of China to all-out resistance."[33] Also *Nihon Rekishi* stated: "The war situation became more and more complicated, and the resistance on the Chinese side grew more intense, triggered by the Japanese Army's atrocities in Nanjing acting as a trigger."[34] These descriptions referring to the Nanjing Massacre were not extensive, and they dealt with the matter somewhat in passing; nonetheless, they represented the view that the event took place in the context of Japan's aggression, involving atrocities committed by the Japanese Army.[35]

Discussions of who actually bore the responsibility for Japan's aggression were another matter, however. All three textbooks basically blamed the military. In other words, the textbooks attempted to address the question of war responsibility, but were not able to go beyond the tribunal court outcomes. For example, in describing the beginning of Japan's aggression against China, *Kuni no Ayumi* stated:

> There was peace for a while after the end of World War I in Europe, but from that time, the atmosphere of our nation gradually changed. In particular, the influence of the military spread throughout the spheres of politics and economy, and society became turbulent, leading to such bloody events as the May 15 and February 26 incidents. Finally, because of the affairs in Manchuria, a troublesome entanglement developed with the Republic of China, and peace in East Asia fell into disarray.[36]

The text also described Japan's defeat as follows: "Our nation was defeated. The people suffered greatly because of the long war. The military's suppression of the people and its waging a reckless war caused this unhappiness."[37] The text did not in any way consider Emperor Hirohito's responsibility for the war. Indeed, at the end of the textbook, the text cited Hirohito's January 1946 statement as a new direction for Japan as a democratic nation. In this statement, Hirohito stressed the importance of rebuilding Japan as a peaceful nation by referring to the Imperial Covenant of Five Articles, the famous oath taken by Emperor Mutsuhito, the Meiji, in 1868 at the beginning of his reign.

The three textbooks were not without their shortcomings. *Kuni no Ayumi* was the most criticized among the three, criticized by both the Japanese left[38] and several foreign countries for failing to completely eradicate the emperor-centered view of history (*kokoku shikan*).[39] Ienaga himself soon admitted its shortcomings. However, in rewriting history, especially wartime history, these authors had only limited sources available to them, since, strictly speaking, no research on the topic had been conducted. In any case, the three last state-authored history textbooks clearly marked the starting point of Japan's postwar historical studies, history education, and textbook controversy.

The 1947 Constitution and the Fundamental Law of Education

The democratization of Japan under the occupation moved along swiftly, at least on the surface. The new constitution, promulgated in 1946 and put into effect in May 1947, offered a picture of nationhood that differed remarkably from the militarist, (ultra)nationalist, and emperor-centered nation of the presurrender period: sovereignty residing with the people (giving the emperor status as a "symbol" of the nation) (Article 1); guaranteeing basic human rights (Article 11); renouncing war (Article 9); guaranteeing academic freedom (Article 23); guaranteeing the people's right to receive an education (Article 26). The constitution thus gave shape to the postwar education.

On March 31, 1947, the Japanese government proclaimed both the Fundamental Law of Education (*Kyoiku Kihon Ho*) and the School Education Law (*Gakko Kyoiku Ho*).[40] The Fundamental Law of Education articulated the key principles of postwar education, including the goal to provide the full development of personality (Article 1), as well as provisions for equal opportunity in education (Article 3) and coeducation (Article 5). Most important, it stated that "Education shall not be subject to improper control, but it shall be directly responsible to the whole people" (Article 10), the concern here being a fear of the potential for oppressive state control over education.[41] The law served, in a sense, as an "educational constitution." As the MOE put it, the legislation was a declaration of new educational ideals in the nature of "an absolutely indispensable law with regard to educational matters" (though the MOE later changed its position on this point). Designed to serve as the foundation of the subsequent course of educational law and policy, the law was to replace the Imperial Rescript on Education.[42]

In contrast, the School Education Law, which dealt with the practical operation of schools, including textbook policy, contained an ambiguity about state control over education. For example, although both the first U. S. education mission to Japan and the Japanese Education Committee (formed to welcome the mission, and chaired by Nambara Shigeru) suggested that textbooks be freely published and freely selected,[43] the School Education Law stipulated that elementary school textbooks were to be screened, approved, or authored by a "competent authority" (*kantoku-cho*, Article 21). The law also stipulated similar procedures for secondary school textbooks. At first, it was understood that not only the MOE but also an education board to be created at prefectural level could be a competent authority. However, in the School Education Law Enforcement Regulations issued in May 1947 (which was not an actual piece of legislation), the MOE defined itself as the sole competent authority for the time being.[44]

Interestingly, the first postwar curriculum policy appearing in the MOE's series of *Instruction Guidelines (gakushu-shido yoryo)* reflected more the democratization ideal of Japanese education than the textbook policy stipulated in the School Education Law. For example, the *Instruction Guidelines: General Guide/A Tentative Plan* (hereafter, the *1947 General Guide*), which was published on March 20, 1947, just before the promulgation of the two laws, criticized Japan's presurrender education over having brought uniformity to schools. It argued, instead, that, within the certain goals and frameworks, each school and teacher should devise educational content and teaching methods appropriate to the needs of their students, school resources, and community environments. As such, the guidelines were tentative rather than prescriptive. The text defined itself as not the teachers' manual of the past, but a "guide" (*tebiki*): "[This text] is written as a guide for teachers to inquire into ways to make use of [ideas for] a course of study that has newly arisen to meet the demands of students and society."[45] In fact, the text generally tended to present the findings of curriculum research rather than statements on curriculum standards. In subsequent years, local schools and teachers, encouraged by the idea of empowering themselves in the domain of curriculum deliberations, made numerous efforts to develop their own curricula to suit their districts and schools.[46]

The Replacement of "History" with "Social Studies"

While the institutional reorganization of Japanese education—in particular, the transition to the 6-3 system[47]—was underway, the idea for replacing history education with a new, integrated subject called social studies (*shakaika*) was being introduced. In September 1946, after the publication of *Kuni no Ayumi*, SCAP allowed schools to resume the teaching of history; about a month later, however, the MOE (with the support of some SCAP officials) announced the introduction of social studies for the 1947 school year.

The new subject would integrate four previously separate subjects—morals, civics, geography, and history—into one subject in which students would explore several major problems in relation to their own experiences. This new curriculum design would basically preclude "systematic learning" (*keito gakushu*), the prevailing approach to organizing curriculum content, and it would not allow teachers to teach history in its chronological narrative forms. The new curriculum approach, thus, sparked a controversy within and outside the MOE. Most historians, for example, opposed the idea of social studies, because they thought that the chronological teaching of history was necessary to explain the origins and developments of historical events. Some CIE officials involved in the state-authored history textbook project also opposed the idea, since it would render the three history textbooks—two of which had just been published and one of which was in the process of coming out—useless after April 1947. The dissent was not, however, powerful enough to reverse the policy.[48]

Just when most people thought they had seen the last of chronological history teaching, however, a certain faction of MOE officials succeeded in having a subject called "national history" (*kokushi*) included in the required subject list for grades eight and nine of the *1947 General Guide* (the MEO's *Instruction Gudelines* prepared in the late fall of 1946 and published in March 1947). An already confusing situation became more so with this insertion, because the volume containing the subject guidelines for "national history," one that was required to immediately follow the *1947 General Guide*, had yet to be developed. That is, the content of "national history" remained undefined and textbook(s) remained unavailable. It was also not clear whether "national history" should mean "chronological history." The MOE was thus compelled to notify the schools that the implementation of social studies would be postponed (until September 1947), and that *Nihon no Rekishi*, the state-authored history textbook for secondary schools, might be used to teach "national history."[49]

In the fall of 1947, the same pro-history faction within the MOE again succeeded in adding "national history" (later renamed "Japanese history") to the required high school subjects. The MOE then created the Committee for Compiling Secondary School National History Textbooks (*Chuto Kokushi Kyokasho Hensan Iinkai*). It invited notable historians of different traditions, not including imperialist and (ultra)nationalist, to join this committee. The MOE's intent was to gather support from these historians for the idea of teaching history within a social studies framework, and to develop national history textbooks compatible with the idea of social studies. This effort failed as the views of most of the committee members differed from the MOE's. Consequently, the committee was unable to develop the textbooks.

Under these circumstances, in the fall of 1948, the MOE revised the high school subject guidelines again and defined social studies as consisting of one required subject (general social studies) and four electives (national history, world history, human geography, and current topics). Although the MOE announced that these subjects would be implemented during the 1949 school year, it failed to issue appropriate instructions on time. The MOE did not complete the subject guidelines for high school Japanese history until 1951 (publishing them in 1952). Because of this, even though it introduced the textbook screening system in 1948, the MOE did not accept manuscripts for high school Japanese history textbooks for some years. In any case, a new situation emerged from the struggle for (and against) a social studies curriculum: while history in elementary schools was replaced with social studies, the idea of teaching history within a framework of social studies did not really materialize at the secondary school level.[50]

How the schools and teachers dealt with the curriculum change from history to social studies varied, especially at elementary schools, where social studies replaced history. According to a memoir written by Kanazawa Kaichi, an elementary school teacher (and later a principal) in Tokyo, Japanese history was not taught at his school during the early years of occupation. Then one year, to his surprise, he found that his students wanted to study Japanese history. As he put it:

On January 8, 1950, after the opening assembly for the [third] term, I asked my sixth-grade homeroom students, "Well now, you have only three months to go as sixth-graders. Let's study hard to be sure that you have nothing to regret later. So tell me what, if anything, you want to be taught before your graduation." One of the students said, "Please teach Japanese history." ... I was shocked because I had not taught anything like history [during the occupation years]. Because other students also said that they wanted to be taught [the subject], for the three months until the graduation, I forgot myself and taught [them] Japanese history. It was during the occupation, when teaching history was not welcome. ... [I used] *Kuni no Ayumi* as a textbook.[51]

Kanazawa was somewhat critical of the way the new subject of social studies was implemented during the occupation. The school next to his school—Sakurada Elementary School—was one of the schools that specialized in the social studies curriculum research, and occupation officials sometimes visited that school.[52] In Kanazawa's view, Sakurada taught social studies "for the United States." One example he gave concerned the story of a street urchin.[53] When the child found a job in the area of Sakurada and wanted to attend school, it refused to admit him on the grounds that "Our school is a school for social studies research ... [and so it] cannot admit street urchins." Hearing this refusal, Kanazawa was left with a poor opinion of the school. As he put it in his memoirs:

If social studies is a subject that is based on the surrounding area, and on dealing with the problems that arise in those areas, the problem of street urchins was the most pressing, real problem [social studies had to address] in [our] area of Shinbashi, Tokyo, at that time. Furthermore, it was a problem that involved children, [one that the students can reflect upon] as their own. I thought that if [Sakurada] had been [truly] a school of social studies research, it should have had been that much more willing to admit the child.[54]

The street urchin ended up entering Kanazawa's class. Kanazawa himself, as he stated, "was not able to adapt to the social studies [practiced] during the occupation." The subject, in his view, was U.S.-oriented rather than one that addressed the problems facing the Japanese people.[55] Whether or not Kanazawa's critique was overstated, the MOE's implementation of a policy mandating the teaching of social studies seemed to have been met with resistance on the part of some (conscientious) teachers.

The Introduction of Postwar Textbook Screening

In September 1947, the MOE announced that it would introduce a textbook screening system in 1948 (for the 1949 school year textbooks), without clarifying that it would halt the publication of state-authored textbooks. The MOE formed several committees to develop ideas and policies for the system, and it was on (relatively) good terms with the Japan Teachers Union (hereafter JTU), which sent its representatives to the committees. Furthermore, around this time, the MOE suggested that schools, in consultation with the teachers, select textbooks appropriate to their own educational needs, though it failed to legally define who would have the authority to adopt these textbooks.[56] Many concerned with education, including teachers, scholars, and the editorial staff of publishing houses, welcomed the MOE's position, and immediately initiated a number of new textbook projects. Even the JTU launched its own textbook projects, and eventually submitted nearly sixty textbook manuscripts for screening.

Textbook screening under the occupation was a complicated and convoluted, twofold process. Publishers were required to submit both Japanese and English versions of manuscripts, and the MOE screened the Japanese manuscripts. In the MOE's screening process, five commissioned examiners evaluated the manuscripts, and sixteen appointed committee members made decisions regarding approval. The CIE screened English-language versions of MOE approved manuscripts. Then, if the CIE requested a revision, the publishers/authors had to revise and resubmit the manuscript to the MOE's committee. The 1948 textbook screening was a rushed process, and only a small number of textbooks gained approval. As of August 11, 418 of the 584 textbooks submitted had passed the MOE's screening, and only 90 of those gained CIE clearance.

From August 25, the textbooks that had passed the screening process were displayed in local school districts. Only 62 textbooks were ready in time for this stage, including two written by the JTU. Many teachers visited the display halls and examined the texts; the atmosphere of the display areas was one of excitement and enthusiasm, an attitude that continued in subsequent years. Tokutake Toshio, then an editorial staff member of the Chukyo Shuppan publishing house, recalled later: "I visited the display hall every day. It was around the time of 1950–55. There were always groups of teachers examining, comparing, and discussing the textbooks."[57]

In general, teachers preferred the "non-governmental" (*minkan*) textbooks, and so the state-authored textbooks lost a significant share of the market. In 1950, the MOE announced it would cease writing textbooks. It made one last futile attempt to reintroduce its own "standard" (*hyojun*) textbooks in 1952, but after this attempt failed, the MOE finally decided to stop publishing state-authored textbooks (which was indeed a gradual withdrawal process, beginning in 1953 and taking several years to complete). This did not mean, however, that the MOE would abandon its control over textbooks, but that it began to influence textbook content by way of textbook screening and other means.

The Content of Non-governmental History Textbooks

Many textbooks that were not state authored represented Japan's war with China (and Japan's occupation of many regions on the Asian continent) as Japanese "aggression" (*shinryaku*). For example, a survey of fifteen junior high school textbooks on Japanese history published in the early 1950s (ones examined by the author for this volume) revealed that twelve used the term "aggression" in one way or another to describe Japanese military conflicts with China that took place in the early 1930s, indicating that Japan's aggression against China began with the events of this period. This was especially true of descriptions of the Manchurian Incident of 1931—when Japan conquered Manchuria, established a puppet government of Manchukuo, and appointed Henry Pu-yi, the heir to the Manchu dynasty, as "provisional president."[58]

Several textbooks also included descriptions of the Nanjing Massacre of 1937. *Gendai Nihon no Naritachi* (The Formation of Contemporary Japan), a high school textbook published in 1952, contained the line, "The Japanese Army's ways of pillaging and assault, including 'the violent incident of Nanjing,' brought it worldwide notoriety."[59] *Gendai Sekai no Naritachi* (The Formation of Contemporary World), another high school text published in 1952, read: "The occupation of Nanjing resounded throughout the world because of the notoriety of 'the violent incident of Nanjing,' so called because of the Japanese Army's destruction of the city, its pillaging, and its assaults."[60] Another text, *Chugaku Shakai* (Junior High School Social Studies), published in 1954, provided even more details of the massacre:

> As the war spread, the [Japanese] army occupied northern China within the year and captured Nanjing. At the time [of capturing Nanjing], the army, entering the fortress Nanjing in triumph, inflicted severe acts of violence on the civilians. Because of this, the people of the world increasingly denounced Japan and sympathized with China.[61]

Moreover, some textbooks also recognized Japan's aggression in other Asian regions. *Chugaku Shakai*, for example, made the following references to Japan's war crimes and the anti-Japanese resistance in Southeast Asia. Its description read: "Because the Japanese forces committed violent acts in various territories it occupied, it incurred [native] inhabitants' enmity. In places such as the Philippines, Malaya, Indochina, and Indonesia, the inhabitants sustained covert resistance movements for independence from Japanese occupation."[62] These textbook descriptions suggest that early postwar textbook authors recognized Japan's war atrocities as war crimes, and understood the importance of representing them as such in school textbooks. In other words, there were clear signs suggesting that the authors were interested in increasing coverage of Japanese aggression in future editions.[63]

The non-governmental textbooks published in the early 1950s, however, did not pursue the question of war responsibility to the extent that a contemporary critic might wish. Many framed their discussion around the results of the Tokyo war tribunal. In this regard, their perspectives were limited, as were those of the three state-authored history textbooks discussed earlier. Most textbooks blamed the military for aggression in Asia and tyranny in Japan, but none questioned, or referred to, Emperor Hirohito's war responsibility. Several textbooks represented Hirohito as a figure whose authority and power were exploited by the (fascist) military leaders, and as a monarch who, in the end, suppressed the pro-war military and ordered the war's end.

Nor did the textbooks explore the issues of the responsibility of the Japanese citizens for the war. Instead, they generally represented the Japanese people as having been deceived by propaganda filtered through the military's control of the media, education, and other information outlets. For example, the 1955 edition of *Atarashii Shakai* (New Social Studies) referred to the civilians twice in its section on the Asia-Pacific War. One reference appeared in the textbook's discussion on the rise of the Japanese military dictatorship during the early 1930s. It explained the relation of the ordinary Japanese to the military dictatorship as follows:

> Around this time, the political parties lost the trust of the people because they connected with the *zaibatsu* [financial conglomerates] to pursue only their own interests and ignored the people's sufferings. The military cleverly took advantage of this and attempted to end the party system and impose a military dictatorship. ... After the February 26 incident, members of the armed forces secured all important political positions. ... Even the liberals and those believing in democracy, not to mention socialists, were denounced as traitors to the nation. In this way, the people were gradually driven into war.[64]

A second reference appeared in the textbook's discussion of the Pacific War, specifically its description of the people's lives during the war's final phase:

> The people's lives were unusually difficult. They faced starvation, their houses were burned down, and they lived on a day-to-day basis with the fear of air raids. They came to hope that the war would end. However, the military did not listen to the people's wishes and only clamored for the decisive battle on the homeland.[65]

These descriptions did not portray people as active participants of history but, instead, as people who were manipulated, had no voice, and were forced to obey. This image, while not entirely false, was a selective representation of a rather heterogeneous population, many of whom were, in fact, strong-minded ultranationalists (or their enthusiastic supporters) at the grassroots level.

Ienaga's High School History Textbook and the Re-militarization of Japan

After the introduction of textbook screening, the Sanseido publishing house asked Ienaga to author a high school history textbook, and, since his *Shin Nihonshi* was already out of print, he agreed. Through the publisher, he submitted the revised manuscript to the MOE in 1952. Ienaga's text was rejected when one of the five examiners gave the manuscript extremely bad marks (in this period a text was evaluated by a team of five examiners); however, when he resubmitted it with no changes to a different team of examiners, it was approved. His textbook was eventually published in 1953.

In this process, Ienaga was disturbed by some of the reasons the MOE gave for the initial rejection of his text. For example, one of the faults was the description of fifth-century diplomatic relationships between Japan and China, in particular, the description of Japan's envoy bringing tribute to China. Such an account, the MOE stated, would cause students to suffer a sense of inferiority. The MOE also argued that too much space had been given to the Pacific War and that, since the students had experienced the war, the entire description should be dropped. Other perceived faults included the description of women's status during the ancient and early modern periods and the descriptions of poverty and peasant rebellions in the early nineteenth century.

Ienaga reported the MOE's criticisms of his textbook in his article published in *Asahi Shinbun*, a major newspaper in Japan.[66] Ienaga was concerned about the future of history education—and his fears were justified. The recovery of Japan's right-wing, including ultranationalists, was well underway in the early 1950s. With the victory of the Chinese revolution and the outbreak of the Korean War, the U.S. occupation policy elevated the importance of anti-communism above democratization in Japan. SCAP ordered a "red purge" (purge of communists) in 1950, with more than 10,000 people, including a significant number of teachers, being purged from public office and private employment.[67]

In 1951, SCAP also began to de-purge many of those who had been purged earlier because of their cooperation in carrying out Japan's war activities. After the San Francisco Peace Treaty became effective, the Japanese government repealed the laws to purge militarists and ultranationalists, and some of those purged in the earlier postwar years were then appointed or elected to important governmental posts. In the MOE, for example, one such person replaced a high official who had been in charge of primary and secondary education and the direction of postwar democratization of education.

Educational policy took an overtly conservative turn after the Ikeda-Robertson talks of October 1953. Ikeda Hayato was then the head of the Policy Research Committee of the Liberal Party (*Jiyuto*, hereafter LP), which was then in power.[68] Walter Robertson was the U.S. Assistant Secretary of State. At their meeting, the United States demanded the re-militarization of Japan. Both the LP and the U.S. government saw Japanese education as one of the major obstacles to Japan's re-militarization and agreed that the Japanese government would make sure that education and the media would propagate a spirit of patriotism and self-defense. In 1954, the

Self-Defense Force (*Jieitai*) was established. It was already a substantive military force consisting of an army, a navy, and an air force—and its constitutionality would become a consistent point of controversy in the following decades.

These conservatives began to attack peace education curricula, accusing the JTU of promoting a communist agenda. At the same time, the Yoshida administration succeeded in passing a series of new laws: the first, in 1953, to empower the Minister of Education with the authority to screen textbooks; another, in 1954, to limit the political activities of public school teachers; and a third, also in 1954, to ensure the political neutrality of compulsory education.[69]

In the general election of February 1955, followed by the collapse of the Yoshida administration, the revision of the 1947 constitution—especially, its renunciation of war—was at stake. Textbook policy also became a major issue, as Nakasone Yasuhiro of the Democratic Party (*Minshuto*, hereafter DP), formed in the fall 1954, advocated a more centralized system for publishing and adopting textbooks. The election results marked a clear political division. Out of 467 seats, the DPs won 185 and the LPs 112, compared to 156 for the Socialist Party (*Shakaito*, hereafter SP).[70] With one third of the Lower House seats, the SP held enough votes to block the initiation of any amendment to the 1947 constitution it considered undesirable. Thus the battle over the constitution was over (at least for this round), but the battle over the textbooks was not.

The Attack on Textbooks, the Formation of a Conservative Power Bloc, and the State's Efforts toward the Reversal of Postwar Education Reforms

The first postwar attack on textbooks took place when the Diet opened in June 1955, and it became a model for later attacks. The right wing (with members in the LP and the DP) launched an attack on education by inviting Ishii Kazutomo, a former official of the JTU, to the Diet to testify on the alleged bribery of local school officials in charge of textbook adoption.[71] The move served as the occasion for launching an attack on textbooks, since Ishii's main topic turned out to be "biased textbooks." He targeted the social studies textbooks, including history textbooks, accusing them of promoting a left-wing, anti-capitalist agenda. Ishii was soon working secretly with the DP on the publication of a series of brochures entitled *Ureubeki Kyokasho no Mondai* (The Deplorable Problems of Textbooks), which directly attacked textbook descriptions written by authors close to the JTU. According to the brochures, the first of which was published in August 1955, there were four types of "biased" description: one supporting the teachers' union and its political activities; one stressing the poverty of the Japanese workers and promoting their labor movement; one praising the U.S.S.R. and the People's Republic of China; and one teaching communist ideas.

Not every conservative politician supported the attack on textbooks. For example, Matsumura Kenzo, a respected conservative and then Minister of Education, was not in favor of the attack. After the first publication of the brochures, the JTU officially entered a protest with the DP against the brochures and asked Minister Matsumura to investigate the source (Ishii's authorship had not been disclosed). When the JTU officials met with Matsumura, he was apparently troubled by the attack, and explained that the attack had been launched without his knowledge. He also assured the JTU officials that even though the DP had designated some textbooks as "biased," the teachers' use of those textbooks would be no problem, since the MOE, having found no biases in the textbooks in its screening, had certified them.

Even if he was troubled, though, Matsumura did not call a halt to the attack on textbooks mounted by his party (DP). The attack was supported in part by some LP politicians, and a merger of DP and LP—the formation of a larger conservative power bloc—had been underway at the time, with Matsumura serving as one of the most effective power brokers. Oppositions such as the right and left factions of the SP had already succeeded in reunifying, so the demands by business and industry for the DP and LP to merge were stronger than ever. Finally, in November, the DP and the LP merged and formed the Liberal Democratic Party (*Jiyuminshuto*, hereafter LDP), which would remain in power without interruption until 1993.[72]

In 1956, the Hatoyama administration of the LDP submitted three bills intended to give the state more control over education. The first would halt the local election of school boards, allowing the MOE to appoint them. The second would establish a special council for educational reform (i.e., to change the Fundamental Law of Education), and the third would enforce stricter policies for screening and adopting textbooks. The protest against these proposed measures was immediate and strong, and it arose not only from intellectuals and educators, but also from the public—in what was to date the biggest protest in postwar education history. The administration brought a police force into the Diet,[73] and it succeeded in forcing the first measure through, although it could not save the second and third. It would have been very difficult for Ienaga to have won the ground-breaking Sugimoto Decision of 1970 (see Chapter 2) if the third bill, which concerned textbooks, had been passed.[74]

Meanwhile, by 1956 the MOE had already tightened criteria for screening textbooks and brought more conservatives into the textbook screening committee (*kentei shingikai*).[75] After the 1956 Diet, the LDP administration, rather than resubmitting the textbook bill, shifted its tactics to strengthen control over textbooks through "regulation" instead of legislation. In 1956, the MOE rejected eight social studies textbooks for their "bias," and required authors to make revisions that included eliminating negative references to Japanese wartime conduct.[76] The MOE also implicitly pressured some textbook companies to remove certain authors from their projects.[77]

Moreover, while increasing the number of textbook screening committee members to add more conservatives members, the MOE made the textbook examiners (*kyokasho chosakan*) full-time employees (this was approved by a Cabinet meeting), and hired, or transferred, several people who held the emperor-centered view of history into social studies textbook examiner positions.[78] In addition, in 1957 the MOE stopped sharing its documents and lists that explained the conditions for approval with authors. Instead, it began to limit its "comments" (*iken*) concerning revisions to oral form only. Apparently, MOE officials wanted to keep their words invisible.[79]

These changes in the textbook authorization system took place side-by-side with the course of reversing curriculum policy. In 1952, in amending the law (the Law of Establishment of the Ministry of Education) concerning the function and administration of the MOE, the state had modified one of its supplementary provisions and made the MOE the only authority for developing instructional guidelines.[80] In 1955, the MOE had removed the term "tentative plan" from the titles of the 1955 *High School Instruction Guidelines*, which signaled that these guidelines were now "requirements" rather than "suggested ideas" for instruction. In 1958, the MOE issued a ministerial ordinance in which it declared that it would regard its instruction guidelines as official pronouncements from then on, and that as such the guidelines would have legal force. In the same year, in an official bulltin, the MOE published a revised series of the *Instruction Guidelines*, in which it identified schools (rather than teachers) as being in charge of composing the daily curriculum and defined schools as administrative bodies rather than an educational ones where teachers work collectively.[81]

Finally, in 1963, a bill was passed making textbooks free to all students in grades 1-9 (i.e., compulsory education). This bill, however, further consolidated the process for adopting textbooks for those grades. In the new arrangement, county-level school boards (consisting of several local school districts), rather than local schools, were to select the textbooks. In effect, compulsory education teachers—who were mostly JTU members—lost control over the textbooks, and the monopolization of the textbook industry was set in motion.

In the late 1950s, the MOE rejected many textbooks, especially in its screening of the textbook manuscripts submitted in 1958 (33 percent of which were not approved). The examiners not only checked textbooks for accuracy, but also evaluated the level of patriotism of each text. The number of textbooks rejected in 1958 was the highest at any time excepting only the first year, when the screening system began, and more than a few publishers decided to discontinue some of their textbook series.[82] The textbook screening system became a de facto process of textbook censorship maintained by the imperialist and right-wing nationalist groups, and the 1960s saw them wield overwhelming influence over textbooks, especially history textbooks.

The Effects of the Reverse Course on Textbooks

The "reverse course" of education policies, especially with regard to textbooks, directly affected elementary and junior high school textbooks. In 1955, for example, 33 junior high school social studies textbook series were competing for the market, but by 1965 the number had been reduced to 14, and in 1969 to 8.[83] (The number of high school Japanese history textbooks remained more or less the same, in part because the free textbook policy was not applied to them.)[84] The discontinued books included some textbook series containing textbooks with descriptions of the Nanjing Massacre. Overall, state control over textbooks became easier and more complete, since the number of textbooks had become smaller than ever. The textbook production and adoption system had, in fact, become very much like that of the state-authored textbook system in place during World War II. In other words, the strategy of the MOE was to write and rewrite history by way of textbook screening, and it made the most of this strategy.

What kinds of language did the MOE employ to criticize the texts? The MOE openly questioned the legitimacy of "scientific" history, which was seen as the main characteristic of postwar history research and education. As mentioned above, following the attack on textbooks, the MOE created its own full-time textbook examiner positions, and it filled the social studies positions with people who held emperor-centered view of history. One such examiner commented on a history textbook he examined as follows:[85]

> [The book] is as a whole too scientific in its descriptions. This is especially true of its description of history since the Meiji period [beginning in 1868], which takes the lack [of the spirit] of independence too far, to the extent to which [I] sometimes took it for the textbook of a foreign country, and wondered whether it was a social studies textbook for Japanese junior high school students or for certain [foreign] countries.[86]

While the MOE's comments touched on the contents of different historical periods, one of the areas receiving the most intense scrutiny was descriptions of Japan's war(s) in the twentieth century, especially the last of those, which ended in Japan's defeat. For the MOE, "literature," not "science," seemed a model for history textbook writing. For example, in the 1955–1956 textbook screening, the MOE commented: "Do not write bad things about Japan in [describing] the Pacific War. Even though they are facts, represent them in romantic [language]."[87]

To be sure, what the MOE wished to accomplish by attacking "history as science" was a revision of the texts toward emperor-centerd nationalist, views of history. Other comments given in these years included:[88]

It is not good only to see Japan's past war(s) as imperialist war(s). It is inadequate to say that Japan ruled China and made it miserable.

"The Pacific War" is not a historical term.[89] Call it the "Great East Asian War."

[The textbook examined here] says, Our country gave various Asian nations immeasurable suffering and damage, especially through the Pacific War. ... Eliminate this description, since a view even exists that [Japan] presented the chance of independence for various Asian nations [from their Western colonizers] through the Pacific War.

[The textbook examined here], in its treatment of the [last] war, describes it as if Japan were unilaterally bad; it is not grounded in a background of world history such as the international situation of the time.[90]

After the MOE created full-time positions for its textbook examiners, the examiners continued to give these criticisms one-sidedly, and when meeting protests from publishers and authors, it merely continued to call their texts "biased," or "useless for cultivation of patriotic spirit."[91] Insofar as the MOE was not able to suggest a total abandonment of "history as science," and its comments in part needed to sound "scientific," there was—theoretically, at least—room for publishers and author(s) to fight back. However, such space, if there was any, seemed very limited in those years. The effects of the imperialist and (ultra)nationalist power upon actual textbook contents—especially in the area of World War II-related materials in history textbooks—were clear even in those textbooks that survived the years of conservative restoration.[92]

For example, *Atarashii Shakai* (New Social Studies), a junior high school social studies textbook series published by Tokyo Shoseki, was one of the two larger market-share series of those years.[93] The series survived the period, but not without major changes. Among them was the use of the term *shinryaku* (aggression, or invasion). The 1955 school year edition of *Atarashii Shakai* had included the following passages about the 1937 Japanese invasion of Northern China, in which the term was used three times:

Japan further attempted to move from Manchuria to take the aggression into northern China. The Chinese Nationalist Government ... joined hands with the Chinese Communist Party and countered Japan's aggression. In this strained situation, in July 1937, near Beijing, an encounter took place between the Japanese Forces and the Chinese Forces. Taking the opportunity, the [Japanese] military ... expanded its military activities. In this way, a large-scale aggression against China was put forward, and the Japanese Army occupied major cities in China.[94]

The 1962 edition of the same book did not use the term in describing the same event. Instead, it employed the term *shinshutsu* (to advance, or advancement). As this edition put it:

In China, the Nationalist Government, even after its establishment, continued a civil war with the Chinese Communist Party. However, since the Japanese Army was attempting to advance into northern China, Chiang Kai-shek, [the head] of the nationalist military, decided to end its conflict with the Communist Party and prepare for the Japanese advancement. In this way, the Japanese and Chinese Armies entered into intense confrontation with each other in northern China, and in July 1937, an encounter of the two armies took place in a suburb of Beijing. Taking the opportunity and not following the [Japanese] government's policy of not widening the front, the Japanese military rapidly expanded the battle line there.[95]

There were further changes from the 1955 to 1962 edition of *Atarashii Shakai*. For instance, the number of descriptions of atomic bomb damage was reduced. The 1955 edition included the following description of atomic bombing in its main text: "The atomic bombs were dropped, targeting Hiroshima and Nagasaki. The damages and misery caused by only one atomic bomb made people cover their eyes."[96] The reference included a footnote:

On August 6, 1945, an atomic bomb was dropped in Hiroshima, and the areas within a diameter of 4 kilometers from the hypocenter were immediately reduced to ruins. Hiroshima then had a population of 400,000, of which the lives of approximately half, over 200,000, were lost in a moment. Then, on the ninth, [another atomic bomb] was also dropped on Nagasaki, resulting in the death of over 100,000.[97]

The 1962 edition wrote of the same event in the main text, as follows: "[T]he United States on August 6 dropped an atomic bomb in Hiroshima. ... Then, on the ninth, another atomic bomb was dropped on Nagasaki."[98] No footnote was added to the text, but two photo illustrations were included. One was a newspaper report of the atomic bombing of Hiroshima, and the other showed the ruin of Hiroshima, and the caption read: "Hiroshima then had a population of 400,000, of which the lives of approximately half were lost in a moment."[99]

In contrast to the above examples, which were removed or reduced, there was a new line that appeared in the 1962 edition, concerning Emperor Hirohito's role in accepting the Potsdam Declaration.[100] The line read: "Finally, Japan decided to accept the Potsdam Declaration, and on the fifteenth, in a radio broadcast, the emperor informed the people that the war was over."[101] In the 1969 edition, the line was expanded to stress the emperor's leading role in the event: "Finally Japan decided, by the emperor's decisive judgment (saidan), to accept the Potsdam Declaration, and on August 15 it informed the people through the emperor's radio address."[102]

It should be noted here, that in spite of the reverse course of these changes, some evidence suggests that certain publishers and authors struggled against the MOE's revision orders. For example, one change in the description of the 1937 Japanese invasion of northern China replaced the term "aggression" with that of "advancement" (see above); however, the author (s) simultaneously introduced a change in illustration(s). The 1955 text included a photo of the *konichi* (anti-Japanese resistance) movement: the photo itself had no detailed captions but in the picture was a billboard reading "Let's Overthrow Japanese Imperialism" (in Chinese letters, which Japanese students could read).[103] The photo was not likely to have impressed the textbook examiners favorably.

In the 1962 edition, three illustrations replaced the photo. Interestingly, one of them was a reduced-sized (seemingly woodblock) print entitled *hainichi* (anti-Japanese) movement.[104] The title for the print did not have an explicit connotation of the struggle of a nation against aggressors; however, its caption (in small print) stated: "This is a print entitled 'Let's fight for the [Chinese] people,' made by a Chinese person around the time of the [1937] incident. As well as soldiers, the picture depicts old people and children."[105] The text was subtle, but suggested resistance on the part of Chinese people, including young and old, to fight against the Japanese invasion.

In fact, a few years later, the 1966 edition used the title *Konichi* Movement for the same illustration print, and stated in its caption: "This is a print made by a Chinese person around the time of the [1937] incident. The [Chinese] soldiers fighting [against Japan] are supported by the old people and children."[106] In a sense, the original term and messages (of the 1955 edition) were restored. In a similar vein, several descriptions of atomic bombing eliminated in the 1962 edition (see above) were restored in the 1966 edition.

The textbook authors and publishers did not seem to give up their struggle to maintain the integrity of their textbooks during these years. Nonetheless, the power of the MOE was tremendous, with its entire institutional arrangement developed around the goal of reversing the course of educational policy. The revisions of history in the textbooks were obvious and overwhelming.

The postwar reforms in Japan that took place at the very beginning of the occupation instituted new social frameworks, centered on terms such as "democracy" and "freedom." In particular, the reforms called the "democratization of Japanese education" opened up a space which made possible the initiation of struggles for the nation's alternative and oppositional narratives (and identities) coming from different social locations. However, these struggles were taking place in a largely unknown terrain. The last state-authored history textbooks, while attempting to develop new national narrative(s), left some of the important aspects of war responsibility untouched. These included, for example, the emperor's as well as the people's responsibility. It could be expected that there would be ambiguities regarding the question of national identity in the three state-authored textbooks, since a sense of who "we" are cannot be changed overnight.

Textbook production through the government textbook screening system, which allowed private publishing houses to write and publish textbooks, resulted in substantive developments in both the variety and quality of textbooks. The textbooks produced by the commercial publishers showed signs that the question of war responsibility, and thus of national identity as well, would be further explored, and that insights would be deepened in the future. However, in the later stages of the occupation of Japan, the United States changed its policy from an emphasis on the de-militarization and democratization of Japan, including education, to an emphasis on developing an anti-communist bloc, allowing the remilitarization of Japan. This enabled Japan's imperialists and right-wing nationalists to recover. Japan's conservative power bloc gained control of the state during the 1950s, and, although it fell just short of changing the 1947 constitution, succeeded in reversing many postwar educational reforms either by legislation or by regulation.

Through the years of conservative restoration in postwar Japan, many history textbooks that included references to the Nanjing Massacre were discontinued, and those that survived the textbook screening process showed the scars of their struggle to get through it (e.g., the number of descriptions of atomic bomb damage was reduced, and lines were added to stress "the emperor's judgment" in accepting the Potsdam Declaration). Because of the institutional arrangement developed in the post-occupation period, the MOE had the upper hand in the struggle. In other words, the late 1950s and 1960s saw the textbook production and adoption system becoming more and more like the state-authored textbook system that had been in place during World War II.

Yet, as we have seen, a few textbook descriptions indicate that individual textbook authors (and staff members of publishing houses) did not give in entirely. They were attempting to recover—however small and partial–some pieces of the territory they lost in those battles. That is to say, signs of their agency were still there, and, in fact, Ienaga Saburo was one of the textbook authors who were increasingly determined to fight back. In 1965, Ienaga filed his first textbook lawsuit to challenge the state through the courts, and his action was about to bring a new aspect to the struggle. The next chapter discusses and explores extensively Ienaga's journey to his court challenge, its features as legal and educational games of truth, its impact upon Japanese social movements, and the effects it brought to Japanese education.

2 The politics over education

Oppositional forces and Ienaga Saburo's first and second textbook lawsuits, 1950s–1970s

Men make their own history, but they do not make it just as they please in circumstances they choose for themselves; rather they make it in present circumstances, given and inherited. Tradition from all the dead generations weighs like a nightmare on the brain of the living. And just when they appear to be revolutionizing themselves and their circumstances, in creating something unprecedented, in just such epochs of revolutionary crisis, that is when they nervously summon up the spirits of the past, borrowing from them their names, marching orders, uniforms, in order to enact new scenes in world history, but in this time-honored guise and with this borrowed language.

Karl Marx, *The Eighteenth Brumaire of Louis Bonaparte*

Ienaga Saburo was one of a very few leading Japanese scholars of the 1960s who clearly recognized the dual aspects of the war experience of ordinary Japanese—that of having been both assailant and victim—and who unequivocally argued the need for the Japanese themselves, through their own judiciary, to pursue the issue of war crimes and address the matter of war responsibility.[1] We should not assume here, however, that his view came naturally, with Japan's defeat in World War II. Instead, we need to understand it historically, or examine it genealogically. As Foucault argues, consciousness—including, I would say, the feeling of guilt—is a form of knowledge and has its own history.

As discussed below, Ienaga wrote as early as 1953 about the need for the Japanese, or at least Japanese alternative and oppositional forces, to "dauntlessly confront" the conservative and right-wing nationalist forces succeeding, to an increasing degree, in reversing the direction of the postwar social and educational reforms. He saw their actions as inciting people to make the same mistake they made during the war—"down the road to ruin" (see below for the entire quote). His criticisms were acute. It should not, however, be too readily assumed that his critical consciousness naturally brought him to take his own legal action. Nor should it be assumed that this consciousness gave him clear ideas of what he (and others who shared the same concern) could do to fight against the conservative political bloc and the state it captured.

While the larger framework of oppositional politics provided a context, the development of Ienaga's idea(s), consciousness, and actions needs to be examined as having multiple origins through his involvement in various activities—intellectual, political, educational, or otherwise. How were oppositional social and political struggles taking place in the 1950s and 1960s, particularly in the field of education, and how did Ienaga reach his idea of challenging the state through its judicial system and decided to act upon the idea? In particular, how did Ienaga link all aspects of his life: academic work as a historian; his involvement in several court cases—some related to education and others to larger justice issues—as an expert witness and supporter; and his experience as a history textbook author?

The court battles Ienaga initiated developed into a complex game of truths with its own twists and turns. How did he and his lawyers develop the basic strategies and arguments over the course of court proceedings stretching from the late 1960s into the 1970s? In particular, when Ienaga filed the first lawsuit, he thought that he would fight it on his own as an individual, since not many moderates, not to mention leftists, of the time, including well-respected intellectuals, had given their all-out support to his plan; however, by the time he filed his second lawsuit, he won support from many people across the nation. It is important to examine the lawsuits themselves as a growing force in the sphere of cultural politics. As such, the lawsuits developed their own logic, strategy, and history.

It is also important to assess the significance of Ienaga's textbook lawsuits in terms of the oppositional politics of the period. Ienaga's court challenges disseminated and practiced an oppositional national narrative, which speaks of the people's educational rights and freedoms, and by doing so, I would argue, constituted one of the most important dimensions of Japanese counter-hegemonic politics. In this regard, we should look at the arguments and strategic choices made by Ienaga and his lawyers; the court decisions concerning his cases during the 1970s, including the Sugimoto decision of 1970, the first decision ever made on his lawsuits, which declared the people's right to educational freedom; and Ienaga's achievements during the late 1960s and the 1970s in general, along with the impact and implications that Ienaga's victory in the Sugimoto decision held for Japanese educational policies as well as larger social movements in particular.

Ienaga Saburo and Research on the Constitution and the Judicial Power

Ienaga admits in a later publication, *Senso Sekinin* (War Responsibility), that it was not until several years after Japan's surrender that he came to recognize the need to address the question of war responsibility. In retrospect, he states, it was the reverse course of postwar Japanese politics, which began in the early 1950s, that first made him aware of the mistake he had made during the war. That mistake was his indifference, in having looked on and done nothing to stop the war, his primary commitment then being to his scholarly work.[2]

As early as 1953, Ienaga had determined to fight against the conservative and right-wing nationalist restoration. As he wrote:

> I have heard that a great scholar once said that those who pursue scholarship must keep in mind that they should endeavor to become even *fuju* (useless scholars). In Japan, where too many are *neiju* (scholars currying favor with the powerful), becoming fuju might even constitute one form of resistance. However, could it really be the [proper] attitude for those who pursue scholarship to remain indifferent, saying that they have their own specialized work to do, while witnessing their society tumbling down in ill-fated directions? During the period of the Pacific War, I escaped from becoming a neiju by becoming a fuju. Now, however, I feel remorse for my having been one of the war criminals in a passive sense, meaning that I was a *fusakuino* criminal, those who [are guilty of] having neglected the duties of preventing the war. I would not like to repeat this repentance twice, and this time I will not. We must, I think, dauntlessly confront the force[s] that urge our fellow [citizens] down the road to ruin.[3]

At this point, however, Ienaga did not seem to have even the slightest idea of the lawsuits he would eventually bring against the state. Rather, with his newly gained consciousness, he became interested in conducting theoretical and historical research in the area of the constitution, judicial power, and basic human rights. For example, Ienaga argued for "the freedom of critique of trial" in relation to the Matsukawa Incident Case, in which twenty union workers, including some Japan Communist Party (*Nihon Kyosanto*, herafter JCP) members, were falsely accused of wrecking a train in 1949.[4] The union workers were found guilty in the lower courts, and several were sentenced to death (in 1950 and 1953). The mass media reported the case very uncritically, based entirely on information supplied by the police and prosecution, since a presurrender policy that prohibited the critique of trials, even though it had been officially abolished, continued to affect the minds of people. In the fall of 1953 (after the second death sentence), however, two writers began to examine the court documents of the case closely, including the judgments, and published a series of articles critical of the adjudication. Then the Supreme Court Chief Justice commented on the reports, stating that trials should not be critiqued outside the court, which triggered a larger public debate over the issue. Ienaga joined the debate, arguing the notion of "the freedom of the critique of trial," and eventually won the debate.

Meanwhile, in the late 1950s, a large support group was formed for the workers. In 1963 all twenty workers were found not guilty.[5] Witnessing the development of the Matsukawa Incident Case (and other court cases he supported), Ienaga came to believe that the judicial system could serve as an avenue through which the people could win a struggle against the powerful, especially the power of the state. As he put it later:

> Around that time, I began little by little to have something like a firm belief that through a trial [we] could gain certain [good] results if [we] worked hard to some extent, even though [we] could never place [our] entire trust in the court, and even though [we] cannot delude ourselves about the court.[6]

At the same time, Ienaga became more and more interested in the study of the history of modern Japanese thought regarding state power and human rights. In 1956, when the Hatoyama administration created a committee for the examination of the 1946 Constitution (in order to change it), progressive scholars such as O'uchi Hyoe, Nambara Shigeru, and Wagatsuma Sakae formed a group called the Constitution Issue Study Group (*Kenpo Mondai Kenkyu-kai*), and Ienaga joined the group. In the early 1960s, Ienaga was no longer a historian of ancient Japanese culture. In 1960, he published *Ueki Emori Kenkyu* (A Study of Ueki Emori), a study of the ideas of Ueki Emori (1857–1892), who was a leader of the democracy movement in the Meiji period. Ienaga pointed out that Ueki regarded human rights as the highest value, which even the state could not violate, and argued that this value was the central theme in Ueki's thought.

In subsequent years, Ienaga also published two volumes of his study of the ideas of Minobe Tatsukichi (1873–1948), a constitutional legal scholar whose idea was suppressed during the war. Ienaga argued that Minobe was significant in the history of Japanese constitutional thought, in that he pointed out limitations to the state's power imposed by international laws, internal laws, specific national customs, and general human knowledge(s). Ienaga gave high marks to Minobe's thought, because Minobe actively argued against the state's improper use of its power. Through these studies, Ienaga learned (and constructed) the languages and vocabularies of Japanese critical thought, especially those that were necessary for struggles against state power.

Ienaga and the "Education Trials"

It was also Ienaga's choice to be involved as an expert witness in several "education trials" (*kyoiku saiban*) that took place in the early 1960s, and these prepared him more directly for his own court challenges. During the late 1950s and 1960s, while the state succeeded in gaining control over schools and textbooks, opposition from various segments of society intensified. Public school teachers, particularly, resisted the state's reverse-course policy. Some of the teachers leading the resistance were arrested and prosecuted, while others were submitted to disciplinary actions. The upshot was a number of court cases, called "education trials."

The most famous education trials were the *kinpyo* trials. *Kinpyo* was the teachers' accountability evaluation system, introduced by prefectural school boards in the late 1950s. Ehime Prefecture in 1957 became the first prefecture to decide to introduce an evaluation of accountability as a part of its plan to overcome its financial difficulties. Other prefectural school boards soon followed, with strong support from the Ministry of Education (MOE).[7] The introduction of the accountability evaluation was opposed by teachers nationwide. The JTU and other unions supported the teachers' opposition,[8] and teachers took "leave"—as a substitute for going on strike. Some of the teachers were arrested and prosecuted on the grounds that their action constituted going on strike, which the law did not allow civil servants, including public school teachers, to do. Other teachers met with disciplinary measures. In the nation as a whole, more than 200 teachers were arrested, and more than 2,500 were subjected to disciplinary action.[9]

Many progressive lawyers committed themselves to defending those teachers arrested and punished, and many intellectuals were involved in the trials as expert witnesses. In particular, the Tokyo Metropolitan Teachers Union case became the locus of the earliest and largest of the kinpyo trials,[10] and the court admitted a large number of expert witnesses, including Ienaga Saburo. In the court(s), the main arguments focused on Japanese educational policies before and after World War II. The trials took on the appearance of passing judgment on the state's educational policies (rather than on those arrested and disciplined), and in many cases the teachers (the accused) won.

Other education trials were called *dentatsu-koshukai* trials. In 1958, in an attempt to promote its nationalist and capitalist agenda, the MOE added a new subject, called moral education (*dotoku*), to its *Instruction Guidelines.* Under the authority of its pronouncement defining the *Instruction Guidelines* as having legal binding force, the MOE ordered teachers nationwide to attend in-service training concerning the content and methods of moral education. A large number of teachers nationwide opposed the implementation of the moral education in-service trainings (*dotoku koshukai* and *dentatsu koshukai*). Their resistance resulted in a number of arrests and disciplinary punishments, and thus in many criminal cases and administrative suits.

As a series of the educational trials began, concern and interest in the legal framework of education began to emerge. The year 1958 saw the formation of the Education Law Study Group, consisting of educational researchers, law scholars, and lawyers.[11] It was the first scholarly group to conduct research on the relationship between the state and education, and it began its inquiry by attempting to clarify the meaning of Article 10 of the Fundamental Education Law. The group hoped to establish a legal consensus—at least among the progressives—with respect to the interpretation of one particular part of the article, which stated that "Education shall not be subject to improper control." The group concluded that the intent of Article 10 was to guarantee the freedom and autonomy of teachers in their teaching, and to restrict the power of the state, including the MOE, over education. It held that the MOE's *Instruction Guidelines* were limited to setting only the most general standards (*taikoteki kijun*).

The efforts of the Education Law Study Group bore some fruit in still another series of education trials, called *gakute* trials, which were fought in the early and middle 1960s. In 1961, the MOE decided to implement a nationwide achievement test (*gakute*) of all eighth- and ninth-graders. The purpose of the test was to find "human resources" at early stages and give certain students an elite education (i.e., tracking of students). It also aimed at testing whether the teachers were teaching in accordance with the *Instruction Guidelines*. In other words, it attempted to control schools and classrooms through achievement testing.

The JTU strongly opposed the first testing in 1961, and in some prefectures the teachers refused to implement the test at all, resulting in 49 arrests and more than 3,200 disciplinary punishments. A number of court cases were fought simultaneously nationwide, and the main focus of the courtroom debate became the interpretation of Article 10 of the Fundamental Education Law. Along with other progressive scholars, Ienaga was also involved in the gakute trials as an expert witness. Several lower court decisions were made against the state, and, even when finding the teachers guilty of charges, many courts held that the state power to meddle in curriculum content should be limited. The MOE was apparently shaken by these court decisions, though it still insisted on the legitimacy of the testing.[12]

Meanwhile, the testing was causing considerable confusion in many classrooms. The mass media reported, for example, that in some prefectures, because the school boards asked teachers to raise student scores, the teachers had begun teaching to the test, cutting other materials. Moreover, in the worst cases, some teachers were instructing academically weaker students not to attend classes on the day of testing, and they were even encouraging students to cheat. *Ehime Shinbun,* a local newspaper, reported the concerns of a parent on July 1, 1962:

> My child is an eighth-grader. The other day, when the achievement test took place, my child came home and said "our teacher gave us the answer for the first question of the science test." I asked more and [my child] said "During testing, our teacher walked around the classroom, fluttering the paper on which the answer was written so that all of us could see it. The answer was in full view. The purpose of showing the answer to us all in such a way would be to raise the student score of the school." I thought, "It cannot be," but it seems that it was the case, since [I] asked two or three of [my child's] friends and they were telling [the same story]. . . . In spite of myself, I shivered. Does [the school] have to raise its score even if it means resorting to such mean tricks?[13]

The opposition and criticism of the public toward testing was growing year by year, and the MOE had to discontinue nationwide testing in 1966.

Ienaga's Decision to Bring his Court Challenges

When Ienaga submitted a revised edition of *Shin Nihonshi* (a high-school Japanese history textbook for which he had been a solo author) to the MOE in 1955, it was approved on condition that he make 216 changes. Ienaga made the changes, and the textbook was published in 1956.[14] However, he immediately had to re-revise the textbook when the MOE issued the new (1955/56) *Instruction Guidelines*. His newly revised text was rejected in 1957, then conditionally approved in 1958. It was eventually published in 1959 after still another revision. Ienaga revised the textbook again a few years later, but when he submitted it to the MOE in 1962, it was again rejected (in 1963). This time the MOE disclosed only twenty or so of its reasons. Ienaga, who had to guess at most of the MOE's criticisms, revised the textbook yet again (there were in fact 323 items altogether, something that became known only later, in the course of his court battle). That revision was approved in 1964 on condition that 293 items be changed. He altered the text accordingly, and it was approved and published.

By that time, Ienaga was convinced that textbook screening was a form of censorship that was both unconstitutional (e.g., a violation of free-dom of expression and scholarship) and contrary to the Fundamental Law of Education (i.e., a violation of the principle protecting education from improper control). His belief that the MOE would not change its prac-tice without a court battle became stronger than ever, and he privately began to look for lawyers who would commit themselves to his case. At the same time, he published the MOE's comments on his textbook manuscripts and his own arguments against the textbook screening.[15] While many progressives, including intellectuals and union activists, expressed sympathy with his concerns, many saw a lawsuit as a risky prospect. Some legal scholars pointed out that almost no legal theories had yet been developed in the area, not to mention that such a suit would be unprecedented. Others worried that Ienaga might lose, and pointed out that if he did, its impact would be damaging to the democratic social movement(s).[16]

Ienaga did not waver, however. His biggest concern at that point was, he recalled later, whether he could find lawyers and afford court costs.[17] Four lawyers (Morikawa Kinjyu, Arai Akira, Imanaga Hiroaki, and Oyama Hiroshi)—most of whom he had met through his involvement in several education trials—agreed to take his case, and on June 12, 1965, Ienaga filed his complaint, a compensatory damage claim suit, against the national government with the Tokyo District Court (in its third division of civil court). At this time, only the damage compensation suit was possible, because some matters Ienaga wished to take to the court would have been ruled out by statutory limit if he had brought other kinds of suits such as an administrative suit.[18] He expressed his determination in his public statement on that day. As he put it:

For over the [past] ten years, as an author of social studies Japanese history textbooks, I myself experienced many times how very illegal textbook screening is. I cannot help but think that in the screenings of the 1963 and 1964 [fiscal] years it reached an extreme stage, and that I would no longer be able to endure it. I dared to take my case to the court of law in order to restore justice. ... I cannot fall silent and overlook the present state of the screening, which tramples the Constitution and the Fundamental Law of Education underfoot and attempts to nip off the spirits of peace and democracy from the consciousness of people.[19]

Much to Ienaga's surprise, support for him was immediate, and came from a wide range of people. As many newspapers reported his filing of the suit, he began to receive personal letters and calls expressing support for him, sometimes with small contributions. (In fact, he received more than 200 letters in a short span of time.) Others wrote to the "voice of readers" sections of their newspapers, expressing not only their approval of Ienaga's action but also their will to support him. Because of these responses from their readers, some major newspapers such as *Mainichi Shinbun* and *Asahi Shinbun* ran articles and/or editorials reporting and discussing Ienaga's actions in more detail. In these articles, his actions were generally presented in a good light.[20] The unions that had already been opposing the state textbook screening, such as the JTU and the Publishing Workers' Union, were quick to announce their organizational support for Ienaga's actions. Ienaga had been prepared to fight alone, but it was apparent from the beginning that his lawsuit would become the center of a large social movement.

These responses were very encouraging for Ienaga's lawyers also, as they recognized the importance of organizing supporters for their client and fighting the lawsuits both inside and outside the court. In retrospect, Ienaga's case became more than a front of oppositional struggle—it became a major anchoring point of oppositional forces in the existing and forthcoming social, political, and educational struggles. Ienaga's case made it clear to everyone that education (and its content) is a contested arena between competing social forces and their visions of the nation's future. (In this sense, it is little wonder that, while his struggle at this early stage focused on issues of the citizen's educational rights, as time went by, Ienaga's challenge to the state became more and more a struggle over the narratives of the nation, in particular, over the interpretation of the history of the Asia-Pacific War. This aspect will be discussed in the following chapters.)

Ienaga's Legal Arguments

The first oral proceedings were held on July 21, 1965, with a small group of the public on hand.[21] Only Ienaga's lawyers presented a case. The state, the defendant, was expected to respond at that point, but was unable to do so because of lack of preparation. Neither had Ienaga's legal team resolved all the legal issues, technical, strategic, or otherwise, by the first proceeding.

Textbook screening as an institution had weak legal grounding.[22] Neither the 1947 Constitution nor the Fundamental Education Law referred specifically to textbook screening (the main focus of each being the guarantee of fundamental rights and freedom of people). The term "textbook screening" (*kyokasho kentei*) figures only marginally in the two pieces of legislation, the School Education Law and the Law of Establishment of the Ministry of Education, where it appears without defining specifics such as purpose, criteria, and procedure. Furthermore, the state had attempted to legislate a textbook bill and had failed, and that failure—an important victory for Japanese progressives—constituted the major legal weakness of textbook screening (see the previous chapter). The practice of screening was grounded almost entirely on ministerial ordinances and notifications.[23]

Ienaga's legal team basically asserted three major legal arguments. The first of these arguments was the "unconstitutional institution" (*seido iken*) argument, which held that textbook screening in and of itself, as an institution, is unconstitutional. The central assertion of the argument was that state textbook screening violated Article 21 of the 1947 Constitution (the guarantee of freedom of expression and prohibition of censorship). This argument also asserted that screening violated other articles of the 1947 Constitution, including Article 13 (the individual's right to life, liberty, and pursuit of happiness), Article 23 (academic freedom), and Article 26 (the people's right to receive equal education). In addition, it stated that screening violated Article 10 of the Fundamental Education Law (the prohibition of improper control of education).

The second argument put forward was the "unconstitutional application" (*tekiyo iken*) argument. It aimed at winning the point that, even if state textbook screening itself was held to be constitutional, the screening as applied to Ienaga's textbook was unconstitutional. The major question posed by this argument concerned the kind of power with which the state was entrusted in its screening of textbooks, and the extent to which it might exercise that power. This second argument, citing the same specific articles as those in the first argument, held that according to the 1947 Constitution and the Fundamental Education Law the state did not have the power to alter the actual content of textbooks, since such state action constituted the censorship of ideas. Therefore, the state's screening of Ienaga's textbook should be ruled unconstitutional.

The third argument put forward by Ienaga's lawyers was called the "improper use of the power of discretion" (*sairyoken ranyo*) argument. This argument was based on the idea that even if state textbook screening was constitutional, and even if the Minister of Education was entrusted with the "power of discretion" to request a revision of textbook content, the exercise of that power must not be arbitrary and groundless, and it should follow the spirit of the existing legislation on education (e.g., the Fundamental Education Law and the School Education Law) and ministerial ordinances and regulations. It also held that, in this regard, the MOE had overstepped its authority and violated its own regulations in the way it had conducted screening of Ienaga's textbook.[24]

The Consideration of Strategies

In the many months of preliminary hearings (which took place over a period of more than two years), Ienaga's legal team weighed the three arguments. The legal team felt that while the three arguments could be put forward simultaneously as legal arguments, they were nevertheless somewhat at odds. Namely, while the first and second arguments both argued in one way or another the unconstitutionality of state meddling in textbook content, the third accepted, at least to some extent, the constitutionality of the state's power to control textbook content. This third argument was more limited, or qualified, in its scope and argued that the state had wielded that power improperly in Ienaga's specific case.[25]

To make the first and second arguments central meant that the main debates would primarily concern the larger educational question regarding the relationships between the state, the people (including textbook authors), and the schools (and textbooks). In essence, the question of censorship depended on who had the right and the power to decide textbook (curriculum) content—the state or the people.[26] According to the theory upon which Ienaga's complaint was based, it was the people who held that right. This theory was at the time quite new, and if Ienaga and his legal team chose to argue this view, they would have to prove that the state violated people's rights when instituting the textbook screening system and/or violated Ienaga's right when requesting changes of his textbook content. A potential dilemma existed in this approach, however. Making this argument meant that Ienaga and his legal team would have to refrain from arguing (and proving) that the state promoted inadequate kinds of educational contents—since such an argument would result in another form of censorship, one that the court, or the judicial system, would conduct on the state's ideas. In other words, they would have to give up proving a point that many of the state comments on Ienaga's text were clearly flawed—a point which they believed to be the case.

To make the third argument central meant that the main debates would focus on the adequacy of the state's requests, or suggestions, in its screening of Ienaga's book. Ienaga's legal team saw this course as dubious, since, given the ambiguity of the MOE's screening regulations and *Instruction Guidelines*, it would be difficult to prove the "overstepping" of state authority. (In addition, they disliked the idea of the constitutionality of state power to interfere with textbook content.) The advantage of the approach, however, was that many of the state comments on Ienaga's text were apparently inadequate. Such an approach would result in each specific comment by the MOE becoming a point of struggle—in particular, a struggle over whose knowledge was valid, or true, the state's or Ienaga's (provided that school textbooks were to contain true knowledge). This question was (and is) central to the area of historical science; the problem was that it was unclear at that point how the question would fit into the courtroom battle and how scholarship on history in general could help Ienaga's case.

Meanwhile, outside the court, several important organizations supporting Ienaga formed quite rapidly. In August 1965, for example, approximately forty people, including legal scholars, educational researchers, historians, and teachers, gathered for a preparatory meeting to establish a nationwide support organization for Ienaga's lawsuit. In October, the National League for Support of the School Textbook Screening Suit (*Kyokasho Kentei Sosho o Shiensuru Zenkokurenrakukai*, hereafter NLSTS) was established, with approximately eighty initial members. From that time on, the NLSTS supported various phases of Ienaga's court challenges, including collecting signatures, holding study meetings, contacting union members, establishing local branches, attending hearings, publishing a periodical newsletter, and planning mass demonstrations. As of June 1966, the NLSTS had 1,256 individual memberships and 203 group memberships, and had collected 10,951 signatures.[27]

In addition, a number of historians and their associations expressed support for Ienaga, and the Association of People Involved in Historical Studies and Supporting the Textbook Screening Lawsuit (*Kyokasho Kentei Sosho o Shiensuru Rekishigaku Kankeisha-no-kai*, hereafter APIHS) was formed in Tokyo in September 1965. The members were mainly historians teaching at the college level with various perspectives, but included Ienaga's colleagues, e.g., philosophers and economists, at his university.[28] Even a number of Marxist historians who did not share Ienaga's empirical approach to the study of history joined the group. As of 1966, the group had 430 members. At this early stage in the legal process the organization did not make use of its members' specific training as academic historians, primarily because of the strategy employed by Ienaga and his legal team (as explained below). However, this organization later took on a crucial role in the process, working with Ienaga's legal team in matters specifically related to history, including writing some portion of court documents, and selecting and supporting expert witnesses (membership remained at approximately 550 until the resolution of Ienaga's third lawsuit in 1997).

The Choice of Strategy

Although Ienaga and his legal team stressed the third argument at the earliest stages of the legal process, as the preliminary hearings progressed they were more inclined to see that winning the case on the strength of the first argument—or, if not, the second—was desirable for Ienaga. In the fourteenth oral proceedings (the last preliminary hearing), they dropped the third argument almost entirely, and proposed to demonstrate that state screening of textbooks was unconstitutional and contrary to the Fundamental Education Law, while demanding financial compensation for the psychological duress caused by the screening process. They applied for submission of items of evidence. These included more than seventy documents and more than forty witnesses.[29] (Ienaga's second suit, filed in June 1967, followed this same basic legal strategy. The third argument became central only later, in Ienaga's third lawsuit. See Chapter 4.)

To prove the unconstitutionality of state textbook screening, or at least that of the screening process of his text, Ienaga and his legal team decided to demonstrate many instances of state censorship and its harmful effects—indeed, as many as possible. Prior to this, they had demanded that the MOE explain all the reasons for its rejection of Ienaga's manuscript. By the end of the preliminary hearings, the details of the textbook screening process and the exact reasons for the rejection of Ienaga's textbook manuscript had been emerging, despite the MOE's resistance. The standards for approval, the existence of two kinds of MOE pressure ("requests" and "suggestions"), the 1,000-point scale by which textbooks were graded (800 and above was considered passing), and the existence of an official file on each textbook all became public knowledge.

In particular, the state was forced to disclose the actual process by which it had censored Ienaga's textbook, and to explain the reasons for its rejection, along with the names of the examiners and the committee members who had vetoed the textbook. For example, the main reason for the 1963 rejection was "flaws in both accuracy and choice of contents"; the number of "inadequate" items was 323; and the mark was 784. In 1964, the text just scraped through the screening, with 73 requests and 217 suggestions.

While further demanding that the MOE submit its internal reports, memos, and documents concerning the screening of Ienaga's manuscript, Ienaga and his lawyers decided to dispute in the trial stage almost all of the points in terms of state censorship, but not in terms of accuracy of the historical knowledge the state attempted to promote.[30] Some of the points were related to the depiction of the Asia-Pacific War. For example, in the textbook, Ienaga had included a line "most [Japanese] citizens were not informed of the truth of the war, and so could only enthusiastically support the reckless war." The MOE had insisted that calling the war "reckless" was a value judgment, and that it was inappropriate to make such value judgments about contemporary events. The MOE had also declared that the manuscript contained too many illustrations of the "dark side" of the war, such as an air raid, a city left in ruins by the atomic bomb, and disabled veterans, and so had asked that some be removed.[31]

Other criticisms made by the MOE were more related to contemporary matters. For example, Ienaga's reference to the U.S. military bases in Japan was disputed. His text, which the MOE conditionally approved in 1964, had included the following phrase in a section explaining the San Francisco Peace Treaty: "[B]ased on the Japan–U.S. Security Treaty, the US military force has continued to station troops in Japan, and retained many bases in various places across the nation." The MOE had requested that Ienaga change the term "base" to "facility and area," because the latter terms were the exact ones used in the Security Treaty.[32]

Ienaga's Second Lawsuit

While advancing his arguments in court, Ienaga attempted to reinstate in the 1967 edition of *Shin Nihonshi* six of the phrases that he had altered for the previous edition. In response, the MOE held that his desired changes could not be regarded as "improvements" (which in its view was the purpose of revision). In response Ienaga filed a second lawsuit in June 1967, at the Tokyo District Court (this time, with the second division of its civil court). This second lawsuit was an administrative lawsuit requesting that the Minister of Education revoke the MOE's decision on the grounds that the rejection of Ienaga's revised version was unconstitutional and contrary to the Fundamental Law of Education. The chief objective of the second lawsuit was the same as the first, and the second suit had two major advantages: (1) because it was an administrative suit, the legal procedure was less complicated than that of the earlier "damage claim" suit, and (2) it involved only six specific points (a contingency, but one that turned out to be a better strategy in the court battle that followed).

One of the specific points in the second suit dealt with Japan's earliest history, particularly the characterization of myths contained in two eighth-century texts, *Kojiki* and *Nihon Shoki*. Ienaga had stated that "all [of the myths] were composed in order to justify the origin of its rule, after the imperial family had integrated Japan." The MOE had ordered him to eliminate these lines, and, as a result, the textbook represented the myths as if they were facts. Another contention concerned a description of the 1941 Japan–U.S.S.R. Neutrality Treaty. The MOE had ordered Ienaga to add the line "Japan entered the treaty as the U.S.S.R. proposed," and it suggested the elimination of a footnote that read:

> After the German army invaded the Soviet Union, Japan collected its army close to the border under the name of the "Kwantung Army special maneuvers," and was preparing to invade Siberia in the event that the situation became advantageous to Japan.

The MOE's intent seemed to be to create an impression that the Soviet Union's declaration of war against Japan in 1945 was the sole violation of the treaty.

The nature of the second suit as an administrative suit kept the debate focused and resulted in short preliminary hearings lasting for only five months (ending in February 1968). Ienaga and his legal team were able to utilize almost all the arguments they had developed for the first suit and their presentation of arguments was more to the point. As in the first suit, they made the MOE explain the reasons for its rejection of six points, and further demanded that it submit to the court its internal reports and documents related to the screening of Ienaga's text. The legal team also applied for the submission of items of evidence: namely, more than 170 documents, including testimonies given for Ienaga in the first suit, and more than twenty additional witnesses. Ienaga's legal team felt that having the second suit would increase their chances of winning. Moreover, the second division of the civil court at the Tokyo District Court had been known to be more progressive than others. The state, in contrast, perhaps saw weaknesses in its situation, and attempted to incorporate the second suit into the first and try them together, but failed. The trial hearings of the two suits thus progressed side by side in the late 1960s.

The Stages of the Two Trials

From the time the first suit was filed, Ienaga's textbook lawsuits were regarded as a successor to a series of education trials that took place in the 1950s and 1960s. Ienaga and his legal team made it clear that this was the case by making the question of censorship central, concerning the people's right to, and the state control over, education. The feature of the first and second suits as centered on education and schooling (rather than the issues of the historical facts) became even clearer in the development of the trial stage of the hearings.

The trial stage of the first suit began in November 1967, with testimony for Ienaga from two witnesses: Nambara Shigeru, a political scientist and ex-chancellor of the University of Tokyo who played an important role in the postwar educational reforms, and Munakata Seiya, a researcher in the area of educational policy and administration and professor at the University of Tokyo. Both of these were well-respected intellectuals of the time, and the court admitted twenty-seven more witnesses for Ienaga, mostly educational researchers and teachers as expert witnesses (there were only three historians called, as Ienaga's legal team strategically chose not to try the inaccuracy of the state's historical knowledge). From that stage on, the courtroom became what some called "a great symposium" on the issue of state power and education, with increasing numbers of the public, for the most part supporters of Ienaga, in the gallery. (The NLSTS and other Ienaga support groups called on their members to attend the trial hearings in order to prevent the right-wingers from harassing Ienaga and his witnesses.)[33]

The state began by arguing against the submission of a large number of witnesses, and only applied for seven witnesses, including Morito Tatsuo, the ex-Minister of Education under a short-lived socialist administration during the occupation. At the time Morito was the president of Nihon Ikueikai, a government subsidiary organization to manage a financial assistance program for economically poor students. In the middle of the trial hearings, however, the state changed its strategy, adding more than ten witnesses. The state also placed more emphasis than did Ienaga and his lawyers on proving that its comments on Ienaga's text were adequate, and that it had thus used its authority properly.

The trial stage was not simply "a great symposium." It also involved another important struggle concerning the state submission of MOE's internal documents to the court. Recall that, by the end of pretrial hearings, it had become known that the MOE had kept reports, memos, and documents detailing its objections to Ienaga's textbook. Ienaga and his legal team recognized that the disclosure of the documents would help Ienaga further validate his claims concerning the MOE's censorship, and requested the court to order the MOE to submit them. Ienaga's request for a court order to hand over the documents was granted in part (in 1968), but the state insisted on the need for confidentiality and refused to submit these documents, appealing the disclosure decision to the higher court (and eventually to the Supreme Court). At this point Ienaga's first suit began to appear stalled, though "the great symposium" continued.

Meanwhile, the second suit proceeded comparatively quickly. Eighteen witnesses gave testimonies for Ienaga, and this time more historians and history educators were included (primarily because Ienaga and his lawyers were able to use the testimonies given in the first suit as evidence, which concerned education more generally). The state, as it had in the first suit, argued against inviting a large number of witnesses; after seeing how well Ienaga's witnesses performed, however, especially in responding to the questions from the judges, the state attempted to prolong the trial by adding more witnesses. The state view was that the judges were too liberal, and so decided to prolong the trial, hoping that the judges would eventually be transferred as part of the regular redeployment process. The state's effort failed, however, since, while admitting the additional witnesses for the state (in total the state had fourteen witnesses), the judges decided to hold the hearings twice a month to speed up the process (they originally held a hearing only once a month).

Ienaga and his legal team were also careful not to prolong the hearings—in fact, in the second suit they gave up the struggle over the MOE's internal documents. As it had in the first lawsuit, Ienaga's legal team requested that the MOE submit its internal documents to the court. The court, admitting Ienaga's request in its entirety, ordered the MOE to submit the entire set of documents requested (in 1968). The state then appealed the decision to the Tokyo High Court, which sided with the state. Ienaga and his lawyers weighed the importance of the internal documents in the second suit (administrative)–which was, in their view, less than in the first (the damage claim suit)–and the importance of having the ruling of the current judges, and decided not to appeal the Tokyo High Court decision to the Supreme Court.

The climax of the second suit came in July 1969, when Ienaga himself took the witness stand. Ienaga's supporters had camped in front of the court for two nights in order to get tickets to the gallery to hear his testimony. Ienaga's support groups, the NLSTS in particular, mobilized them, in part because a newly formed right-wing nationalist group, called the Group to Defend Textbooks (*Kyokasho o Mamorukai*), had indicated a possible attempt to stop Ienaga by physically harming him. When the members of the Group to Defend Textbooks showed up, no more tickets were available; then, after they made a noisy protest, the court issued additional tickets, which delayed the opening time.

Taking the witness stand slightly later than scheduled, Ienaga began by testifying about his childhood school experience in the presurrender period, and went on to describe his adult experience, including writing school textbooks and being censored. In the end he expressed his reasons for bringing the suit. As he put it:

> Because of that reckless war, hundreds of fellow countrymen of my generation died miserable deaths in such places as the wild fields of the [Asian] continent, the bottom of the deep sea, or the depths of the jungle ... I am only a feeble citizen, but I dared to take the plunge on this lawsuit because I feel that I would like to atone for my sin ... of not having been able to oppose the war.[34]

When he finished, there was applause, which even the judges did not try to stop, and some of the audience members were weeping.[35]

The Sugimoto Decision of 1970

In 1970, the Tokyo District Court, with Chief Justice Sugimoto presiding, ruled in Ienaga's favor. Recognizing the people's educational rights and freedoms, the Sugimoto decision ruled that in the case of Ienaga's textbook, the state had clearly exceeded its authority, and that while government screening as an institution could not be considered unconstitutional (as long as it only corrected obvious mistakes), it could be unconstitutional when it ordered a change in educational content. In short, the Sugimoto decision took the unconstitutional application argument (i.e., Ienaga's second argument), and ruled to revoke the MOE's rejection of all six points in its 1968 screening of Ienaga's manuscript.[36]

In ruling on the case, the decision examined all legal arguments (and theories) put before the court and stated its opinion. The Sugimoto decision interpreted Article 26 of the 1947 Constitution as guaranteeing the people's—and in particular every child's—right to receive an education, and regarded that right as one of the basic human rights. It thus declared, "the primary responsibility for educating the child and guaranteeing his or her right to learn falls upon the people as a whole, and upon parents in particular." The decision defined that right to education and the responsibility for it as the "people's educational freedom."[37]

The decision (re)defined the role of the state as one which did not necessarily include the rights to interfere with educational content. It held instead that the state was to establish and maintain various conditions for the development of such education as guaranteed by the 1947 Constitution, and that decision-making concerning educational content (curriculum) was essentially incompatible with the way party politics and majority rule worked. In this regard, the Sugimoto decision adopted the theory developed by the Education Law Study Group arguing that the intent of Article 10 of the Fundamental Education Law was to limit the power of the MOE over educational content to allow it to set only the most general standards.[38]

The Sugimoto decision also framed teachers as professionals and teaching as a "scientific undertaking" involved with understanding children's physical and mental development and their psychological and social environment. In this sense, the decision viewed teachers as researchers, and held that scholarship and teaching are essentially inseparable. Thus teachers' educational freedom was in fact an academic freedom, so that the guarantee of academic freedom by Article 23 of the 1947 Constitution should be applied. The decision sharply criticized the state's control over the teachers' academic and educational freedom. As it stated:

> [I]t must be said that such activities of the state as the one-sided imposition on teachers of a duty to use textbooks, the limiting of their participation in the selection of textbooks, and the restriction of the teacher's freedom in the schools by giving the *Instruction Guidelines* legally binding force, are inappropriate.[39]

The Sugimoto decision was not clear-cut with regard to the freedom of textbook authors, however. It fell slightly short of declaring the state textbook screening unconstitutional as an institution. Instead, it basically held that the people's educational freedom as guaranteed by Article 26 of the constitution did not necessarily translate as freedom concerning textbook writing. In other words, it held that the freedom of expression in textbook writing and publishing could be restricted to a reasonable and necessary extent by the state's pursuit of the common good.[40]

The decision did find, however, that state textbook screening as practiced in Ienaga's case violated Ienaga's freedom of expression (the freedom stipulated by Article 21 of the Constitution). The decision recognized the people's right to know the truth, and it recognized teaching the truth as one of the essential aims of education. The decision regarded textbook authoring as one form of presenting academic views and truths and stated that "it is natural that the freedom of textbook writing and publishing of scholars must be guaranteed." It further stated that in writing textbooks, authors—not the state—should make their own judgments and consider the educational appropriateness of their texts to child's development.[41]

The Sugimoto decision significantly shocked the government (and the LDP). Tanaka Kakuei, then the chief secretary of the LDP (who became Prime Minister later in 1972) criticized the decision in the press conference, stating: "[I'd] like to say [you, the judges, are] damn fools." The Minister of Education immediately—in a move that was highly unusual—instructed the local school boards to disregard the decision. The Minister of Education appealed the Sugimoto decision to the Tokyo High Court. Therefore, Ienaga also appealed.

The Protracted Court Battles and the Entry of Historians as Specialists

In October 1970, at the appeals court (Tokyo High Court) in Ienaga's second lawsuit, the state submitted three "expert opinions" written by academic historians.[42] The state, having lost its case with the Sugimoto decision, attempted to recover from the discouraging situation by offering arguments grounded in historical research. As discussed above, academic historians formed the APIHS, one of Ienaga's support organizations, when Ienaga filed his first lawsuit; however in the late 1960s, they more or less limited themselves to disseminating information and calling for support. The state's new strategy changed the nature of their involvement. In countering the state's action, the APIHS distributed the copies of the state's expert opinions to historians attending meetings and conferences held by several major organizations for the study of history, e.g., *Rekishigaku Kenkyukai* (The [Japanese] Society for History Studies). Many historians, with varied special interests and training, were more than willing to hold extra meetings to examine, discuss, and critique the content of the state's expert opinions.[43] The study of history as a discipline appeared to become more interested in Ienaga's textbook lawsuits.

The first suit became also active (once again) in the early 1970s. After the Supreme Court dismissed the state's appeal against disclosing the MOE's internal documents (in 1971), and after considerable public pressure, the state submitted its file on the case—which was more than 100 pages long. The ruling was a significant victory for Ienaga. Previously the undemocratic nature of the textbook screening system had been known only through (informal) complaints made by textbook authors and publishers' staff, but now the MOE's own documents revealed an arbitrary process, rife with abuses of power.

The involvement of academic historians in Ienaga's first lawsuit was also strengthened by the disclosure of the MOE's documents, since the historians were again more than willing to examine the adequacy of the MOE's criticisms on Ienaga's text. When the court called the MOE's textbook examiners to testify for the state, several historians, prepared through the study meetings held by the APIHS and other academic organizations, joined and advised the legal team in court to cross-examine the witnesses. In 1973, when Ienaga's legal team submitted the documents (incidentally, the last documents to be submitted at this stage) to the district court to refute the MOE's reasons for rejection one by one, more than thirty historians were directly involved in authoring them, delivering "the fruits of current studies of history ... to the maximum extent."[44]

In May 1974, the first suit finally concluded its proceedings. The suit had lasted over nine years, with the chief justice on the case changing four times. A few months later the Tokyo District Court delivered the judgment (the Takatsu decision). Although the MOE's file actually substantiated Ienaga's argument and testimony, the court handed him only a partial victory. The court found some abuse of power in the requests made by the MOE on eleven specific items (out of the 293 that Ienaga had contested), but it affirmed the state's right to regulate the content of education, and declared state textbook screening constitutional. Ienaga appealed to the higher court, and the state also appealed, in order to revoke the eleven points it had lost.

At this point, Ienaga and his legal team began to realize that the first suit would run for a long period of time, in part because of their strategy of calling a large number of expert witnesses and disputing more than 200 points. While the strategy had certain merits, such as gaining support from a wider range of the concerned public as well as historians and disseminating progressive views on education, certain disadvantages also seemed inevitable, including a loss of focus and the changes of judges because of their rotation. Nonetheless, Ienaga's legal team did not reformulate, or elaborate, its basic strategy (primarily because it underestimated the power of conservative and right-wing forces within the judicial system).

Meanwhile, the situation of Ienaga's second lawsuit, at the Tokyo High Court, was not looking particularly good. The Chief Judge, Hosui, expressed his feeling against the Sugimoto decision explicitly before the hearing began, stating:

> We [the judges] would like to get the case out of the way as fast as possible. After the [Sugimoto] decision, there seem to be various theories emerging, but [we] don't accept those peculiar [theories]. [We] thus may not reach the peculiar decision like the decision handed down at the District Court. To put it extremely, [we] can write our decision without examining [further] evidence.[45]

The chief judge, while admitting additional witnesses for Ienaga and the state, continued to behave indifferently. He even fell asleep and snored loudly during the hearing. Ienaga's legal team challenged the judge, and, even though the legal team's challenge failed, Hosui resigned.

The new Chief Justice, Azegami, was not enthusiastic about the case either. Without completing the scheduled hearings, the judge asked both parties to come to an amicable settlement. His proposal was rejected by both parties. In 1975, with Chief Justice Azegami presiding, the court dismissed the state's appeal, while avoiding a direct judgment on the constitutionality of government screening. Although the decision was less clear-cut, Ienaga had won again. The Education Minister appealed the decision to the Supreme Court.

Every indication in the late 1970s suggested that Ienaga's court challenge would be a protracted one. In those years, while the basic legal strategy remained the same, the involvement of academic historians as specialists became more and more significant. After the Takatsu decision, for example, the APIHS sought a better way of disputing numerous points. It categorized all of the more than 200 points of disputes in terms of eight topics (e.g., "ordinary people's history" and "women's history"), and organized eight study groups, called Working Groups, to examine those eight topic areas closely. In 1979, when Ienaga's legal team submitted its sixth set of documents to the Tokyo High Court, the documents were written by historians of the Working Groups and totaled 765 pages. In other words, by the end of the 1970s, historians were directly involved in the legal processes, and this was a new aspect, one that had developed through the court battles and would become crucial in Ienega's court challenges of the 1980s.

Ienaga's Achievements Outside the Court

From the beginning, Ienaga's court challenge, attracting strong public interest, helped ordinary Japanese citizens become aware of their constitutional rights and freedom of education. Although the 1947 Constitution defined the sovereignty of the people and their right to education, in the commonsensical view of the 1960s, schooling was still seen as something that the state provided, and thus as something only the state had the right to supervise and control. In other words, the presurrender view that people cannot criticize schooling granted by the (successive) emperors remained dominant.

Ienaga's lawsuits informed ordinary citizens of new theories concerning schooling that argued for empowerment of people with the authority for educational decision-making. Soon after Ienaga's initiation of lawsuits, numerous grassroots citizen groups were formed to examine school textbooks and to study education policies, something that was unprecedented. The NLSTS, Ienaga's main support organization, encouraged local citizens to form their own groups and establish regional branches. As the previously hidden state textbook screening processes were made public through the court hearings, many people became concerned with and disgusted by this process.

Then, the Sugimoto decision of 1970 gave legitimacy to the new theories about education. As the NLSTS summarized: "This [Sugimoto] decision, which denied the state the right to control education and declared the educational freedom of people, turned the [people's] 'common sense' upside down, and as such it gave a refreshing shock to everyone in the nation."[46]

The membership of the NLSTS in 1969 was 6,299 (4,765 individual and 1,534 corporate members); by the end of 1971, it had climbed to 11,605 (9,178 individual and 2,427 corporate members); by 1973 to 18,772 (15,229 individual and 3,160 corporate members).[47] The members not only took part in letter-writing campaigns and fund raising, but also held study meetings to inform members as well as the general public about the significance of Ienaga's textbook lawsuits and the idea of people's educational rights. For example, after the Sugimoto decision was handed down, the *Kanagawa Shimin-no-kai* (Group of Kanagawa Citizens) decided to have regular monthly study meeting targeted at homemakers.[48]

In the mid-1970s, Ienaga's court challenges continued to make a difference outside the courts. Various groups of parents, teachers, publishers' staff, and researchers who had been struggling to establish alternative and oppositional narratives in textbooks were empowered through a new-found consciousness of their educational rights and freedom. As Yamamoto Aya, one of representatives of a women's organization, put it:

> [I] was greatly encouraged by the victory in the decision of [Ienaga's] second textbook lawsuit at the district court, which made it clear that the educational right resides with the people. At the moment when the Tanaka [Kakuei] administration brings up the spirit of the dead Imperial Rescript, and attempts to (re)militarize education, [I would like to] strengthen the movement based on that historical victory and gather the power of women caring about children.[49]

Especially encouraged in the 1970s appeared to be history textbook authors and publishers' staff, who in general wished to include the findings of the research on various phases of the Asia-Pacific War, especially with respect to Japan's war crimes and atrocities. There was a clear sign of the impact of the victories in Ienaga's second lawsuit on school textbooks, in particular, his winning of the Sugimoto decision of 1970, as the MOE, following the Sugimoto decision, relaxed its criteria for screening. As we shall see in more detail in the next chapter, the authors and the staff of publishing houses were swift to move to recover from the setbacks they had experienced during the period of the conservative restoration of the late 1950s and the 1960s, and to go beyond them. The timing seemed perfect, since the 1970s were also the years during which much new research on various phases of the Asia-Pacific War was surfacing.

While experiencing the state's textbook screening process of the 1950s and the early 1960s and feeling that his freedom of expression as a textbook author had been violated, Ienaga Saburo spent years exploring his options to fight back. In these years, he shifted his focus of research from the ancient Japanese cultural history to the area of modern Japanese thought concerning the constitution and the power of justice system. He was, however, also involved in many court cases as an expert witness which gave him some sense of the possibility of court challenge. In 1965, after changing nearly 300 items of

Shin Nihonshi for state approval, Ienaga concluded that a court battle would be the most effective way for him to fight.

Although Ienaga's lawsuits against the state textbook screening process surprised a great number of people, in large part, because such an idea, and such an action, was new, his activities in the 1950s and 1960s reflected a number of alternative and oppositional struggles that took place throughout Japanese society in the political, legal, and educational spheres. In this sense, Ienaga's ideas (and his court challenge) originated in the multiple social struggles to counter the conservative power bloc that had captured the state.

Of course, we cannot overlook the fact that in his heart of hearts, Ienaga deeply regretted having failed to oppose the war, and that he was determined not to make the same mistake again. But such a critical consciousness was also a historical product. Even given that firm consciousness, it had taken him more than a decade to develop his idea(s)—consulting the writings of past (modern) Japanese thinkers such as Ueki and Minobe, borrowing their language and vocabulary, and remaking them as tools for contemporary struggles—and to act upon them.

Having said this, it is true that, while Ienaga's textbook lawsuits took place at the intersection of many alternative and oppositional social, legal, and educational struggles of the time, many viewed them as successors to the education trials—a series of the court battles over the educational right and freedom of people, including teachers, to educate youth. Ienaga and his legal team made that connection clear by framing the issue as a question of censorship, orienting their argument in terms of the people's right to education, and to the limitation of the state control over schools and school textbooks. Moreover, because of the legal strategies taken by Ienaga and his legal team, the courtroom debates and testimonies in Ienaga's first and second suits were geared more towards the "education question" than, say, the "history question," which would become more central only later, in his third lawsuit.

Ienaga's lawsuits went beyond the previous education trials in at least two major ways: First, in these lawsuits the state was the defendant (his suits were civil procedures), whereas in previous education trials (which were in most cases criminal procedures), the state was the accuser. In other words, the tables were turned (though the nature of the trials, civil or criminal, was different). Second, in Ienaga's lawsuits, the main issue was the interpretation of the 1947 Constitution, and the suits themselves were centered on the practice of freedom and the rights guaranteed by that constitution, whereas the disputes of the previous education trials concerned mainly the interpretation of the Fundamental Education Law.

While still in its early stages, Ienaga's court battles already made significant differences in the cultural and educational politics of the 1970s, both inside and outside the court. Ienaga's lawsuits attracted strong public interest and succeeded in increasing general awareness of school textbook issues. The two suits, particularly the first, brought the state textbook screening system, which had been hidden from the public, into the open.

The battle over the submission of the MOE's official file on each textbook and Ienaga's (partial) victory in that battle was a milestone in the larger struggle over education, particularly with respect to school textbooks. The undemocratic nature of the textbook screening system had been criticized by both textbook authors and the staff of publishing houses. Up to this point, the MOE had been able to dismiss these criticisms as "rumors," but now the MOE's own documents confirmed its abuses of power.

The oppositional narrative of the nation, which spoke of the people as holders of educational rights and freedom, is what Ienaga insisted on, acted upon, and battled for in the court. The Sugimoto decision of 1970, which in part supported the narrative he brought, compelled the MOE to relax its criteria for screening. Various grassroots struggles for establishing alternative and oppositional narratives in textbooks became empowered through a new-found idea of people's educational rights and freedom. Textbook authors were willing and happy to take the opportunity to include a wider range of material concerning Japanese wartime atrocities. The middle and late 1970s saw increasingly greater inclusion of alternative and oppositional narratives of the Asia-Pacific War in history textbooks (see Chapter 3).

I am not suggesting here that we credit Ienaga with all the gains made in education, in particular school textbooks in the 1970s. I am merely positing that his success in disseminating and legitimizing the oppositional narrative through his court challenges seemed to open up a space for various kinds of counter-narratives of the war. In other words, while Ienaga's achievements at this early stage were impressive, their value might have been diminished without the struggles of socially subordinate groups attempting to give voice to their own knowledge, and without the struggles of other critical scholars, journalists, and educators to recognize and help circulate such voices from the margin. It follows that the latter component of the period, in particular, the voices of subordinate groups and the research—be it journalistic or academic—on the war needs to be examined carefully in its own light. This is the topic of the next chapter.

3 Counter-memories of the Asia-Pacific War

The history controversy and school textbooks in the 1970s

In the production of the nation as narration there is a split between the continuist, accumulative temporality of the pedagogical, and the repetitious, recursive strategy of the performative. It is through this process of splitting that the conceptual ambivalence of modern society becomes the site of *writing the nation*.

Counter-narratives of the nation that continually evoke and erase its totalizing boundaries—both actual and conceptual—disturb those ideological maneuvers through which "imagined communities" are given essentialist identities.

[T]he national narrative is the site of an ambivalent identification; a margin of the uncertainty of cultural meaning that may become the space for an agonistic minority position.

Homi K. Bhabha, "DissemiNation" (emphasis in the original)

While a single war in the sense of actual military conflict usually ceases at some point in history, the same war in the arena of representation and consciousness can continue forever. A "war" almost always defines the boundaries of nations, states, and forces—enemies or allies—in actual as well as in imaginary geography. The binary of "us" and "them" in terms of the nation-state is easily constructed in this kind of geography, and it is precisely for this reason that a "war" is often an essential theme and topic at the site of "writing the nation."[1]

Sometimes at the site of "writing the nation" we can observe a struggle even in such matters as naming a war, which suggests that the particular name a nation wishes to give to a war is—at least in part—indicative of their view of the war (as well as of themselves and their social relations). A case in point is the naming of the war that resulted in Japan's defeat in 1945. Japanese historians now often use the phrase *Ajia Taiheiyo Senso* (The Asia-Pacific War)—the phrase that appears in the title of this chapter. However, this phrase is relatively new and might not yet be commonplace. In many writings and conversations, especially among those who experienced it, it has been referred to simply as "the war." There seems to be some difficulty in reducing their war experiences to a single phrase—perhaps because there are too many meanings involved.

The name officially used during the late war years (and the one still used by right-wing nationalists) is *Daitoa Senso* (The Great East Asian War).[2]

This was replaced by the name *Taiheiyo Senso* (The Pacific War), which was coined and promoted by the United States and became popular among the people of Japan (see Chapter 1). The problem with the latter is that it does not really denote that Asia was the main place Japan invaded and where most of the battles were fought.[3] To overcome these short-comings, Japanese scholars forged the phrase *Jyugo-nen Senso* (The Fifteen-Year War), which explicitly considers the war to have started in 1931 with Japan's invasion of northern China, and to have ended with its defeat in 1945. The term was not easily accepted either by the status quo or by the general public.[4] Scholars sometimes used the phrase *Nicchu Senso* (The China-Japan War), but only for referring to the conflict in China. The recently coined *Ajia Taiheiyo Senso* more directly signifies "Asia" as Japan's main target of aggression and at the same time incorporates some sentiments and nuances involved in the term *Taiheiyo Senso*.[5] Of course, in postwar Japan, not only the name of the war but also the entire history, or representation, of the war has been at issue in the sphere of culture, including education and school textbooks. It is this topic that is discussed in the present chapter.

Some recent research in history suggests that the late 1960s and 1970s saw a change—though by no means a drastic change—in Japanese views on the war, in which more and more Japanese began to recognize the suffering Japan caused Asian people and countries during the war.[6] However, as discussed below, those years also saw a controversy over some events in the war (e.g., the Nanjing Massacre and the Okinawan "mass-suicides") emerge in public discourse. This chapter examines this new phase concerning Japanese cultural politics, when issues of Japan's war responsibility began to be raised again in public. This was the first time the Japanese themselves began to deal with the issues. The chapter focuses on the forces and actors in the controversy—both those bringing counter-memories of the subordinate groups and the right-wing nationalists' insistence on the "traditional" history—and the arguments and methods of argumentation employed.

How did the changes in international and national geo-politics in Asia—mainly in terms of the Vietnam War, the Japanese anti-war movement in the 1970s, and signs of peace—trigger journalistic and academic research on Japan's war atrocities during the Asia-Pacific War, and how did they influence the public consciousness? How did the right-wing nationalists begin to launch a counter-offensive, in particular with two major frontal attacks (i.e., the denial of the Nanjing Massacre, and the downplay of the murder of Okinawans committed by Japanese forces in the Battle of Okinawa)? The major strategy was making the topics controversial—how did it work?

History textbook descriptions concerning Japan's wartime conduct changed significantly after the Sugimoto decision of 1970, which handed Ienaga Saburo a total victory. As discussed below, Ienaga's textbook lawsuits and the oppositional cultural politics of the 1970s had a strong impact on the way the history of the Asia-Pacific War was written in school textbooks (e.g., more references to Japan's war crimes in Asia). Does this mean that no ambiguity existed in the (re)emerging oppositional and alternative narrative (s) of the nation? Do we find any uncertainty concerning war responsibility, including the involvement of Emperor Hirohito and ordinary Japanese citizens in the pursuit of the war?

Growing Interests in the 1970s in Research on Japan's Wartime Atrocities

In the late 1960s and early 1970s, an increasing number of people involved in the anti-U.S.–Japan Security Treaty and anti-Vietnam War movements came to recognize Japan's part in the U.S. war against Vietnam, especially in the intensive air war. (Most of the bombers flew from Okinawa.) In retrospect, this realization served as the beginning point for many Japanese in shifting their understandings of the past and current war(s). That is, viewing the events of current wars (e.g., the impact of U.S. air raids and other assaults upon the Vietnamese) through the lens of their own experiences in the last years and months of the Asia-Pacific War allowed them to recognize more clearly two basic aspects of war—that of the victim and of the aggressor.

The recognition did not bring immediate awareness regarding the role of ordinary Japanese as assailants in the war. Nevertheless, various grassroots oral history projects, often with some support from the municipal governments, were launched to record the accounts of ordinary Japanese concerning their war experiences (e.g., U.S. air raids of many cities, the atomic bombs dropped on Hiroshima and Nagasaki, and the Battle of Okinawa). As an outcome of these projects, many Japanese gradually came to feel the need to address a previously neglected aspect of the Japanese war experience, i.e., Japan as aggressor.[7]

Some changes in international relations in the 1970s also stimulated many Japanese to reexamine Japan's past. In particular, the (re)establishment of Japan's diplomatic relations with the People's Republic of China (which took place finally in 1972) gave many Japanese a strong incentive to revisit the question of Japan's war responsibility. In addition, Emperor Hirohito's visits to Europe (September to October, 1971) and to the United States (September to October, 1975)—despite the fact that he was officially welcomed by the host countries—were met in many places with resentment, and thus served to remind the Japanese that the issues surrounding the war were not yet fully resolved.

These events triggered scholarly and journalistic interests as well. For example, historian Inoue Kiyoshi conducted the first serious scholarly research on the role of the emperor in the pursuit of the war,[8] and, as discussed below, journalist Honda Katsuichi reported on Japan's war crimes in China.

The 1970s saw most Japanese appreciate, or at least acknowledge, significant developments in various areas of studies of the Asia-Pacific War, indicating some changes in commonly held Japanese view(s) on the war. Counteracting those trends were right-wing intellectuals who began to mount efforts at discrediting the research and journalistic findings. In particular they attempted to make two topics controversial: the Nanjing Massacre and what has been called the Okinawans' "mass suicide," which took place during the Battle of Okinawa.

The Beginning of Research on the Nanjing Massacre

The Nanjing Massacre had been completely concealed within Japan throughout the war period by strict control over the media and through the prohibition against discussing the subject that was placed on Japanese soldiers returning from China.[9] Most Japanese learned of the massacre only through the testimonies given at the Tokyo tribunal court. However, the impact of those testimonies on the public, particularly on ordinary Japanese, was limited, and did not lead to an investigation of further details. In part this was because many Japanese, after initially welcoming the tribunal, eventually came to see the tribunal as somewhat one-sided, which left them with mixed feelings. Above all, the priority for most ordinary Japanese in the late 1940s was to survive and rebuild their lives.

In the 1950s, the best-known sources of information on the massacre were the translations of Edgar Snow's *The Battle for Asia* and a few other publications.[10] Some lines of Snow's description of the "sordid story" of the Nanjing Massacre read as follows:

> According to an estimate given to me by members of the Nanking International Relief Committee—which was, incidentally, headed by a German business man, Mr. John H. D. Rabe, who wore Hitler's highest Nazi decoration—the Japanese murdered no less than 42,000 people in Nanking alone, a large percentage of them women and children. It is estimated that 300,000 civilians were murdered by the Japanese in their march between Shanghai and Nanking, a number roughly equal to the casualties suffered by the Chinese armed forces. Anything female between the ages of 10 and 70 was raped. Discards were often bayonetted by drunken soldiers. Frequently mothers had to watch their babies beheaded, and then submit to raping.[11]

Other sources available in the decade included *Gaikokujin no Mita Nihongun* (The Japanese Forces Witnessed by a Foreigner) and *Sanko* (Three Lightnings). The former was a translation of H. J. Timperley's book *What War Means: The Japanese Terror in China*, which was seen as somewhat unreliable at the time because the original English book and translators were both unknown, and because the Japanese translation was, itself, a translation from Chinese.[12] *Sanko* was a volume written based on Chinese material that consisted of the confessions of Japanese war criminals detained there. While readers found its contents shocking, the book included few descriptions of Japan's major war crimes. Even so, the publisher soon stopped printing it because of threats from the right-wing.[13]

The first scholarly work by Japanese historians on the subject appeared in 1967, when Hora Tomio took up the subject and included a chapter entitled "*Nankin Jiken*" (The Nanjing Incident) in his book.[14] It was the work of Honda Katsuichi, however, that captured the nation. Honda, a journalist in his late thirties working for *Asahi* newspaper, had already earned several awards for his documentary work. His work included a series on Canadian Eskimos living in the Arctic Circle, as well as reports from Vietnam on the lives of people in local villages being dragged into the war. In August 1971, Honda began a series of newspaper reports entitled "*Chugoku no Tabi*" (A Journey in China) on the Nanjing Massacre and other Japanese war atrocities. The reports were primarily based on interviews with survivors he had met in China in the summer of 1970. In this sense, Honda's work, with his critical perspective, brought Chinese voices to a Japanese audience.

According to Honda, his series on Japan's wartime atrocities in China was motivated by several factors, the first being timeliness. The series was published just before the establishment of Japan's diplomatic relations with People's Republic of China (the relationship began in 1972), and he thought a true friendship with China would be impossible unless the Japanese were to reflect on their past aggressions against China. He also realized that the mass media had not yet reported any of the concrete details of Japan's wartime atrocities, and that therefore the nation only knew them in the most general terms. As a result, he saw, Japanese were unable to understand why China was so wary of Japan's remilitarization. Finally, Honda was impressed by U.S. media coverage of the Vietnam War, especially on the atrocities committed by the United States forces, and he thought he should cover Japan's wartime wrongdoings in China in a similar manner.[15]

Honda's newspaper pieces instantaneously produced a great, nationwide sensation, and he received numerous "strong and serious responses of a kind he had never had before" from readers. The main theme of the responses was dismay, accompanied by statements from readers that they had never known that the Japanese forces had perpetrated such cruel acts. Approximately 95 percent of the responses were positive, expressing the view that Japan had made a huge mistake, and that the nation must admit it as fact. As a whole, more letters came from males than females, and the majority of letters came from the younger generation, including high-school students. (In the case of high school student letters, more letters came from females than males.) The negative responses were often anonymous, or gave false names and addresses. These included some threatening letters, which most typically expressed a view that reporting Japan's wartime wrongdoings was exposing the shame of its past, and was therefore undesirable.[16] With the overwhelming reader support he received, Honda was able to publish his reports as a book, *Chugoku no Tabi*, published in March 1972. The volume went to a seventh printing by the end of May.

The Right-wing Campaign to Deny the Nanjing Massacre: Making it Controversial

The great influence of Honda's book on the public apparently prompted right-wing intellectuals and writers to launch their own campaign. As early as 1972, they began to openly deny the Nanjing Massacre by disseminating a theory that characterized the Nanjing Massacre as an illusion. The center of the right-wing publications was *Shokun*, a journal of right-wing opinion that was founded in the summer of 1969 by Bungei Shunju in order to counter the counter-hegemonic movement's opposition to the renewal in 1970 of the U.S.–Japan Security Treaty. Bungei Shunju had been a publishing house during the war period, particularly active in supporting and helping instigate aggression against China (and Asia as a whole) by publishing the government propaganda newspapers and battle reports. It had escaped being questioned about its responsibility for the war, however, and by the late 1960s was again an active proponent of nationalist discourses.[17]

Most of the right-wing articles attempting to deny the Nanjing Massacre were published in *Shokun*. In January 1972, a writer, who called himself Izaya Bendasan (a Jewish name in Japanese) and who did not show himself in public, published a critique of Honda's work in *Shokun*, arguing that after such a long time Japan was no longer obligated to apologize to China. (Bendasan was already the author of a best-selling book entitled *Nihonjin to Yudayajin* [The Japanese and the Jews], in which he associated the uniqueness of the Japanese with that of the Jews, and argued—in a racist way—that both ethnic groups were disliked by others, but that the Japanese should not worry, since they would be successful as the Jews had been.)[18] While Bendasan was no specialist in areas such as cultural anthropology (in fact, he made many mistakes in his descriptions of Jewish culture),[19] his Jewish name gave legitimacy to his argument.

Pendasan's critique of Honda's work drew a good deal of attention from the public, in part because his arguments were provocative and in part because of he was a best selling writer of "mysterious" identity. In November 1972, his articles were published as a book, *Nihonkyo nitsuite* (On Japanism), translated by Yamamoto Hichihei, a bookstore owner. Eventually it became known that Yamamoto was in fact Bendasan. While he did not disclose the reason(s) for his use of a Jewish name, he admitted he was the author. Yamamoto continued to write pieces in *Shokun* denying the Nanjing Massacre, and Bungei Shunju published his books as two volumes entitled *Watashi no nakano Nihongun* (The Japanese Military within Myself).[20]

Another famous right-wing writer of the period was a journalist whose pen name was Suzuki Akira. (It is perhaps important to note the anonymity of this case as well as Bendasan's case.) In April 1972, in *Shokun*, he published an article entitled "The Illusion of the Nanjing Massacre," in which he demonstrated that the story of "two Japanese soldiers who competed to kill 100 enemies in Nanjing" was invented (or extremely exaggerated). The story was a well-known newspaper report that had been used to show the "strength" of Japanese soldiers during the wartime.[21] Suzuki, by showing the ways through which it had been invented, suggested—with some slippery arguments and emotionally charged styles—that other stories of the Nanjing Massacre could have been inventions, and that therefore the massacre itself could have been a fiction. Suzuki published a book with the same title in March 1973, which became a milestone piece for the denial of the Nanjing Massacre.[22]

Honda rebutted the right-wing writers by pointing out the manipulative nature of their arguments,[23] but it was the historian Hora who was most effective in discrediting Suzuki's work. As already mentioned, Hora had been investigating the Nanjing Massacre, and was just then publishing the results of his work, including his book *Nankin Jiken* (The Nanjing Incident) and two volumes compiling various historical sources on the subject.[24] In 1975, Hora himself wrote a book refuting Suzuki's arguments, while preparing more publications on the subject.[25]

Thus, in the late 1970s, the writers gathering under *Shokun* had a poor chance of winning the argument on a scholarly level, but they continued to hold to the theory of the Nanjing Massacre as an illusion. In a sense, their strategy was simply to make and keep the subject controversial. In fact, as discussed below, a similar kind of strategy—making and keeping the subject controversial—can be found in the right-wing nationalists' arguments in the debates concerning the "mass suicides" of Okinawan civilians in the Battle of Okinawa. The counter-memories and narratives of the battle, however, surfaced and were brought to light in somewhat different ways than those of the Nanjing Massacre, because of the different circumstances surrounding Okinawa in postwar Japan.[26]

The Search for the Meaning of the Battle of Okinawa in the 1950s

Okinawa was the only place—the first and last—in Japan proper where the Japanese wartime doctrine of *gyokusai* was put into practice upon the civilian population. The term translates literally as "to break [die] like gem stones," and it meant to fight to the death, with no surrender. In practice, it resulted in a high number Okinawan civilian casualties, as the Okinawans were caught in the fighting between the Japanese and U.S. forces. A significant number of Okinawans were also robbed, murdered, and raped by Japanese soldiers and officers. Further, the no-surrender gyokusai doctrine resulted in some Okinawans killing their own families, as well as fellow villagers, and in committing suicide. Even at the time of the battle, some of the ruling Japanese elites in Tokyo already knew of the Okinawan civilian suffering, but did nothing. Okinawa was a "sacrifice" made for the sake of gaining the time needed to allow Japanese forces to prepare for the "decisive battle" that was to defend Japan's main islands.[27]

After Japan's defeat in the Battle of Okinawa, all Okinawans spent at least the first several postwar months in camps. Most of them were able to return to their homes by March 1947, when the daytime ban on travel was lifted. For the rest of the 1940s, the Okinawans themselves remained largely silent about their experiences during the battle. Accounts of the battle published during the early postwar years were written by Japanese soldiers who had survived the war, and these described little about the lives and sufferings of the Okinawans during the battle.[28] It gradually became clear, however, that the postwar Okinawan politics would inevitably involve a struggle over the meaning of the Battle of Okinawa. In particular, at the end of 1940s, when faced with the Japanese government's intent to continue to allow U.S. military control over Okinawa (in exchange for its peace treaty with the Allied forces), Okinawans were appalled, and some began to examine their experiences in the battle.

Tetsu no Bofu (The Typhoon of Iron), the first volume written on the battle by Okinawans themselves, included many survivor accounts. It was edited and published by the Okinawa Times, a newspaper company.[29] On balance, the book aimed not so much at condemning Japanese war conduct as urging readers, primarily Okinawans, to remember "the past nightmarish war" so as not to repeat "the folly" again. One of the topics it covered was gyokusai— Okinawans' killing of each other in the battle—and it coined a new phrase, *shudan jiketsu* ("mass suicide"), to refer to the event. Despite the fact that the survivors were still calling it "gyokusai," the editors chose to use the new phrase, in part because the old term carried more imperialist and militarist connotations.[30] The new phrase was problematic in its own way, however, since it signified that the deaths of Okinawans were the results of their own free will.[31] Nevertheless, the new phrase became commonplace in the late 1950s, when the Japanese government, in its attempt to include Okinawan civilian casualties of the "mass suicide" in the category of the fallen soldiers, adopted it (in 1957) as an official name for the event.[32]

Tension regarding the meanings of the battle was developing throughout the 1950s. As the Japanese media began to represent the Okinawan civilian deaths as "lofty sacrifice," some bereaved Okinawan families accepted the interpretation, other Okinawan survivors disagreed (though modestly). Two compilations of notes taken by survivors on their war experiences were published early in the decade: *Okinawa no Higeki* (The Tragedy of Okinawa) in 1951 and *Okinawa Kenjitai* (The Okinawan Healthy Boys' Troop) in 1953. While, coincidentally, the editors of both books stressed that their work was an attempt to document the facts, both volumes delivered more than just facts. Whether intentional or not, explicit or not, an anti-war perspective was central to both texts.[33] In contrast, *Minnamino Iwao no Hateni* (The End of the Southern Steep Mountains), published at the end of the 1950s, was oriented more toward honoring (and so beautifying) the Okinawans' deaths. The book was a collection of notes from those who had not survived the battle, edited by two Okinawans who had not experienced the battle themselves (though one of them had lost his younger sisters in the battle).[34]

The Struggle over the Meaning of the Battle of Okinawa, 1960s–1970s

The 1960s saw an "Okinawa boom" in Japan because the possible reversion of Okinawa became an important political and diplomatic agenda. Among the narratives of the Battle of Okinawa in circulation were two that were becoming increasingly divergent: one defending the conduct of the Japanese force and so praising and glorifying the death and suffering of Okinawans, the other representing the atrocities committed by the Japanese military from critical perspectives, and naming the Japanese military as the party directly or indirectly responsible.

For example, *Okinawa Homen Rikugun Sakusen* (The Army Campaign in and around Okinawa), published in 1968 by the War History Office of the Japan's Defense Department (*Boeicho Boeikenkyujo Senshibu*), took the former position. An entry of the record of the Battle of Kerama Islands in the book read:

> The landing of the U.S. military in the Kerama Islands invited a tragedy of the mass suicide of the young and elderly in Zamami and Tokashiki villages. ... The basic reason for this mass suicide was that the people at that time were full of the spirit of a special [suicide] attack corps and they disdained to surrender to the enemy even though they were not combatants. [The islanders,] including even elementary school students and women, cooperated during the battle, became one with the Army, and together attempted to defend their fatherland. Those unable to make a contribution to the battle had no place of refuge, and in order to eliminate the burdensome encumbrance [they might cause] for the combatants, some took their own lives in a lofty spirit of self-sacrifice.[35]

At the end of the entry a reference to the names and ages of three commanders in the Kerama islands—Umezawa, 28 years old, Noda, 26, and Akamatsu, 25—appeared. The entry noted "sympathy" to these young officers. As it put it: "Sympathy to these young commanders who had gone there to do special [suicide] attacks. For them the ground battle with a large number of residents and with no preparation at all was too heavy a burden to carry."[36] While it is somewhat unclear whose sympathy the War History Office represented, the record did not express sympathy for the Okinawans being killed in the Battle. Nor did it refer to the responsibility of the leaders of the Japanese military as well as its ultimate leader, Emperor Hirohito, who sent these inexperienced young officers to fight against the U.S. landing operation.

It is not just the War History Office that took a view defending the conduct of the Japanese force—some Japanese popular writers did as well. As Okinawa attracted public interest, Tokyo-based novelists also took up "the Battle of Okinawa" as the main topic or motif of their work. Among these was Sono Ayako, who published three volumes in the early 1970s.[37] Sono, once a liberal writer, was becoming part of the status quo around that time, and the main themes in her novels dealt either with the "complicity" of the Okinawan victims in their own deaths (since they wished to be killed) or with the "mass suicide" survivors as "perpetrators" (since they killed family members and fellow villagers). While both themes had some value, especially given the genre, Sono undermined them by ultimately defending the Japanese Army's conduct during the Battle.

In particular, in her volume *Aru Shinwa no Haikei: Okinawa Tokashiki no Shudan Jiketsu* (The Background of a Certain Myth: The Mass Suicide of Tokashiki, Okinawa), Sono specifically dealt with the "mass suicide" that took place on Tokashiki Island, and attempted to disprove the commonly held view—"myth" in her term—that the event took place under the orders of the commander of the Japanese forces that occupied the island. Her approach suffered from a central flaw. In the name of "fairness" she represented the voices of surviving Japanese officers and soldiers without juxtaposing Okinawan voices critical of the conduct of Japanese force.[38] Some Okinawan writers, such as Ota, who coined the term "mass suicide," criticized Sono's approach, but she insisted on the legitimacy of her investigation.

Meanwhile, the second, critical view of the Battle of Okinawa began to circulate widely—put forth by critical scholars and educators—in Japan in the middle of the 1960s. Ienaga, for example, in his book *Taiheiyo Senso* (The Pacific War) described the battle in the Kerama Islands in quite a different way than the account given by the War History Office:

> Garrison commander Akamatsu Yoshitsugu of Tokashikijima [Tokashiki Island], Kerama archipelago, Okinawa, ordered local inhabitants to turn over all food supplies to the army and commit suicide before U.S. troops landed. The obedient islanders, 329 all together, killed each other at the Onna River with razors, hatchets, and sickles. U.S. forces occupied nearby Iejima and used some of the local people to take surrender appeals to Akamatsu's unit on Tokashikijima. Akamatsu's men killed the emissaries and many members of the island's self-defense unit for allegedly violating orders. On another Okinawan island, Zamami, unit commander Umezawa ordered the island's elderly and children to commit suicide in front of the memorial to local war dead from the

Sino and Russo-Japanese Wars. The remaining islanders were forbidden to pick up potatoes or vegetables. Thirty persons who violated the order were starved or shot.[39]

Ienaga was one of the earliest historians to represent the critical view on the "mass-suicides" of Okinawans in an academic piece on the history of the Asia-Pacific War. In fact, in writing the book, he recalls, he made extra efforts to incorporate new materials and knowledge(s) just coming out around the time in various publications. Because of the "Okinawa boom" new materials were increasing, and the area of the critical research on the subject just opened up.[40]

Importantly, interest in the Battle of Okinawa was growing in Okinawa. This was in part because many Okinawans felt works such as Sono's were far from an adequate representation of the facts. A research project funded by the Okinawa government was launched to publish two volumes of the records of Okinawans' personal accounts of their experiences of the battle. The initial planning of the project began around 1965, with the project team consisting of historians interested in "regional history" (Okinawan history in this case). The team conducted a critical review of the existing literature on the topic and decided to write the (oral) history from the perspective of the Okinawan civilians, who had suffered so much during the battle.[41] Actual research activity began in 1967, and the project results were published in the early 1970s as a part of a series entitled *Okinawa Prefectural History.*

While the (oral) history project was moving well, nothing was as significant in terms of its influence upon the project as the reversion of Okinawa to Japan in 1972, after twenty-seven years of U.S. occupation. The reversion—or, more precisely, the discontent it brought to Okinawans, especially teachers and intellectuals—became a driving force behind the project. Around the time of the reversion, the struggle over the meaning of the Battle of Okinawa then became even sharper as the Japanese government began to station Japan's Self-Defense Force in Okinawa. Despite the opposition of many Okinawans, the government enforced this move, saying that Okinawa should be equal to Japan. In fact, however, the Japanese government's arrogance and ignorance made many Okinawans recall the conduct of Japanese imperial forces in the Battle of Okinawa.

As the social and political struggle against the enforcement of the Self-Defense Force station began, the Okinawa Teachers' Union created the Committee for the Pursuit of War Crimes, and published *Korega Nihongun da* (This Was the Japanese Military).[42] This publication strongly denounced the acts of the Japanese military during the Battle of Okinawa as war crimes. It was, in fact, the first publication to make the point so explicitly and pointedly in postwar Okinawa. In short, a new narrative of the Battle of Okinawa began—as a new struggle against Japanese control over Okinawa. "The meaning of the past experience," a notable Okinawan critic put it, "can [only] be grasped through the present struggle," and as the struggle continued, the controversy over the Battle of Okinawa continued into the 1980s.[43]

"Okinawa" in Japanese Textbooks and Ienaga's Textbook Lawsuits

It should be noted that, by the time of Okinawa reversion, the Japanese government already had (indirect) control of an important area of education in Okinawa—the school textbooks. Since 1948, Okinawan teachers had successfully resisted the U.S. education policy in Okinawa education, preventing the use of Ryukyu (the native Okinawan language, linguistically very close to Japanese) as the language of instruction and the use of textbooks developed under supervision of the U.S. military government. In the 1950s, Japanese control over textbook content was not an issue, however, because the major Okinawan struggle of the 1950s was against the U.S. occupation, in which Okinawa's identification with Japan played a crucial part.

Okinawans gradually began to voice their opinions about the textbooks produced in Tokyo, however. In 1960, the Ryukyu government sent those involved in the production of social studies textbooks in Japan a letter requesting more inclusion of Okinawa-related contents. In particular, it asked them to note the fact that Okinawa was a part of Japan proper, even though it was currently under U.S. administrative control.[44] In the following years, Okinawan activists involved in the Okinawa reversion movement continued to express their desire to see more Japanese textbooks with references to Okinawa, especially about the problems caused by the U.S. occupation and military base.[45]

The fact that there were few references to Okinawa in Japanese textbooks was due in part to the Tokyo-centered production system. The publishing industry was (and still is) heavily concentrated in the Tokyo area. Written and edited by authors and publishers' staff living, for the most part, in the main Japanese islands (usually living in cities), and authorized by the Ministry of Education (MOE) in Tokyo, these textbooks tended to reflect the experiences, values, and concerns of mainland Japanese. Very few history textbooks referred to Okinawa in their modern and contemporary history sections.[46]

Another reason for this silence, however, was the Japanese government's active attempts to keep the younger generation on the mainland uninformed about the situation of Okinawa. The existence of U.S. military bases in Japan had already been an issue, giving rise to the largest political protest at the conclusion at the 1960 U.S.–Japan Security Treaty, so that representing the issue as still unsettled was a thing the Japanese government very much wished to avoid. Not surprisingly, one of the MOE's main approaches to the issue was to use its textbook screening processes to remove references to the existence and problems of U.S. military bases in Okinawa.

For example, a section on Okinawa in one junior-high school geography textbook rejected during the 1960s (rejected probably because of its overall critical approach to social issues) read:

The Okinawa Islands are part of Japanese territory; however, after being occupied by the United States during the World War II, the United States continued to control it to date, and a large military facility exists on the Okinawa Islands. Currently, it is governed by the Ryukyu government, under supervision of the United States, and it is treated as being outside Japan, to the extent ... that passports are required when traveling between Japan proper and Okinawa. However, many residents seriously hope for the return of Okinawa to Japan proper, and for unrestricted travel between them.[47]

In contrast, one geography textbook that won the MOE's approval around the same time explicitly stated the contributions of the United States to Okinawa's modernization, including the building of waterworks and power plants, as well as economic aid from the Unites States and Japan.[48]

Ienaga's filing of two textbook lawsuits against the Japanese state impressed Okinawans, who almost from the very beginning showed strong interest and support.[49] To be sure, no dispute in Ienaga's first lawsuit (or his second) was directly related to Okinawa, but some points of his dispute came close to addressing the concerns shared by many Okinawans. One such example was the dispute concerning Ienaga's reference to the U.S. military bases in Japan in general. His text, which the MOE conditionally approved in 1964, included the following phrase in a section explaining the San Francisco Peace Treaty: "[B]ased on the Japan–U.S. Security Treaty, the U.S. military force has continued to station troops in Japan, and retained many bases in various places across the nation." The Ministry requested that Ienaga change the language "base" (*kichi*) to "facility and area" (*shisetsu*) because, it argued, the latter terms were the ones used in the Security Treaty. (The MOE's argument was not exactly correct, as the 1952 Security Treaty between the United States and Japan, which Ienaga's text discussed, did not include the terms *facility* and *area*. The MOE's real motive was perhaps to avoid the former since it clearly signifies "military base" in Japanese; the latter is a more neutral term with multiple meanings.)[50]

Several Okinawans almost immediately became members of Ienaga's support organization, the National League for Support of the School Textbook Screening Suit (*Kyokasho Kentei Sosho wo Shiensuru Zenkokurenrakukai*, NLSTS, hereafter), and asked the NLSTS to invite the Okinawan Teachers Association into its organizational membership. In August 1966, the NLSTS sent a letter of invitation to Yara Chobyo, the chairperson of the Association. Okinawan teachers organized support groups in their schools and circulated information about Ienaga's lawsuit and its development. In 1967, a regional branch of Ienaga's support group was organized.[51] The NLSTS newsletter featured issues related to U.S. military bases and the remilitarization of Japan (which as a matter of course referred to the situation in Okinawa). The Sugimoto decision of 1970, which was a victory for Ienaga on the grounds of Japan's 1946 Constitution, was also impressive in the eyes of Okinawan alternative and oppositional forces inclined to square off against the Japanese government. The hope was that Japan's undemocratic policies, on education or otherwise, could be changed by popular movements.

As of June 1971, when Okinawa reversion was a foregone conclusion, the number of NLSTS member in the Okinawa prefecture was 769 (746 individuals, mostly consisting of teachers, and 23 organizations), making it the 5th largest member group.[52] Some Okinawans, increasingly aware of Japan's reactionary social and educational policies, saw themselves as caught between the United States and Japan, "a tiger and a wolf," and saw fighting Ienaga's struggle together with Japanese counter-hegemonic movements as a realistic way to overcome their predicament.[53] Ienaga and his supporters needed that kind of reinforcement, and soon after the reversion, the NLSTS sent its secretariat to Okinawa to meet the Okinawa union leaders and citizens' groups. Those meetings strengthened their solidarity.

In an essay that was run in the NLSTS's newspaper, Miyayoshi Chiyo, a homemaker and widow, expressed her support of Ienaga's textbook lawsuit as follows:

> [During the war] we were taught "to lay down our lives for the emperor," or "admirable Japanese are just those who die for the country." ... I was told that an admirable Japanese mother was one who encourages her son and tells him to die in the war and serve the country, when he does not die a glorious death in the battle and does not render distinguished services. I felt that way at that time. ... When I realized that such education had caused me to make a huge mistake, it was already after I lost everything and was deprived of my precious husband and child(ren). ... The state seems to be in the process of changing piece by piece, without letting [us] know, the textbooks in such a way ... that allows it to restore an education that was in place before and during the war. ... We have to support the textbook lawsuit and see that it wins.[54]

Many Okinawans were determined to reject the revival of Japan's emperor-centered and militarist education. The memory of the war, in particular the Battle of Okinawa, was clearly the point from which those Okinawans drew their political will. In 1973, when Ienaga himself visited Ishigaki Island, one of the Okinawan Islands, for the first time, the whole island was full of standing billboards with the phrase "Let's support Ienaga's Lawsuits."[55] In the early 1970s, Ienaga's textbook lawsuits came to be well incorporated into their agenda, and theirs into Ienaga's. It is no coincidence that in his third lawsuit filed in 1984, Ienaga chose to include the MOE's objection to his description of the Battle of Okinawa as one of his major contentions (see the chapters that follow).

For some critics, Ienaga may look unique in that he made a commitment to the issue of peace and justice education, and combined his specialties as historian, textbook author, and plaintiff in his court challenges to the state. It is perhaps true that he was very unique in bringing lawsuits against the state, but his court challenges need to be understood in relation to various counter-hegemonic struggles that took place in postwar Japan. As discussed above, there were many intellectuals who attempted to write and disseminate alternative and oppositional narratives of the nation during the period, and Ienaga was merely one of them. Also he was one of many textbook authors who attempted to represent the counter-narratives in school textbooks. Below I would like to examine the history textbooks of the 1970s, as their content drastically moved to a critical direction after 1970, the year Ienaga won a victory in his second lawsuit.

Textbook Reference to the Japanese Aggression against China and the Nanjing Massacre

As discussed above, the late 1960s and 1970s was the period during which the landscape of Japan's cultural politics significantly shifted to include references to Japanese wrongdoings during the war. In particular, the counter-memories and histories of the Asia-Pacific War came to be recognized and represented in the public to a greater extent than ever. It can be suggested that even the right-wing denial of Japanese war atrocities (e.g., the Nanjing Massacre and the Okinawan's "mass-suicides") was a response—perhaps with a feeling of crisis among nationalists—to the larger cultural (and so political) shift.

In terms of textbook descriptions concerning the war, however, it was after Ienaga's victory in his second lawsuit at the district court (the Sugimoto decision of 1970) that we see a change—and in fact, a sea change. In 1973, Ienaga's revised *Shin Nihonshi* passed the screening process, even though it contained additional detailed descriptions of Japan's invasion of China and of its colonial policy in Korea. Ienaga was not alone in taking an opportunity presented by the Sugimoto decision. Some textbooks that passed the screening in the early 1970s clearly showed an eagerness on the part of most of the textbook authors to take critical perspectives in assessing Japan's wartime conduct. The MOE had no choice but to relent from its hard-line approach to textbook screening policies.

In the 1972–1973 screening, for example, a high school Japanese history textbook containing a reference to the Nanjing Massacre was approved. The book referred to the Japanese occupation of Nanjing in its main text, and included a footnote, which read: "Because at that time a large-scale massacre of civilians took place, the consciousness of Chinese people to resist (Japan) escalated further."[56] Moreover, that same text now employed the term *Nicchu Senso* (the China-Japan War) as a title of the section discussing a series of Japanese military actions in China in 1937 and thereafter. The term was meant to signify that conflict as part of a full-scale war. In fact, the text referred to it as "a war without declaration." In the previous edition of the textbook, the language used had been *Nikka Jihen* (the China-Japan Incident), which had both under-represented the scale of Japan's military activities and helped the question of war responsibility to be overlooked.[57]

Other textbooks quickly began to change their content also. In the 1973–1974 screening, for example, two junior high (social studies) history textbooks that included descriptions of the Nanjing Massacre passed the screening: the 1975 editions of *Chugaku Shakai* (Junior High Social Studies) and of *Hyojun Chugaku Shakai* (Standard Junior High Social Studies).[58] In its main text, *Chugaku Shakai* used the phrase *Nicchu Senso* to characterize Japan's military activities in China in the 1930s. Where it referred to the Japanese occupation of Nanjing, it appended a footnote, which read:

> At the time [it occupied Nanjing], because there were those [Chinese] who attacked and shot [the Japanese Army] outside the battle lines, the Japanese Army killed 42,000 civilians, including women and children. There were numerous small-scale incidents similar to this.[59]

The number of victims and the scale of the massacre cited by the text were smaller than those given in today's standard descriptions, which was probably a reflection of insufficient research on the topic in the 1960s.[60] Nonetheless, the change clearly marked a (re)emergence of counter narrative(s) of the nation that spoke of Japan's war crimes, and that opposed the interpretation given to the war by the imperialist and (ultra)nationalist narratives.

By the late 1970s, some textbooks containing more details about the Nanjing Massacre appeared on the market, updating their content by research in the area. For example, the 1974 edition of *Atarashii Shakai*, a junior high history textbook published by the Tokyo Shoseki, contained a line stating "[The Japanese Army] captured Nanjing, and caused terrible damage to lives of Chinese people in various places,"[61] whereas the 1978 edition of *Atarashii Shakai* expanded the line: "[The Japanese Army] captured Nanjing, took the lives of numerous Chinese civilians throughout China, and caused enormous damage to their daily lives." Moreover, the line was footnoted as follows:

> Immediately after entering the city of Nanjing, the Japanese Army killed and wounded an enormous number of Chinese people, including women, children, and soldiers who were either no longer armed or wearing civilian clothes. For its actions in this incident, [Japan] met with criticism from various foreign countries, which denounced [the incident] as the Nanjing Massacre, but ordinary Japanese were not informed of the facts [of the event].[62]

By the early 1980s, almost all the school textbooks for Japanese history came to include some description of the massacre, and it should be noted that the inclusions were decided on in spite of the continuing efforts of the right-wing writers to deny that the Nanjing Massacre had ever taken place. (Incidentally, Ienaga's *Shin Nihonshi* first included the specific reference to the massacre in its 1978 edition.)[63]

Textbook Content Related to Other Wartime Issues

History textbooks in the 1970s began, in their respective ways, to cover other issues concerning Japanese wartime wrongdoings as well. For example, references to the forced laborers brought to Japan during World War II came to be included in many textbooks. The 1969 and 1972 editions of *Chugaku Shakai*—the texts of which were prepared at the end of the 1960s— included the line "Many Koreans were conscripted for labor [and sent] to [mainland] Japan" in a section entitled "The Lives of People During the War."[64] The 1975 edition of the same book expanded that line to read: "Approximately 700,000 Koreans were conscripted for labor," and added a note to further explain the event, reading: "[This was] the forced labor (*kyosei renko*). [In addition,] approximately 40,000 Chinese were also taken to Japan from the farms and streets, and were forced to work relentlessly."[65]

The 1978 edition of *Chugaku Shakai* represented the number of Korean forced laborers as "approximately 1,500,000," with a footnote presenting the number of Chinese force laborers as approximately 50,000.[66] In its 1981 edition, the same book gave a description of the forced labor in its main text, which referred to the number of forced laborers as being more than 700,000 (the number close to the earlier version) but gave fuller explanation of the event:

> To make up the shortage in the labor force [during the war], more than 700,000 Koreans were forced to come to Japan (mainland). Then they were made to work under strict supervision in places such as coal mines, other mines, and construction and civil engineering sites, while they endured hunger, fatigue, illness, and cold winter. Approximately 50,000 Chinese were forced to come to Japan from the farms and streets, and were made to work in a similar manner. Later, the military draft was [also] implemented in Korean and Taiwan.[67]

Other textbooks of the 1970s came to include references to the issue. For example, *Atarashii Shakai* began to refer to the event in the main text of its 1975 edition: "[The Japanese government] forcibly compelled numerous Koreans and Chinese to come [to Japan], and they were forced to engage in hard work under harsh conditions in places such as mines."[68] The *Hyojun Shakai* included a reference in the main text of its 1975 edition: "To make up the shortage in the labor force [during the war], [the Japanese government] took Koreans and Chinese to [Japan] and forced them to work in coal and other mines."[69] By the early 1980s, descriptions of Korean and Chinese forced laborers had become commonplace for those writing Japanese history of the period for school textbooks. At least all of the textbooks of the late 1970s examined for the present study included either reference to, or description of, the event.[70] (Interestingly, Ienaga's inclusion of the reference was in his *Shin Nihonshi* was in its 1977 edition, later than some textbooks.)

References and descriptions concerning the Battle of Okinawa also began to emerge in the textbooks of the 1970s. The reference to the murder of Okinawan residents by the Japanese forces was yet to come (see Chapter 4), but the 1975 edition of *Atarashii Shakai* came very close. On one page it featured a boxed article, entitled "War and People's Lives," that contained several specially written or illustrated materials aimed at having students imagine the war experience. One item included was an excerpt from *Okinawa Prefectural History*, in which an Okinawan woman spoke about her experience of being dragged into the battle:

> Because the [U.S.] shells fell [on us] very hard, too hard, ... [we] gathered things in a bag, took it, and headed to the South [to flee]. ... First, [we] moved into an empty house. ... Then two or three days later, [we] were attacked [by the U.S. forces] very hard [so we fled]. Finally, we found a natural trench just in time, and entered there with many others. Then four or five days later, our troops [i.e., the Japanese Army] came and ordered us to leave, saying that the soldiers would use the trenches, and, therefore that the refugees [should] move out. [This] caused chaos [among us].[71]

By the early 1980s, the wartime issues emerging and re-emerging in the textbooks included, but were not limited to: Japan's colonial policies (e.g., the educational and cultural assimilation policy in Korea); Japan's war crimes in China as well as in other parts of Asia, the anti-Japanese resistance that occurred in these places; the number of war victims in (major) Asian countries; and the sufferings of ordinary Japanese (in events such as Great Tokyo Air Raid and the atomic bombings).[72] Clearly, the new composition of textbook content in the 1970s represented not only a recovery by the critical textbook authors of lost territory of the 1960s (see Chapter 1), but also the steady development of alternative and oppositional perspectives, and new power alignments, in Japanese history writing of the Asia-Pacific War.

The Question of Emperor Hirohito's War Responsibility

In spite of these advances, however, other important wartime issues remained more or less untouched, or ambiguous. One, in particular, was the question of Emperor Hirohito's war responsibility. Of course, if authors had attempted to refer to this directly, their texts would probably not have passed the screening process, since legally the emperor had been found to bear no responsibility. The Japanese presurrender constitution exempted him from legal responsibility for any matters, the Tokyo war tribunal exempted him from prosecution, and the Japanese government accepted the outcome of the tribunal at the San Francisco Peace Treaty. In the late 1940s, some Japanese intellectuals argued that the fact that the emperor could not be tried did not mean he did not bear legal, political, and/or moral responsibility. In the course of history, these arguments were not developed; instead, the question of the emperor's war responsibility itself became a sort of taboo.[73]

However, since the emperor's involvement in the pursuit of war had begun to be studied in the 1970s, it may be asked whether textbook authors of the period might have been able to include at least some nuanced references to the matter. In fact, however, none of the history textbooks of the 1970s among those examined for the present study referred to the emperor's role in the conduct of the war. None of the events of the Japanese war period (i.e., 1931–1945) described in the textbooks included any reference to him as an active (and indeed powerful) participant—with only one exception. The sole reference to the emperor playing a role at all came in regard to Japan's defeat, and his role, as described in many textbooks, was represented as a kind of peacemaker, who decided to "accept the Potsdam Declaration" and informed the nation about it. (Note that "the acceptance of the Potsdam Declaration" has been a euphemism for Japan's surrender to the Allied powers, so that the texts also make somewhat ambiguous the relation between the emperor and Japan's defeat in the war.[74])

As discussed in Chapter 1, during the late 1960s the emperor's involvement in the decision-making that led to Japan's surrender came to be stressed as the "decisive judgment" of the emperor. At the beginning of the 1970s, the phrase was still common in many textbooks. For example, the 1972 edition of *Hyojun Chugaku Shakai* (the manuscript of which was prepared at the end of 1960s) included the phrase "decisive judgment" in describing the event:

> Although there was a movement among the military to continue the war, the [Japanese] government stopped this [movement] by seeking the decisive judgment of the emperor and decided to accept the Potsdam Declaration to surrender to the Allied powers, and, on August 15, the emperor, in a radio broadcast, announced this to the people.[75]

The passage was revised in the 1975 edition of the same book, however, in which the phrase was removed to read:

> Although there was a movement among the military to continue the war, the [Japanese] government decided to accept the Potsdam Declaration and surrender to the Allied powers. On August 15, the people learned of the end of the war in the emperor's radio broadcast.[76]

Notice that the final line in both passages, in its reference to the emperor's radio announcement of Japan's defeat to the nation, was also modified grammatically. Whereas in the 1972 edition, the subject of the sentence is "the emperor," in the 1975 edition it is "the people," suggesting that the author(s) struggled to find the (right) way to describe the event, which inevitably expresses the relations between the state, the emperor, and the people in the event. We should note that the struggle here was in a sense a new type, since it was no longer about inclusion or exclusion of the event, but about its meaning and how to express it. Interestingly, the struggle seems to have been one which the author(s) needed to work through within themselves, rather than one that took place with regard to state imposition.

Another textbook, no doubt struggling with the same problem, represented the event in still other grammatical forms. The 1972 edition of *Chugaku Shakai* represented the same event, in which "the Japanese government" is the subject of the sentence, as follows: "The Japanese government ... accepted the Potsdam Declaration and surrendered to the Allied powers, and the next day [August 15] informed the people of it through the emperor's [radio] broadcast."[77] The 1975 edition of the same textbook began with almost the same sentence, but changed the subject to "the people," rendered in passive voice: "The Japanese government ... accepted the Potsdam Declaration and surrendered, and the next day the people were informed of it through electrical transcription of the emperor's [radio] broadcast."[78]

Yet "Japan" was also employed as the subject of the sentence in other textbooks. For example, the 1975 edition of *Atarashii Shakai* read: "On August 14, Japan finally decided to accept the Potsdam Declaration, and on August 15, [Japan] informed the people of it through the emperor's radio broadcast."[79] In its previous editions, the book had used different grammatical constructions. In its 1962 edition, for example, it had stated: "[F]inally Japan decided to accept the Potsdam Declaration, and the emperor informed the people through his radio broadcast that the war was over."

The manner in which the event was to be expressed became a point of subtle struggle in the textbooks of the 1970s, and the unresolved character of the descriptions indicates the opening of a space in which the struggle concerning the question of war responsibility could be fought. No doubt, there are questions like "If he was able to stop the war in the end, why he had not done so at the beginning?" To represent the emperor's radio broadcast that took place at Japan's defeat would at least potentially have led textbook authors (and readers) to question the role played by Emperor Hirohito in the entire pursuit of the war. (In this connection, interestingly, no edition of Ienaga's *Shin Nihonshi*, written in the 1970s, referred to the event at all, which suggests that Ienega was deliberating the issue.) In any case, the reference to the emperor's radio broadcast became commonplace among the textbooks of 1980s.[80]

The Question of Ordinary People's War Responsibility

Another wartime issue about which the textbooks were ambivalent was the role played by the ordinary Japanese citizens in the war. To be sure, the war experience of ordinary Japanese not only differed greatly on an individual basis but also was complex and contradictory. Some Japanese were victims, some were assailants. Still, in most cases, the experience was a mixture of the two (e.g., the poor rural peasant male who was drafted into the military and sent to Asia was often the oppressed and the oppressor at once). Thus, defining the role of the ordinary Japanese is no simple task, especially when we consider addressing it in the limited space of history textbooks. This is a necessary task, however, if issues of Japan's war responsibility are to be sincerely and fully considered from different angles.

The history textbooks of the 1970s came to include more references to ordinary people and their lives during the war, especially in comparison to those written in the 1950s. Some textbooks attempted to include information explaining the people's involvement in the pursuit of the war. The 1975 edition of *Atarashii Shakai*, for example, included a reference to those people who supported the growing militarism in the 1930s: "The exercise of strict control over ideas that opposed militarism became more severe. ... [N]ot only the communists and socialists but also the liberals were subjected to oppression. [T]he [people] supporting the ways the military [led the country] increased in number, however, since after the Manchurian Incident of 1931 business was gaining with the prospering of the military industry."[81]

For the most part, however, the textbooks persistently portrayed people as passive participants in the course of history. For example, the description of preparations for war against the United States (and the Allied powers) during the late 1930s and early 1940s read as follows in the 1975 edition of *Atarashii Shakai:*

> In 1940, all the political parties disbanded. ... The labor unions also disbanded. ... It became impossible to oppose the war. Furthermore, on the basis of the government's announcements and the reports of controlled media such as newspaper and radio, the greater part of the people believed in the victory of the war and had no doubt about the continuation of the war.[82]

The same book presented almost the same image of ordinary people in its description of the last phase of the war, which began with the following passage:

> As the war intensified, the sufferings of the people grew. ... [T]he supply of everyday goods fell short, the prices of commodities rose, and people's lives became extremely difficult. Males were drafted one after another and taken into the military services, and [male] students went to the front before graduation.[83]

The description ended with the following passage:

> In this way, Japan lost almost all its power [to continue] to fight the war; however, most people were not able to know the real situation of

the war, and so [continued to] work [hard] in their respective positions, while enduring their difficult lives.[84]

The view of ordinary Japanese as being taken in, having no voice, and being forced to follow remained dominant in the textbooks. While the image is not entirely false (and may offer some truths), it has troublesome consequences. For one, it undermines the grounds for considering the possibility (and the nature) of ordinary people's responsibility for the war—if people are never represented as active participants in the event, they cannot be held responsible. For another, it misses representing one important connection of the people to the war—that the majority of the soldiers (and many officers) who committed many of the war crimes were ordinary citizens who had been drafted into service (though, as imperial subjects, they did not have the same rights as Japanese citizens have today). While representing war atrocities such as the Nanjing Massacre as something that "took place," or that "the Japanese military" committed, most textbooks fell short of explicating one of the critical points—that those atrocities were carried out by ordinary Japanese men. The representation of relations between the state (including its military force) and the people during the war was something that had yet to be worked out.

The 1970s were also years of new research on the various phases of the Asia-Pacific War from peace and justice perspectives, with a movement toward increasingly critical views that included the perspectives of marginalized groups in Japan and colonized and victimized peoples in other parts of Asia. No cases show the point more clearly than the research on the war in China, particularly on the Nanjing Massacre, and the Okinawan "mass-suicides." It is important to note that the voices of the victims played significant roles in both cases. While some academic research began to explicate the facts of the Japanese war atrocities in China, including the Nanjing Massacre, it was Honda's work which, by introducing the Chinese voices (with some photos of their faces), shook the entire nation. In the case of Okinawa, it was Okinawans themselves who raised objections to the dominant interpretation of "mass-suicides."

It is also important to note the roles played by specialized intellectuals such as historians with critical perspectives in the subsequent development of the struggle(s) over history. The forces struggling to recognize, or reconstruct, counter-memories and counter-narratives met right-wing nationalist offensives. While the nationalist forces attempted to deny the (historical) facts, or to make them controversial, specialized intellectuals in the struggle chose to refute the nationalist arguments one by one, through empirical studies of history. This was in a sense a move to make the struggle more explicitly into a cultural and political struggle in the name of truth, or "the game of truth," over the unresolved issues of war. While the link between social force, power, and truth in the struggle is clear here, we also begin to see two distinct forces—one that "respect[s] the strategy of argumentation and its rules," and the other that "simply want[s] to impose [its] power."[85] This distinction would sharpen in the subsequent developments of the struggle.

The examination of history textbooks shows that Ienaga's court challenges, when combined with the development of research on the Asia-Pacific War, brought significant changes—both quantitative and qualitative—to the descriptions of, or references to, Japan's wartime wrongdoings in the history textbooks written (and published) in the 1970s. While various citizen groups flourished in the years following the Sugimoto decision of 1970, gaining strength in the struggle for alternative and oppositional narratives in textbooks, those who were perhaps most immediately encouraged were textbook authors who wished to include some of the findings of the research on various phases of the Asia-Pacific War in their texts, especially with respect to Japan's war crimes and atrocities. An analysis of history textbooks written and/or published in the 1970s clearly shows that the textbook authors took sides, in that they preferred to include passages on Japan's wartime wrongdoings. The setbacks they had experienced during the period of the conservative restoration in the late 1950s and the 1960s were not only recovered but surpassed in the 1970s.

It is also clear, however, that textbooks remained somewhat silent or ambivalent about certain issues of war, notably questions regarding Emperor Hirohito's war responsibility as well as the war responsibility of the ordinary Japanese. The Tokyo war tribunal had basically avoided these two questions, and they remained more or less unexamined—having become "taboo"—in the early postwar years. The 1970s saw some serious attempts—though they were only the beginnings—both by journalists and academics, to document (and so reconstruct) wartime events involving the emperor and ordinary people. It is undeniable that both were (major) actors in the war, and it was the aim of this new effort to develop insights capable of addressing those questions. Of course, some critics wonder if the researchers, or the Japanese in general for that matter, will ever be able to overcome the uncertainty of the cultural meaning of the war, since the national narrative is perhaps always "the site of an ambivalent identification" (see the opening quote from Bhabha). But I would suggest that this does not preclude the possibility of settling some ambiguities, or reaching some consensus, even though doing so means to invite a new kind of uncertainty.

In summation, the Japanese cultural politics of the 1970s contained many new developments in the struggle over national narrative(s). The counter-hegemonic bloc gained considerable strength in the sphere of culture and education, and Ienaga was deeply involved in several important fronts of the struggle. At the same time, there were signs of uncertainty in the act of writing the nation even among the progressives, in particular among the textbook authors. Meanwhile, right-wing nationalist discourses, while hardly winning the academic debates, continued to lurk on the public side of the debate, mainly by way of the right-wing news media. Thus, the politics of truths and the struggle over the narratives of the nation would continue into the next decade and beyond, which will be discussed in the following chapters.

4 Ienaga Saburo's third lawsuit and strategic conjunctures

Changing intra- and inter-national relations and the history textbook controversy in the 1980s

In analyzing the third level or moment of the system of relations of force which exists in a given situation, one may usefully have recourse to the concept which in military science is called the "strategic conjuncture"—or rather, more precisely, the level of strategic preparation of the theater of struggle. One of the principal factors of this "strategic conjuncture" consists in the qualitative condition of the leading personnel, and of what may be called the "front-line" (and assault) forces. The level of strategic preparation can give the victory to forces which are "apparently" (i.e., quantitatively) inferior to those of the enemy.

Antonio Gramsci, *Selections from the Prison Notebooks*

The textbook controversy of the 1980s began with the so-called "second attack on textbooks." The attack was initiated in 1979 and continued into the early 1980s, and it was to some extent a reaction on the part of conservative forces to the advances of Japanese alternative and oppositional forces during the 1970s. At its forefront were right-wing members of the ruling Liberal Democratic Party (hereafter LDP). In the area of textbook screening, passages referring to the acts of the Japanese Forces during the Asia-Pacific War became points of contention between the generally progressive textbook authors on the one hand and, on the other, the Ministry of Education (hereafter MOE) and its conservative, for the most part imperialist and right-wing nationalist, textbook examiners.

One of the items the MOE with its supporting institutions attempted to erase entirely from textbooks was the representation of the Nanjing Massacre. When its attempt met with resistance on the part of textbook authors and publishers' staff members, the MOE attempted to represent the massacre as something that had occurred by chance during the "chaos." The MOE also persisted in its efforts to eliminate all mention of the murder of Okinawans committed by the Japanese Forces during the Battle of Okinawa. The MOE's attempts to revise history in more right-wing nationalist terms eventually caused Ienaga Saburo to file his third textbook lawsuit. This time, however, he and his legal team and support groups took time to consider strategic and historical conjunctures, and framed the suit more in terms of "history on trial."

What kinds of politics and social forces did the attack on textbooks in the early 1980s involve? How did the MOE conduct its textbook screening processes during the period? Two notable texts here were: Ienaga Saburo's *Shin Nihonshi*, and a new text, *Nihonshi*, which was in the process of being published by another publisher and in which one of the co-authors attempted to write about the murder of Okinawans by the Japanese Forces during the Battle of Okinawa. Did the MOE's textbook screening constitute de facto censorship of textbooks of the period, in its efforts to revise texts from right-wing perspectives?

Key topics in this chapter include: the national and international dimensions of the history textbook controversy that developed almost instantaneously when the media reported the results of the MOE's textbook screening in 1982, in particular, protests from other Asian countries as well as from Okinawans; the ways the Japanese government dealt with them; the ways textbook authors responded to the textbook controversy; Ienaga's reaction to the MOE in the textbook screening process of 1983–1984, which eventually led him to file his third textbook lawsuit; and the conscious choice Ienaga and his legal team made strategically—the decision to focus more on disputes concerning the "historical facts" than they had in the first and second lawsuits.

It is also important to examine Ienaga's struggle both inside and outside the court, including the revitalization of the activities of support groups brought by Ienaga's third suit. Among new developments were: the increasing involvement of specialist historians in Ienaga's court challenges; and the renewed public interest in textbook issues. I would suggest that Ienaga's third suit can be seen as a historical event that articulated various social movements that had taken place somewhat independently since 1945. In doing so it projected a clearer, more focused picture of what these efforts had in common—namely, the counter-hegemonic struggle for alternative and oppositional narratives of the nation's history.

The LDP's Right-wing Nationalist Direction: The Politics and the State at the Beginning of the 1980s

In the late 1970s, the Japanese government and the LDP attempted to regain control over education and to (re)introduce nationalist (patriotic) curricula. For example, when the *Instruction Guidelines* (for elementary and junior high schools) was revised in 1977, a higher official of the MOE inserted the modifier "national anthem," thereby designating the song "Kimigayo" as the national anthem. This occurred with the support of right-wing politicians in the LDP, but without an open discussion, and despite the fact that no legal definition of the Japanese national anthem existed. It also flew in the face of leftists, who disliked the song because it celebrates the eternity of the emperor's sovereignty.[1] In 1977, the MOE rejected five high school textbooks (one on ethics/civics, two on Japanese history, and two on world history), and at about the same time it changed its textbook screening regulations to require authors to follow the *Instruction Guidelines* more closely.

It should be noted here that the struggle for power among various factions within the LDP had intensified in those years. In the mid-1970s, Prime Minister Tanaka Kakuei, once extremely popular as a premier with a humble (*heimin*) origin, was criticized for his plutocracy, and he resigned his position after the LDP lost a number of seats in the election of the House of Councilors (Upper House) in 1974 (though he remained the LDP's most powerful king-maker).[2] Miki Takeo, a reformer of the LDP whose base was a small LDP faction, succeeded Tanaka. In 1976, it became known that Lockheed, the U.S. aircraft company, had bribed several Japanese government officials and powerful right-wing figures to pressure Japanese companies to buy its airplanes. Prime Minster Miki, willing to conduct a full investigation, met with strong LDP protests (Tanaka was one of those arrested), and he resigned after the LDP lost in the election of the Lower House in 1976.[3]

Fukuda Takeo, Tanaka's rival, became the Prime Minister, but in 1978 he lost the majority support of LDP members and was succeeded by Ohira Masayoshi, Tanaka's sworn friend. Ohira turned out to be a moderate on certain issues (e.g., remilitarization) and managed to overcome the oil shortage following the Iranian Revolution. However, in 1979 the LDP was not able to increase its seats in the general election.[4] The defeat rekindled the LDP's factional conflict, and eventually, in 1980, led to the passage of a no-confidence vote in the Diet against the Ohira administration (some LDP members were among those voting for no-confidence). Ohira dissolved the Diet, intending to win support in the election of both Houses on June 22, but died suddenly of myocardial infarction on June 12. Ironically, Ohira's death resulted in the LDP winning both houses by a wide margin. The LDP's factional strife was halted by a truce that was called after the election (though only for a short time).[5]

On the ideological plane, however, the struggle inside (and outside) the LDP continued uninterrupted through the early part of the 1980s. Conservative politicians, especially the LDP's younger hawks, began to mount a more vocal attack on textbooks after the 1980 election. These younger members were eager to strengthen their influence inside and outside of the LDP, and saw the attack on textbooks as something that would serve their purposes well. In the view of these young hawks, most of the changes in textbooks after the Sugimoto decision of 1970 had been biased, e.g., written from a communist perspective, so they attempted to enact stricter legislation for controlling textbook content. A particularly nasty campaign was launched in the LDP's weekly newspaper by Ishii Kazutomo, the same person who took part in the attack on textbooks in the 1950s. This time, in addition to social studies textbooks, Ishii attacked Japanese language textbooks on the grounds that many of the authors had supported the Japan Teachers

Union (hereafter, JTU), the Communist Party, or the democratic education movements.

One example of this was the criticism by the LDP and Ishii of a particular Russian folk tale, "A Big Turnip" (*Okina Kabu*), which in their view promoted a communist agenda. The story was about family members (a grandpa, grandma, granddaughter, dog, cat, and rat) joining hands to pull out a big turnip. It was originally recorded by a Russian folklorist Aleksandr N. Afanase'v (1826–1871), and it had (and has) long been popular reading material for first-grade elementary school students.[6] Ishii and the LDP falsely stated that the story was a *Soviet* folk tale and Afanase'v a *Soviet* folklorist. They also offered an interpretation of the story that perhaps no one had thought of—that it was about the workers, peasants, students, and intellectuals standing together to bring down capitalists. These and other absurd critiques were used in the attack, as they had been in the 1950s, but this time the attack was joined by right-wing intellectuals, economists, and members of big business.

Soon the Science and Technology Agency (*Kagakugijyutsu-cho*), troubled by the anti-nuclear movement, joined the attack by criticizing the junior high school civics textbooks. In 1980, claiming that the textbooks emphasized the negative aspects of atomic power plants, causing everyone to question their safety, the agency pressured the MOE to change the descriptions of atomic energy already in the textbooks. Those descriptions had in fact been approved for use after April 1981, so the MOE could not effect such a change immediately, as it would have been a violation of its own regulations to do so. But party politics intervened, as the Democratic Social Party (Minshato), an opposition party supported by small business owners, joined the attack.[7] In addition, special interest groups joined the attack, as various business groups also lobbied the MOE for changes in the depiction of their industries. Eventually, the MOE had the publishers change the descriptions in question by informally "implying" revisions.

These battles in the political sphere were highly public in nature, but they also took place "behind closed doors" (the term used by Ienaga to describe the history textbook screening that was occurring simultaneously, without attracting serious attention from the general public and mass media). The MOE attempted to revise history within the framework of textbook screening, by stretching the gray areas of the law, to make the most of its ability to request changes or suggest improvements. Ienaga's text, along with a number of others, was targeted in those attempts.

The 1980–1981 Screening of Ienaga's Shin Nihonshi and the Description of the Nanjing Massacre

As the MOE revised its *High School Instruction Guidelines* in August 1978, Ienaga began to revise his *Shin Nihonshi* and in 1980 he submitted the revised manuscript to the MOE. Only two high school Japanese history textbook manuscripts were submitted that year, so Ienaga was one of the first authors to experience the newly revived history revisionist efforts.[8] In January 1981, Ienaga and his publisher were notified that the book had been conditionally approved. When Ienaga, through the publisher, asked the MOE to present those conditions in writing, the request—not surprisingly—was denied.

On February 2, the publisher's staff and two of the book's co-authors went to the MOE for an oral account of the conditions (Ienaga did not attend because of illness). The meeting lasted approximately seven hours, and recommenced on the following day for approximately four more hours, this time with Ienaga in attendance. In the meetings, the MOE's textbook examiner(s) commented on approximately 420 items, and Ienaga, his associates, and the publisher's staff asked questions aimed at clarifying the MOE's positions while arguing in defense of the text. These exchanges were tape-recorded, with permission, and some were published in a booklet.[9]

Among other things, the examiner(s) took issue with the manuscript's representation of the Nanjing Massacre. In the main part of the text, for example, was a passage that read: "The Japanese Forces occupied the [Chinese] capital Nanjing, other main cities, and areas along the main railroad lines."[10] To this passage Ienaga had added a footnote describing the Nanjing Massacre that read: "Immediately after the occupation of Nanjing, the Japanese Forces killed numerous Chinese soldiers and civilians. [This came to be] called the Nanjing Atrocity."[11]

Both passages had passed the previous screening in 1977, but this time the examiner(s) would not approve it. In requesting the change in Ienaga's description of the Nanjing Massacre, the chief examiner offered a detailed explanation, beginning with a reference to his own research of the literature on the subject. As he put it:

> Checking on various writings ... I [now] doubt that [we] can limit the massacre to [having taken place] immediately after the occupation. ... [Doing so] may cause the misunderstanding that [the Japanese Forces] conducted a systematic killing by command. And, [about the term] *numerous* and so forth ... Well, of course, it depends on the meaning of [the term] *numerous*, but [in any case, the MOE] asks for your reconsideration of these matters. [12]

The examiner then continued at some length, citing literature that denied or minimized the extent of the Nanjing Massacre, such as *"Nanjing Daigyakusatsu" no Maboroshi* (The Illusion of the "Nanjing Massacre") and *Shanhai Jidai* (The Days in Shanghai).[13] Then he (implicitly) recommended an alternative phrasing to Ienaga's. As he put it:

> In any case, [I] cannot believe that [the Japanese Forces] conducted the massacre systematically as a military force. ... Er, well, phrases such as

"in the chaos during the Japanese Forces' occupation of Nanjing, numerous Chinese soldiers and civilians became victims" can be definitely stated.[14]

The examiner suggested that the phrase he recommended represented the fact. At the end of his long explanation, the examiner made it clear that his comment was intended as an order to Ienaga to change his description. Ienaga's associate brought up the name of Hora Tomio, whose work on the Nanjing Massacre documented the large scale of the Massacre and was at that time held by many historians to be the most reliable research on the subject. The examiner insisted that, although he had read Hora's book, he found that it gave no definite basis to conclude the time line and the nature of the Massacre (i.e., when it took place and whether it was done by army command).

In the subsequent months, Ienaga's manuscript passed through a complicated, time-consuming series of revisions. Every step required a negotiation with the MOE. First, while making a few changes to other passages, Ienaga wrote a letter refusing the modification orders on two specific items, one of which the MOE permitted. On March 9, Ienaga submitted, through his publisher, the revised manuscript and a letter in which he stated his refusal to carry out some of the changes suggested for "improvement." On March 23, 24, and 25, the publisher's staff went to the MOE to hear its decisions, which they were not permitted to tape-record.

Thereafter Ienaga revised the manuscript again and once again submitted it with a letter stating his refusal to meet some of the MOE's repeated requests. On April 20 and 21, further negotiations took place between the publisher's staff and the examiners, and, on April 27, between Ienaga (along with the staff) and the examiners. In May, after several days of negotiations, the MOE finally passed the manuscript, in which the description of the Nanjing Massacre read: "The Japanese forces, breaking through the strong resistance of the Chinese forces, occupied Nanjing in a rage and killed numerous Chinese soldiers and civilians. This is called the Nanjing Atrocity."[15] The publisher went to great lengths to see that sample copies were available for the textbook exhibits (usually scheduled for the beginning of July). Finally, on July 8, the sample copies were finished and authorized for display—just two days before the opening of the exhibits, which that year were held on a slightly later date than usual. Ienaga's described the 1981–1982 screening as "the longest process ever since 1957."[16]

The textbook screening of Ienaga's text did not receive a great deal of (mass) media attention, however, because the media was highly interested in the screening results of textbooks of "contemporary society." This was a completely new high-school subject instituted by the new instruction guidelines, and the MOE had been checking the texts "very carefully." In fact, the MOE had to delay the textbook display and give authors and publishers involved in producing contemporary society textbooks additional time for rewriting the manuscripts and preparing the sample copies. While this same delay helped Ienaga's textbook meet the date of the exhibition, the events taking place that year clearly suggested that the MOE had considerably stiffened its use of screening criteria, and that Ienaga's text might not have been the only text receiving a damaging critique from the MOE. In fact, there was another good example—*Nihonshi* (Japanese History)—a completely new high school Japanese history textbook that was being published by Jikkyo Shuppan.

The 1981–1982 Textbook Screening of *Nihonshi* and the Description of the Battle of Okinawa

The *Nihonshi* manuscript passed through the screening process on the heels of Ienaga's text. Preparation of the manuscript had begun in 1979, and in March 1981 it was submitted to the MOE. One of the co-authors, Eguchi Keiichi, was a specialist of modern/contemporary Japanese history (especially Japanese imperialism and the Asia-Pacific War). Eguchi was the first textbook author to attempt to include the murder of Okinawans by the Japanese forces. At the time he did not anticipate that his attempt would make newspaper headlines, and that his struggle would become a threshold issue for the textbook controversy of the 1980s.[17]

During the 1970s, history textbooks had begun to include words such as "Okinawa" and "the Battle of Okinawa" in their descriptions of the final stage of the Asia-Pacific War. For the most part, however, these had been references without details, and no textbook had mentioned the murder by Japanese forces of Okinawan civilians. When Eguchi was asked to serve as co-author for rewriting the textbook *Nihonshi*, Eguchi thought that new perspectives and knowledge(s) needed to be included in order for the book to be viable on the market (where it would compete with more than twenty others). His assignment was to cover the period from World War I to the present, and to his passage on the Battle of Okinawa he added this footnote:

> In the battle [of Okinawa] that continued into June [1945], approximately 100,000 combatants and 200,000 civilians were killed. Young teenage boys and girls, who were organized into troops such as the Tekketsu Kin'no troop and the Himeyuri troop, were [some of] the victims. Also, approximately 800 Okinawan residents were murdered at the hands of the Japanese forces for reasons such as being a hindrance to combat.[18]

The entire manuscript of *Nihonshi* was submitted to the MOE for screening in March 1981. The MOE conditionally approved it in September, and in October it held a meeting with the publisher's staff to announce a total of 870 conditions, 231 of which concerned Eguchi's section. Most of the MOE's comments centered on Eguchi's references to Japan's wrongdoings during the Asia-Pacific War, including his descriptions of the Nanjing

Massacre, the forced labor of Chinese and Koreans, and the March First independence movement in Korea. With respect to the description of the Battle of Okinawa, the examiner (who was also the examiner of Ienaga's textbook) flatly denied the truth of Eguchi's reference to the murder of Okinawans by the Japanese forces. The examiner ordered that Eguchi reconsider the entire sentence, stating that numbers such as 100,000, 200,000, and 800 were either inaccurate or without basis, and that the murdering of Okinawans by the Japanese forces was "inconceivable as taking place between Japanese."[19]

Eguchi's decision was to make some concessions but not give up and delete the subject altogether. First, he changed or removed the numbers and altered the last sentence to read: "Also, there was a case in which Okinawa residents were murdered at the hands of the Japanese forces on allegations such as having committed acts of espionage."[20] As altered, the sentence (implicitly) referred to the Kumeshima Incident, an event in which a Japanese troop executed innocent Okinawans. (The event had become public in the 1970s, and it was well-known at the time.)

When the examiner again rejected the text, Eguchi revised again. This time he simply referred to the death of "approximately 94,000" of Okinawa's residents, and modified the last sentence to read: "Also, in the battleground, which was extremely chaotic, more than a few fell victim to the friendly forces (*yugun*)."[21] This time the sentence was based on an account on the Battle given to the collection owned by the Okinawa Prefectural Museum of Peace Prayer. The examiner again rejected the text, this time on the grounds that the account used in the exhibit was not an acceptable source.

For his third revision, Eguchi decided to use *Okinawa Prefectural History* as his source, since the examiner himself once referred to it as a basis for the MOE's argument. Eguchi modified the last sentence to read: "Also, as described in some cases cited in *Okinawa Prefectural History*, [Okinawan] residents became the victims of Japanese forces during the chaos of the battleground."[22] The examiner again rejected the text, saying that *Okinawa Prefectural History* was a collection of personal accounts of Okinawans' experiences of the battle and thus not an adequate source. The examiner requested that the sources be scholarly research texts. At this point, Eguchi realized that the examiner was rejecting his text not on the grounds of accuracy or source, but because the MOE just wanted to eliminate the reference to the murder of Okinawans by Japanese forces. The deadline (for meeting the textbook display of July 1982) was nearing, so Eguchi was compelled to give up the inclusion of the reference.[23]

The 1982 Media Coverage of the Textbook Screening and the Protests inside and outside of Japan

In 1982, as a result of the highly political public textbook attacks of the time generally, and also as a result of the hype created by reports of the 1981 textbook screening in particular, all the major media outlets were extremely interested in the results of the latest round of Japanese history textbook screening. In their top stories, major newspapers such as *Asahi Shinbun* and *Mainichi Shinbun* reported that state control over education had been strengthened and that the depiction of the Japanese wartime invasion of Asian countries had been watered down (even though it was much earlier, in the 1960s the term "aggression" [*shinryaku*] had been replaced by "advancement" [*shinshutsu*]). Almost instantly, these reports triggered strong protests, from both inside and outside the country.

International censure against Japan's history revision came about as the stories were reported internationally, especially in countries throughout East and Southeast Asia. In July, both the Republic of Korea (South Korea) and the People's Republic of China officially reacted with protests to the Japanese government, and some labor unions and social action groups in Hong Kong sent a letter of complaint to the Japanese Embassy. In August, the official party newspaper of the Democratic Republic of Korea (North Korea) criticized the Japanese "official view" on this issue, and at about the same time the Vietnamese government asked the Japanese ambassador for corrections concerning that country. By the end of September, media criticism of Japan's revision of history through textbook screening included nineteen of Japan's Asian neighbors, with the number of newspaper reports totaling more than two thousand.

There were also mounting protests by Okinawans (though the media attention was more focused on the international protests). In July, two major Okinawan newspapers ran a series of articles featuring the excision of Eguchi's description of the murder of Okinawans in the Battle of Okinawa. In many places on the Okinawa islands, movements were initiated demanding the restoration of the description. In September, the Okinawan Assembly held an extraordinary session and unanimously adopted "A Letter of Opinion Concerning Textbook Screening" and presented it to the MOE. A passage of the letter read:

> The murder of the people of Okinawa [by Japanese forces] is an undeniable fact as clear as day. ... [T]he Okinawa Assembly, in order to correctly impart the experience of the Battle of Okinawa and also to prevent [us] from again making tragic, wretched wars, strongly demands the restoration of the description [of the murder of Okinawans by Japanese forces] be achieved in short order.[24]

These inter- and intranational developments were a clear signal that the textbook controversy of the 1980s was not and would not be the same as the previous one. The international and national circumstances surrounding Japan's politics had changed, and Japan's conservative forces had apparently underestimated the extent of the change. Now the Japanese government needed to fix (and contain) the problem—especially the international one. In August 1982, through an "informal talk," the chief cabinet secretary, Miyazawa Kiichi, announced that the Japanese government would fully consider the criticism of its Asian neighbors to promote friendship with them, and that it would take responsibility for "correcting [the textbook descriptions]." The South Korean government essentially accepted the proposal, but the Chinese government insisted that Miyazawa's word was insufficient as a guarantee against future revisionism in textbook screening.[25]

From late October to November, the MOE delivered official declarations of its new arrangements. First, the Minister of Education expressed his expectation for schools and teachers to cultivate a spirit of international understanding and cooperation among students (though his speech did not refer to the MOE's own responsibility in this regard). The MOE then presented additional textbook screening criteria, by which textbooks were to give "necessary consideration, in the perspective of international friendship and cooperation," to addressing the modern and contemporary history between Japan and its neighboring Asian countries. The MOE also noted that it would not ask authors to replace the term "aggression" with "advancement," or add phrasing suggesting that the Nanjing Massacre occurred as the result of a moment of chaos. With respect to authors' references to the number of victims of the Nanjing Massacre, the MOE announced it would only ask authors to provide citations.[26] At this juncture, then, the Japanese government unilaterally declared the (international) textbook controversy settled.

The government's word proved false in that the situation for the textbook authors was not much improved. To be sure, the MOE's policy changes made some difference with regard to its textbook-screening processes. For example, textbooks that referred to the number of Nanjing Massacre victims as being more than 200,000 passed the textbook screening process. (The number was based on the findings of *Ketteiban Nankin Daigyakusatsu* [The Nanjing Massacre: A Definitive Edition], the newest research on the subject at the time, conducted by Hora Tomio.)[27] The MOE also responded to the Okinawan protest by allowing authors to include—though not entirely without restriction—descriptions of the massacre of Okinawans by Japanese forces.

By and large, however, the nationalist orientation and bureaucratic attitudes of the MOE changed very little. Publishers and authors, for example (Ienaga among them), wished to restore descriptions that had been required for the 1980–1981 and 1981–1982 textbook screening processes, but the MOE refused to accept their correction procedure applications (stating that the procedure was for "correction of errors" not for "restoration of passages previously dropped"). It also continued, in its 1983–1984 textbook screening processes, its efforts to censor and remove descriptions of Japan's aggression and war crimes. For example, while allowing the use of the term "aggression," it continued to suggest that textbooks should report smaller numbers of victims in the massacres that took place in Nanjing, Singapore, and Okinawa during the war.

Moreover, Prime Minister Nakasone Yasuhiro, who had taken office and formed his cabinet in November 1982, was strongly interested in the right-wing nationalist reform of education, and in the "reconstruction of a Japanese identity." He called for "neo-conservatism," and defined himself as the Japanese equivalent of U.S. President Ronald Reagan and Prime Minister Margaret Thatcher of Britain. When he saw that his popularity declined because of his explicit militarist language, e.g., "making Japan into an aircraft carrier that will never sink" (against possible Soviet aggression: these were his words in his interview with *Washington Post*), he switched to an emphasis on the importance of educational reform (among other things such as a smaller government).

Nakasone's ideas for a rightist direction for educational reform were radical. For example, he created the *Rinji Kyoiku Shingikai* (Special Education Council) and hand-picked its members. The council was to bypass the MOE's bureaucracy and the Diet politics, recommend policies, move public opinion, and short-change the schools by adding regulatory practices. Nakasone's ideas and policies were too drastic and undemocratic for the moderates and leftists, and so they strongly opposed them. Even some officials in the MOE did not appreciate Nakasone's top-down approach to the reforms. There was, however, no reason for the MOE to stop its de facto censorship of textbooks, since, as we have seen in Chapter 3, Nakasone had been an advocate for the tight state control of textbooks since the 1950s.

The 1983–1984 Textbook Screening and Ienaga's Decision to File his Third Lawsuit

It would be a mistake to view the MOE as the only active force in the textbook screening process of the time, however. Many textbook authors and publishers' editorial staff were ready for waging struggle(s) against the MOE's overt and covert efforts to revise history.[28] Ienaga, for one, seemed to enter his 1983–1984 textbook screening process with a fighting spirit, challenging the MOE by including more controversial matters, and it was this process which eventually made him decide to file still another lawsuit, his third.

To begin with, in the newly revised manuscript of *Shin Nihonshi* Ienaga restored the phrase concerning the Nanjing Massacre that he had had to alter for the 1980–1981 screening. In addition, he added the phrase "among the Japanese officers and soldiers, more than a few raped Chinese women." He also referred to the rape of Chinese women by the Japanese forces in another section, in which he described Japanese aggression in northern China. Ienaga also increased his coverage of the Battle of Okinawa. In a footnote of his *Shin Nihonshi* (which had passed the 1980–1981 screening), Ienaga had written "Okinawa Prefecture became the battlefield of ground-level fighting, and numerous Okinawan residents approximately as many as 160,000—young, old, men, and women—were compelled to die tragic deaths in the war." In the 1983–1984 revision, he inserted an additional phrase at the end of the footnote, reading: "Among these [Okinawans who died], more than a few were killed by the Japanese forces."[29]

On September 8, 1983, the revised manuscript was submitted to the MOE (Ienaga having revised 84 passages). On December 21, the MOE notified the publisher that the revised text was approved with 24 conditions (i.e., it had approved 60 changes Ienaga made but not the remaining 24). On December 27, Ienaga, one of his writing collaborators, and one of the publisher's editorial staff went to the MOE, where the examiner orally stated the specific conditions. The exchanges were tape-recorded, and some of them were later published as a booklet.[30]

Regarding the description of the Battle of Okinawa, the examiner did not argue against the phrase stating that Japanese forces had killed Okinawa civilians, but insisted that Ienaga should refer to the "mass suicide" as a major cause of the Okinawans' deaths in the Battle. As he put it:

> On the issue of the sacrifice of Okinawan residents, ... the point is that we would like you to write about it in a way that the full picture of the Battle of Okinawa can be understood. [You write] "Among these, more than a few were killed by Japanese forces," which is a fact, as you say. But the largest loss in terms of numbers of people, in the case of ordinary civilians who were the greatest number among those who made sacrifices, mass suicide is the largest, so we would like you to mention that first. Of course, the [exact] number cannot be known in this case as [in the other cases of Okinawans' death], but see, for example, *Soshi Okinawa-sen*, published by Iwanami, where mass suicide is the largest in terms of the numbers given. The number commonly referred to is in excess of six hundred in Tokashiki Island and Zamami Village—I am reading the name right, am I not?—together, and as a whole, eight hundred and so on. Even if these numbers are not necessarily reliable, mass suicide is the largest in terms of numbers, so we would like you too add it to this [description]. This is ... the modification comment [i.e., order to change].[31]

Ienaga argued against the comment, the examiner did not concede (though he became somewhat inarticulate), and the upshot was a struggle over the meaning of the Battle of Okinawa, as in the following exchange:

> **Ienaga:** But it [mass suicide] is included in "tragic deaths."
> **Examiner:** Well, well, let me see ... "numerous," and "as many as 160,000 ..."
> **Ienaga:** And [the phrase begins with] "Among these, [more than a few]." I wrote this specifically because the Japanese forces very much

did what they must never do. Regarding mass suicide, it was not necessarily an event that took place only in Okinawa, was it? It also took place in Saipan.

Examiner: Well, let me see, er ...

Ienaga: Thus, [if I were to follow your order] I would be led again into having to write every detail of these [which I hesitate to do].

Examiner: In this case, it [mass suicide] is the largest in number, so the full picture cannot be grasped without writing about it. Therefore, "mass suicide, etc.". . .

An unidentifiable voice: It is included in "die tragic deaths," so ...

Examiner: [We would like you to write like] "as many as approximately 160,000 Okinawan residents ... die[d] tragic deaths, such as [deaths] by mass suicide, [and so forth]" Things like that are [the content] of the modification comment.[32]

On the description of the Nanjing Massacre, while the examiner did not comment on the Massacre per se, he took issue with the description of the rape of Chinese women. While stating that the rape of Chinese women was "a matter for regret" and "must be recognized as fact," he argued that it was another question altogether whether it was proper to include the matter in a textbook, because rape in war was "a practice common the world over since ancient times." He was a little sarcastic, since the citation he referred to here was, in fact, from Ienaga's *Taiheiyo Senso* (The Pacific War).[33] The examiner then continued:

As Professor Ienaga writes, it is widely recognized that [the permissive policy toward sex in the military, e.g., rape during war] is a practice common the world over since the ancient times. In this sense, to write particularly about this only in the case of the Japanese forces is problematic in terms of selection, the selection and organization [of knowledge]. For this reason, [the MOE] would like [you] to remove this [phrase].[34]

Ienaga asked the examiner if this was a "modification comment" (i.e., order to change), and the answer was "Yes." The examiner continued in much the same vein to explain the MOE's reasons for its rejection of other descriptions.

On January 17, 1984, Ienaga lodged an objection with the MOE against seven (of a total of twenty-four) orders to change or remove passages, and on the next day filed his third lawsuit at Tokyo District Court. He felt strongly that the textbook screening of the early 1980s had worsened, and had waited to see if other textbook authors would initiate proceedings. But when no one did, he decided, with his lawyers' encouragement, that he would.

On February 1, the MOE accepted two objections and dismissed five. One of the dismissed points was Ienaga's objection to the order to remove the reference to the rape of Chinese women—at that point, there was no way forward but to drop the description of the rape. Ienaga and his publisher proceeded to the next task together. Ienaga revised the text, and resubmitted it to the MOE, with the description of the Battle of Okinawa reading as follows:

> Numerous Okinawan residents, approximately as many as 160,000—young, old, men, and women—were compelled to die tragic deaths in the war, including being killed by the U.S. attacks and in mass suicide; some were forced out by the Japanese forces from the trenches onto the ground where bullets and shells were fired heavily as rain, and infants who cried and adults suspected of being spies were murdered [by the Japanese forces].[35]

In the middle of February 1984, the examiner orally told the publisher's editorial staff that the revision was still unacceptable. His reason was that the revision was too extensive and many cases of tragic deaths were named and put into one sentence, which was not good prose style. Ienaga again had to change the text. The final text read:

> Numerous Okinawan residents, approximately as many as 160,000—young, old, men, and women—were compelled to die tragic deaths in the war, such as being killed in the shell bombing and being driven to mass suicide, and among those more than a few were killed by the Japanese forces.[36]

The text was approved in April, and the textbook was printed and approved in late May. By that time, Ienaga was fighting his three lawsuits simultaneously.

Ienaga's Third Lawsuit: History on Trial

Ienaga's third lawsuit called for compensation for the damage caused mainly in the 1980–1981 and 1983–1984 textbook screening processes. His chief objective was to prove the unconstitutionality and unlawfulness of textbook screening by disputing specific points (in this case eight) that the MOE requested, or suggested, for revision. In these terms, the dispute of the third suit was the same as it had been in the first and second suits. The only significant difference between his third suit and previous ones was that the points of contention over specific "historical facts" would become more central to the third suit. In other words, the nature of the third suit shifted to a "game of historical truth."

The suit was designed in order to meet several conditions of Ienaga's camp. First, Ienaga was already over seventy years old, so the third suit needed to be planned in such a way as to be concluded in a short time; in other words, it needed a clear focus. Second, Ienaga's legal team as a whole saw that the climate of the justice system, having become more conservative during the late 1970s, were set against Ienaga. Thus, the realistic goal was to win specific contentions in terms of the state's "abuse of (its discretionary) power" (which was the third argument put forward in Ienaga's first and second suits). That is to say, to aim at a sweeping victory in terms of the unconstitutionality of textbook screening in general, or the screening process of Ienaga's textbook manuscript in particular, would not be the actual focus (although these still had to remain the ultimate objective and be promoted as such).

The new legal strategy required a careful selection of several specific disputes over the description of historical events (from all the possible disputes Ienaga could make) in order for Ienaga to have a good chance of winning the game of historical truth. Moreover, Ienaga, his lawyers, and supporters were keenly aware that the court battles must involve, and be involved in, the social, political, and cultural movements outside the court. This meant perhaps including disputes that were part of the larger political context, which might bring a victory for Ienaga outside the court even if he were to lose inside the court.

While the strategic shift might have been somewhat disappointing to Ienaga and his lawyers (because they had fought for years to win a victory in terms of the unconstitutionality of textbook screening), it created more room for the historians supporting Ienaga to make their contributions by using their specialized knowledge and skills. The involvement of academic historians in Ienaga's lawsuits had deepened during the 1970s, and in fact, in filing the third suit it was the members of the Group of People Involved in Historical Studies and Supporting the Textbook Screening Lawsuit (*Kyokasho Kentei Sosho o Shiensuru Rekishigaku Kankeisha-no-kai*, hereafter APIHS), an organization established in 1965 to support Ienaga which consisted mostly of academic historians (see Chapter 2), that selected, in conjunction with Ienaga's legal team, eight points of contention.

The APIHS historians chose the disputes in accordance with the strategy of putting "history" on trial, with the result that more points reflecting the struggle over the memory of the Asia-Pacific War were included.[37] For example, among the eight points were the disputes over the description of the Nanjing Massacre, the rape of Nanjing, and the Battle of Okinawa. Nanjing and Okinawa had already been two quite contentious fronts in the struggle over the memory of the Asia-Pacific War (see Chapter 3), and during the screening processes in question in the third lawsuit Ienaga had strongly resisted the MOE's order to change or remove descriptions concerning those events.

Another two points of contention—the use of the term "aggression" and the case of Unit 731—were also related to the Japanese invasion of China. The MOE's de fact censorship of the use of the term "aggression" to describe the Japanese invasion of China was by this time an infamous point (since the 1982 news media report on the revision of history in textbooks). In the 1980–1981 and 1983–1984 screening processes, Ienaga had insisted on the appropriateness of the term. Although he had not changed the description, despite the MOE's repeated "suggestion" to do so, the point was included in the lawsuit.[38] The MOE had also requested that he remove mention of Unit 731, a bio-warfare unit that had conducted experiments that involved killing live human subjects (mainly Chinese prisoners of war but also people from Korea, Mongolia, Europe, and the USSR).[39] The MOE had argued that there was no credible scholarly research concerning Unit 731 and that it was therefore premature to include the matter in school textbooks. The dispute over Unit 731 was included in the lawsuit because it was seen as one of the most horrible of all of Japan's war crimes.[40]

Disagreement between Ienaga and the state also arose from their divergent perspectives on the Korean resistance to the Japanese invasion of Korea during the Sino-Japanese War of 1894–1895. In his textbook, Ienaga described the event as the beginning of a fifty-year period of Japanese colonization of Korea. He had written that "in Korea, which was the major battlefield of the war, popular anti-Japanese resistance often took place." The screening officials in the MOE requested that he alter the phrase "anti-Japanese resistance," maintaining that the meaning of the phrase was not exactly clear, and so would confuse high school students.[41]

Finally, two further domestic issues highlighted as points in Ienaga's third lawsuit were his questioning of the righteousness of the imperial power—a topic usually avoided by the official narrative. One of the issues was the MOE's order of a change in the description of the volunteer army known as "Troop Somo," which had fought for the (re)establishment of an emperor system at the beginning of the Meiji Restoration but was then quickly suppressed by the Meiji government because of its populist orientation. The historians elected to include this point because it was clear that the examiner had misread the text of the original source.[42]

The other point (and the last of the eight points of contention) concerned the description of a protest made by Shinran (1173–1262) to the Imperial Court against its oppression of new Buddhist denominations that appeared during the Kamakura era. During the screening process the MOE made a "suggestion for improvement," suggesting that Ienaga reconsider his description because there was no historical source demonstrating Shinran protested at the time he met the oppression. The APIHS historians included the point, even though some felt it somewhat weak, because there were no other points dealing with Japan's pre-modern period.[43]

Taken overall, by the time Ienaga filed his third lawsuit, Ienaga, his lawyers, and his supporters were experienced both in the legal game of truth and the larger arena of (cultural) politics surrounding it. They were able to analyze their situation accurately and plan more consciously to take advantage of historical conjunctures. In retrospect, as we shall see below in more detail, with the shift of emphasis from the game of educational truth to that of historical truth, Ienaga's court challenge entered a new phase. In particular, fighting the game of historical truth turned out to be a good strategy. The early 1980s saw an enhanced use of the skills and knowledge of the historians supporting Ienaga, including the APIHS historians, in Ienaga's court battles. Moreover, while decisions in the lawsuits were still years away, Ienaga's third lawsuit turned out to be very timely. It reflected the growing public concern about the issues of textbooks in the early 1980s, and brought about renewed interest in all of Ienaga's textbook lawsuits.

A Joining of the Forces inside and outside the Court: Journalists, Writers, Historians, and Victims of the War

As we saw in Chapter 2, the activities of academic historians supporting Ienaga had gradually assumed an important role in the legal processes of his first and second suits in the 1970s. In particular, they had begun to assist and advise Ienaga's legal team in court, and help author legal documents to refute the MOE's criticisms of Ienaga's text. In the early and middle 1980s, the involvement of historians as specialists increased. For example, between 1981 and 1982 eleven members of the APIHS took the witness stand for Ienaga in his first suit, at the Tokyo High Court. The Working Groups (the study groups the APIHS organized in the 1970s to overcome the Takatsu decision at Tokyo District Court, in Ienaga's first suit) were particularly involved, from the preparation of witnesses' written statements (submitted before the court) to the formulation of strategy, advising lawyers, and coaching the witnesses.[44]

The historians participating in the APIHS activities not only offered their expertise but also learned from the process. For example, one member who joined the Working Groups later reported:

> Personally, [I] learned a lot by joining the discussion and listening to it. . . . Throughout [the Working Groups], both the problem of how to think about the methodology of history as an academic discipline and the issue of its social function were connected and discussed in relation to the reality and as [part of] the courtroom dispute against the [state] screening. In this sense, I really feel that [my involvement in the Working Groups] taught me a lot about forming my own view of the study of history.[45]

In fact, many historians benefited from the discussions that took place in the APIHS meetings, Working Groups or otherwise, in developing their own research and publishing articles in major academic journals such as *Rekishigaku Kenkyu* (The Study of History), *Rekishi Hyoron* (Historical Review), and *Nihonshi Kenkyu* (The Study of Japanese History) in the 1980s.[46]

Ienaga's third suit also instigated a drive to accelerate research on the various unresolved issues of the Asia-Pacific War. In this connection, the involvement of historians took a slightly different shape than it had in the Working

Groups for the first suit. Because Ienaga's third suit was more focused on the disputes over specific historical facts, historians with more specific interests, skills, and knowledge formed kinds of special interest groups. For example, the *Nankin Jiken Chosa-kenkyu-kai* (The Group for Research on the Nanjing Incident) was formed immediately, using the opportunity of a discussion in the NLSTS newsletter on the massacre and rape that took place during the battles by which Japan eventually occupied Nanjing in 1937. Around this time the NLSTS ran articles and features in its monthly newsletter to clarify the points of contention in Ienaga's third lawsuit, and the feature on the Nanjing Massacre was published in April 1984.[47]

While the feature highlighted the conversation between Ienaga and Honda Katsuichi, a journalist who published *Chugoku no Tabi* (A Trip in China) in the 1970s, several others, including two historians and one of Ienaga's lawyers, participated in the discussion. At the end of the discussion, they recognized that the historical research on the subject had not been sufficient, and agreed to have a regular meeting to study the Nanjing Massacre and other Japanese war atrocities such as the rape of Chinese women. Shortly thereafter the group was formed. It included Hora Tomio, a leading scholar in the area since the 1970s (selected to serve as chair), as well as prominent historians such as Fujiwara Akira, and younger historians such as Yoshida Yutaka. During the remainder of 1980s, the group's achievement in research on the topic was enormous, and it refuted completely—at least on the grounds set by historical studies—the arguments that had been advanced by the (ultra)nationalist and imperialist scholars since the 1970s (e.g., that the Nanjing Massacre was an illusion).[48]

Another group of scholars devoted their efforts to research on Unit 731. The effort began, like the one for the Nanjing Massacre, with a discussion on the topic between Ienaga and Morimura Seiichi published in the NLSTS newsletter in January 1984.[49] Morimura was a well-known mystery writer who had begun to interview former members of the Unit in the early 1980s (he succeeded in collecting approximately fifty interviews from the eighty former unit members he approached).[50] He reported his findings in *Akahata* (the official newspaper of the Japan Communist Party), and in the early 1980s published three bestseller volumes entitled *Akuma no Hoshoku* (The Devil's Gluttony).[51] The existence of the unit had been known since the 1950s, but Morimura's volumes, perhaps because of his name value, appealed to a broader audience (much as Honda's report in the 1970s on the subject of Japanese war atrocities in China).

The discussion in the NLSTS newsletter was in fact a successful attempt to capitalize on Morimura's achievement by inviting him to discuss the subject with Ienaga, as it became the occasion when a number of historians became particularly interested in the topic. Among them was Matsumura Takao, a professor of Keio University. Matsumura had been active in research on the history of the Asia-Pacific War for some time, and had organized a study group at his university. As a result of the NLSTS article

Matsumura's group decided to focus on the explication of Unit 731 in more depth. The group succeeded in making findings, old and new, in a more organized, systematic manner. It also clarified the history and state of research on the subject and helped verify that a number of materials and publications indicating the existence of the Unit were available at the time Ienaga included the description in his textbook manuscript.[52]

Ienaga, his legal team, and his support organizations also attempted to incorporate voices of Okinawans in their activities both inside and outside the courts. The dispute between Ienaga and the MOE over the description of the Battle of Okinawa was included in Ienaga's third suit because of Okinawan protest during the textbook controversy of the early 1980s. Research on the subject by the Okinawan historians had been well under way since the 1970s. Ienaga's legal team not only requested the court to call several Okinawans to testify for Ienaga, but also asked it to hold the hearings in Okinawa. In the mid-1980s, the court decided to allow the hearings to be held in Okinawa, and thereafter the NLSTS worked hard with Okinawan supporters to make the hearings a great success. Through these activities, the facts of the murder of Okinawan civilians by Japanese forces during the Battle of Okinawa gradually came to be known throughout the nation.[53]

The Public Response to the Second Textbook Attack and Ienaga's Third Lawsuit

There seems to have been a large, albeit latent, level of protest among the general citizenry against the right-wing attempt to revise history by way of the textbook screening process. The situation in the 1980s, in particular the textbook controversies, caused some of those who had been previously silent to become active participants of the opposition. Two new organizations were formed as the direct results of the second textbook attack and Ienaga's move to file his third lawsuit. One of these, the Association of Citizens Thinking about the Textbook Issue (*Kyokasho Mondai o Kangaeru Shimin-no-kai*), was a group of concerned citizens. The group listed famous scholars and writers (such as Yamazumi Masami, an education professor of Tokyo Metropolitan University) as its leaders, but in practice it was run by women–mostly homemakers–who were concerned about education. The group was open to everyone and published a newsletter *Shimin no Koe* (The Voice of Citizens). It also collected signatures against the MOE's textbook screening processes, and brought them to the MOE.

The second group was the Informal Gathering of Social Studies Textbook Authors (*Shakaika Kyokasho Shippitsusha Kondankai*). Its organizers succeeded in gathering into the group almost all the authors of social studies textbooks within just a few months in 1982, when the textbook controversy became an international issue. The first meeting was held on September 4,

1982, at the Private Colleges Hall (*Shigaku Kaikan*) in Tokyo, with over eighty members attending. The groups' purpose was not only to provide a network for individual authors, but also to take on certain initiatives. After Miyazawa's informal talk, for example, it encouraged each author to request immediately a "correction procedure" that would allow him/her to restore text (s) changed or dropped because of the textbook screening processes. (In fact, Ienaga was one such author who immediately applied for the correction procedure, and the MOE's refusal was included as one of the complaints in his third suit.)

The organization also successfully edited and published *Kyokasho Mondai towa Nanika* (What Is the Textbook Issue?) quickly. The volume collected various textbook authors' first-hand accounts of their experiences of the textbook screening processes and the voices of parents and teachers on current textbooks.[54] The subject areas of the textbook authors included Japanese history, world history, geography, politics and economy, and contemporary society. Although it was no real news that the MOE had been revising textbooks from a right-wing nationalist perspective,[55] this was the first time that particular authors, from across fields, spoke up as a collective. (The organization has functioned well since then as a center for gathering and disseminating information about problems in the textbook screening processes.)

The NLSTS saw a significant increase in its membership in the 1980s. Throughout the middle and late 1970s, the NLSTS's membership had remained at roughly 17,500. During the mass media reports on the MOE's revision of history in 1982, membership increased to over 18,000. Then, just after Ienaga filed his third lawsuit, membership reached 20,000, and thereafter, throughout the 1980s, it increased steadily to a high of more than 27,000 in 1989.[56] This increase in membership indicated the renewed interest among teachers (approximately 60 percent of the members were teachers), those working in publishing houses, and the general public in the issue of textbooks and screening processes.

The NLSTS also rekindled its efforts to win support for Ienaga's textbook lawsuits. It had been almost twenty years since Ienaga filed his first suit in the mid-1960s, and the daily activity of the NLSTS had become somewhat routine in the late 1970s, so Ienaga's third suit provided a good opportunity for it to become more active again. For example, when the NLSTS sent its representatives to the annual national conference co-held by the JTU and High School Teachers Union in Kobe in February 1984, it decided to stress the importance of Ienaga's third lawsuit. The representatives were given the chance to speak in half of the twenty-six sessions held, and there was even a session entitled "Textbook Issues and Course of Study," which discussed, in part, the ways teachers could support Ienaga's textbook lawsuits. The NLSTS also held its own (informal) evening gathering to report on the third suit, and met with good responses (the room was full, with approximately one hundred teachers).[57]

Ienaga's lawsuits also functioned as an anchoring point for those who were generally opposed to Prime Minister Nakasone's educational reforms. Many letters the NLSTS received around the time when Ienaga filed his third suit included criticism of Nakasone's education reforms. For example, a letter written by a person who was probably in his mid-twenties, who decided to rejoin the organization, read as follows:

> Recently, the Nakasone cabinet decided to establish a "Special Education Council," and the reactionary and nationalist [trend] in education is strengthening more and more. In such a context, it gives us great courage to see Professor Ienaga take the plunge in his third lawsuit, and I feel keenly that I should again be active on this issue. ... I would like to ask my friends around me for their participation, too, so I would be grateful if you [NLSTS] can send me about ten copies of leaflets.[58]

In June 1984, approximately 50,000 people took to the street to protest Nakasone's education reforms, and the NLSTS was one of the major co-organizers of the event.

The struggle over textbooks can always be viewed as part of a larger political struggle, a war by proxy reflecting changes in inter- and intra-national relations. In fact, the Japanese textbook controversy of the early 1980s was a series of events that took place at a particular historical juncture, in which the existing social forces (re)connected each other and recreated their respective political blocs. The second attack on textbooks, for example, was initiated by the efforts of LDP's young right-wing members to gain more influence, and it proceeded beyond that point to open up a space for other forces, including other political parties and interest groups, to join and strengthen their power(s). The forces that joined this recreated hegemonic power bloc differed in their immediate concerns and ways to approach the ideological struggle(s), but they agreed on one issue—the control over textbooks. (For example, the MOE was not in perfect concert with the LDP right-wingers, but in the end it used its power quite tactfully to change textbook descriptions to meet their demands.)

The protests from other Asian countries and from Okinawa against the MOE's revision of history by way of its textbook screening suggest a critical conjuncture of the period. The textbook controversy of the 1980s was quite different from the one that took place in the 1950s in that the voices and faces of Asian and Okinawan victims of the Asia-Pacific War were included for the first time. While the textbook attack of the 1950s involved a fierce struggle between right-wing nationalists and counter-hegemonic forces over the national narrative(s) and identity, Asian and Okinawan voices had not been able to enter the theater. It was primarily the Asian peace processes of the 1970s that made it possible for those who had been outside the struggle to show up and be heard. At the same time, it was the efforts of alternative and oppositional forces in the 1970s, including textbook authors, which opened up a space by writing about the war from critical perspectives. Importantly, various postwar struggles for alternative and oppositional national narratives finally came together in this series of events.

The textbook controversy was followed by Ienaga's third textbook lawsuit, and Ienaga and his legal team made a conscious choice to make strategic use of existing historical factors. Namely, they selected points of contention for the lawsuit in a way that clearly reflected the voices from Okinawa and other countries of Asia. In a sense, Ienaga's third suit was an outcome of the historical moment, and at the same time it attempted to capitalize upon (and advance) that moment. Moreover, Ienaga and his lawyers were also aware of their situation. They planned their "strategic conjuncture," in a Gramscian sense, through a consideration of Ienaga's age, the involvement of academic historians as specialists, and the conservative tendency of the judicial system, and decided to fight Ienaga's third suit more as a game of historical truth than they had his first and second suits. Outside the court, the NLSTS (Ienaga's support organization) revitalized its activities by focusing on Ienaga's new challenge to the state, and emerged as a major force capable of mobilizing citizens for social and political protests in the field of education.

In short, there was plenty of evidence suggesting that Ienaga's court challenges found new life in the early 1980s. In retrospect, the historical conjuncture and the new strategies Ienaga and his team developed clearly had a positive impact for Ienaga in his court battles (even though, as I explain in the chapters that follow, the court decisions were in most cases not immediately favorable). In particular, the strategy to utilize academic specialists' knowledge and skills and play the game of historical truths to the maximum extent turned out to be more successful than expected. This does not mean, of course, that there were no twists and turns in the deployment of their strategy. The next chapter examines the game of historical truth fought in Ienaga's third lawsuit. In particular, it concerns the kinds of arguments about "historical facts" advanced by the state and Ienaga, and the consistency of the two parties in approaching two specific points of contention, i.e., Ienaga's descriptions of the Nanjing Massacre and the Battle of Okinawa.

5 What is historical fact?

Dispute over historical research and education in court

[I]sn't the most general of political problems the problem of truth? How can one analyze the connection between ways of distinguishing true and false and ways of governing oneself and others? The search for a new foundation for each of these practices, in itself and relative to the other, the will to discover a different way of governing oneself through a different way of dividing up true and false—this is what I would call "political *spiritualite.*"

Michel Foucault, "Questions of Method"

If the relations of "truth" and "power"—or the "politics of truth"—are constitutive of hegemony,[1] their role in the struggles to build a new (or *counter*) hegemony is equally crucial. Ienaga's textbook lawsuit needs to be examined in terms of the "multiple games of truth" deployed in its process, as articulated by Foucault. For example, should historical narratives in school textbooks be written based on "truths," that is, facts verified by "science"? Here "science"—including "historical science"—means a systematic approach to the knowledge of a given field, one that makes claims of validity by employing a logic of scholarly inquiry shared by scholars of that field in general.[2]

This question, in fact, became the focal point of Ienaga's third lawsuit (as compared to his second and first lawsuits, where the central question concerned education and the right to education), and it is the focus of this chapter to examine the ways in which the questions of "historical research" and "historical facts" were addressed in court.[3] Interestingly, both Ienaga and the state insisted that the narratives in history textbooks should be based on (historical) "facts" (rather than "fiction"). The question thus became: What are historical facts and how can they be obtained? In essence, then, the first game of truth at play in Ienaga's third textbook lawsuit needed to be concerned with the epistemology and methodology of historical research, followed by disputes over the "facts" of specific past events.

What were the epistemological and methodological position(s) held by the Ministry of Education (MOE) with respect to historical studies, history education, and history textbook writing? What were the basic assumptions and position(s) and how did the state use those positions in the actual screening process of Ienaga's textbook? This chapter examines two expert testimonies (in this case, from well-known historians)—one in support of Ienaga, to refute the state's position(s), and the other in favor of the state, to defend its position(s). Their testimonies are analyzed and assessed in terms of clarity, effectiveness, and articulation of the issues involved in historical research (e.g., having a "perspective" and pursuing "objectivity").

The chapter then directs its attention to one of the specific points of contention—the dispute over the description of the Nanjing Massacre and related issues. It (re)presents some interesting moments that took place during the courtroom debates, when two witnesses—one for Ienaga and the other for the state—gave their testimonies. In particular, it examines the witnesses' explanations for using particular methods and methodologies in their research. The chapter suggests that the issues involved in (historical) research methods and methodology, whether or not they were made explicit, were present in these debates over the specific "facts" involved in the events related to the Nanjing Massacre.

The State's Views on History and History Textbooks: Simultaneously "Objectivist" and "Relativist"

Throughout the trial, both Ienaga and the state regarded history as a science. They differed significantly, however, in terms of their epistemological and methodological positions. With respect to history education and the writing of history textbooks, the MOE stressed (and still does) the importance of "objective facts," an "impartial position," a "full picture," and an "undistorted picture." It is safe to suggest that the first characteristic in the MOE's prescription for writing history textbooks is a reference to "objectivity." The MOE's version of objectivity is one where information is obtained through a strict abstinence from value judgments.

For example, in its fifth document, filed before the court as part of a legal procedure, the MOE expressed its policy on textbook screening as follows:

> First, in order to have educational content written [in textbooks] with a basis in objective facts, in cases in which textbook manuscripts are written based on the academic views advanced by only a small group of people, which are hardly recognized as widely held in academia, [the MOE] indicates [to publishers and authors] the necessary points for making the descriptions be ones which are by and large established and which do not leave room for further discussion.[4]

While the MOE did not provide a definition of "objective facts" (or its view on the nature of objective facts), or a discussion of how they might be attained (in terms of epistemology and methodology), we can make further inferences and raise questions regarding some of the MOE's views on this matter.

For one thing, the fact that the MOE simply asserted that "objective facts are (or ought to be) the basis of educational content" suggests that it regarded them as self-evident in some cases, and at least *available* in most cases. Otherwise, it would have been impossible to ask authors to write textbooks based on them. Such a position was advantageous to the MOE in a practical sense as well: since the self-evident could always be controversial, a strict application of the position would narrowly circumscribe the topics and descriptions that textbook writers could cover.

For another, the MOE seemed to equate history writing "based on objective facts" with those writings that present widely accepted, or indisputable, academic views. Several problems can be found with this formula. First, academic views need to be open to criticism and further inquiries, and so in many cases adversarial views exist. From the MOE's phrasing, it is unclear who decides which facts are not "commonly accepted" and what criteria would be used in that determination. Also, things commonly accepted as facts—whether accepted by scholars or not—are, quite simply, not always objective facts. Some facts supported by a small number of academics could turn out to be more "objective" than others. Of course, it also depends on how one defines the "objectivity" of a given research project, something the MOE did not address.

The MOE's methodological position was not only "objectivist," however. Curiously, in cases where, in the MOE's view, a divergence of views on given historical events emerges (i.e., where no established objective facts are found), objectivity is maintained by making no value judgments, by including multiple views. Here, in a sense, the MOE becomes "relativist," celebrating "diversity." As the MOE put it:

> Second, in cases in which evaluations are divided on a given fact and [textbook authors] attempt to write about one view which has not yet come to be established, [the MOE], considering that textbooks are used by children and students who are in the process of mental and physical development, indicates—as occasion demands and as it meets students' developmental stages—the necessary points for making the descriptions ones that allow students to understand that diverse views exist. For example, in cases where multiple views exist, when [textbook authors] attempt to give an account of only one view, [the MOE] directs that other views be included with it.[5]

In a similar vein, to emphasize one fact over others was, in the MOE's view, biased, and so in need of correction:

> Third, in cases where textbook manuscripts are written from viewpoints that distort the accuracy of the full picture by intentionally choosing a specific fact from many facts and writing about it, or by expanding a description of a specific fact beyond necessity, and in a way that cannot be regarded

as impartial, [the MOE] tells [publishers and authors] to make the description impartial and not one-sided, since [such manuscripts] are inappropriate for children and students who are still in the process of mental and physical development, and whose critical ability is not sufficient to prevent their being directly influenced by the content of textbook description.[6]

Taken together, the MOE's statements suggest its essential views on history and history textbook writing:[7] First, history is a series of facts, and the best way to present it is to list all such facts without choosing—or making judgments for—one over the other. In short, the MOE's view on history is empiricist (some critics might say "classic historicist"): facts speak for themselves; if they do not, accumulate them, and they will eventually reveal themselves. The MOE, in fact, often argued that the orders and suggestions it gave during textbook screening proceedings were not based on its specific historical views and understandings, but only on historical data. It argued that its actions followed "the normal course of historical studies."[8]

In its argument concerning the epistemology and methodology of historical studies and history textbook writing, the state took a position that argued either "no values" or "all values" in history research and writing. In other words, when the MOE cannot maintain the empiricist position, its view on history becomes relativist, asking to present multiple views, since no single view is certain. For convenience, the state position as a whole was both empiricist *and* relativist. Note that such a position is subject to close examination with respect to its logical consistency and epistemological assumptions, and the move from "empiricist" to "relativist" may be reasonable in some cases. It is, however, quite possible that it is not a move at all, since the two positions could be two sides of the same coin.[9]

These state positions were repeated by Tokinoya Shigeru, the chief officer in charge of examining Ienaga's *Shin Nihonshi* in its 1980–81 and 1983–84 screenings. Tokinoya appeared as a witness in the third trial, at the request of both Ienaga and the state.[10] Tokinoya explained that the nature of textbook screening was "not an examination of, or scholarly critique of, academic views" but the consideration of "whether [textbooks] were written based on common views, i.e., stable academic views that were generally accepted." Regarding the reasons for the MOE's rejection of the specific textbook descriptions in dispute in the third lawsuit, he took the empiricist position almost from beginning to end, arguing that at the time of the textbook screening, the research on the topics was insufficient because it was still in the process of data collection, or that the MOE had suggested that nothing conclusive be written on those topics because the research had not established its views. It should be noted here that to argue for a position and to do things based on that position (i.e., to practice the position) are often two different things. Some critics justifiably raise the question: In what ways was such logic used to justify the state's rejection of the specific history textbook passages that were in dispute?

The Dispute over the Anti-Japanese Resistance in Colonized Korea

Ienaga and the MOE disagreed on the description of Korean resistance against Japanese aggression in Korea during the Sino-Japanese War of 1894–1895. The description given in Ienaga's *Shin Nihonshi* presented the Sino-Japanese War as part of Japan's colonial war over Korea. His passage read as follows:

> At last, in 1884, the Sino-Japanese War broke out. During the war, which stretched over the next year, the victories of the Japanese military continued, but in Korea, which was the major battlefield of the war, popular anti-Japanese resistance often took place.[11]

During the textbook screening process, the MOE had ordered Ienaga to eliminate the entire passage, including the key phrase, "anti-Japanese resistance." On behalf of the MOE, Tokinoya told Ienaga that the Korean uprising that took place between 1894 and 1895 had been generally known as either the Togakuto Rebellion or the Kogo Peasant War (in either case, the uprising was seen as a rebellion against the Korean government, and Japan's role in this interpretation was to aid the Korean government's efforts in suppressing the uprising). Since Ienaga's description referred to neither event, the historical event that the phrase "anti-Japanese resistance" signified was unclear. He also told Ienaga that none of the history books written for the general public used the phrase, so the term would be incomprehensible to high-school teachers and students.[12]

In his testimony given to the court, Tokinoya defended the MOE's reasons for rejecting Ienaga's manuscript. For example, Tokinoya stated that the MOE saw his writing as based on a view of history that was not generally accepted in academia at the time of the screening. For another, when the state lawyer asked Tokinoya if the MOE had altered its position (since its present position was grounded in the idea that "it is inappropriate to write textbooks based on academic views that are not introduced to the academy"), Tokinoya stated:

> If this [the anti-Japanese resistance] does not signify the Togakuto Rebellion, nor the Kogo Peasant War, then the view can only be one that is peculiar to the author, even if such an event had existed. ... In short, [the MOE's reason] was that "it is not allowed to write about things which are not presented at or introduced to the academy," so there is no change [in the MOE's position].[13]

Ienaga's legal team questioned Tokinoya about whether he recognized at the time of the screening that several instances of popular anti-Japanese resistance took place around the time of the Sino-Japanese War. Tokinoya's response was affirmative, but he insisted that the phrase "Togakuto Rebellion" (the phrase the MOE endorsed) conceptually included these uprisings. Ienaga's legal team then asked Tokinoya whether, if the phrase had been used in other books, such as the series called *Koza Nihonshi* (a highly respected series in historical research in Japan, to which Tokinoya had referred to in the screening process), it would have been permissible in textbooks. Tokinoya avoided a yes or no answer, arguing, instead, that academic work should not be considered in terms of such a simple answer: "It is not such a simple matter. Not a [simple] good or bad [matter]. The scholarship is not such a [simple] matter, plus or minus, yes or no."[14]

The lawyer then asked Tokinoya if he recognized that the Sino-Japanese War was a significant event, one that allowed Japan to complete its colonization of Korea. Tokinoya's response was, "No need to respond."[15] The lawyer asked him further if he understood that the colonization of Korea was against the principle of the self-determination of peoples. His answer was, "Of course, [it] violates [the principle]." The lawyer's last question had to do with which of Ienaga's texts, before or after the screening, "represent[ed] more clearly the meaning of the Sino-Japanese War [and] the impact of Japan's policy upon Korea." Tokinoya's response was: "Such a thing cannot be put simply."[16]

The Dispute over the Nanjing Massacre and Rape

Regarding the Nanjing Massacre, Ienaga had originally written (in a footnote in his 1980 manuscript): "The Japanese forces killed numerous Chinese soldiers and civilians immediately after the occupation of Nanjing." The MOE had objected to the sentence because it gave the impression that the Japanese forces carried out a systematic killing ("systematic" meaning by command), and ordered Ienaga to alter the sentence either to "Chinese soldiers and civilians who were involved in the chaos (or confusion) were killed," or "Chinese soldiers and civilians were killed by the Japanese forces during the chaos (or confusion)." Ienaga finally changed it to "The Japanese forces, breaking through the strong resistance of the Chinese forces, occupied Nanjing in a rage and killed numerous Chinese soldiers and civilians," and the MOE approved this.[17]

In the sixth statement that the state filed with the court, the MOE held that Ienaga's manuscript could be read as reporting that "the Nanjing Incident" was "the action of killing that the Japanese Army committed systematically, by command, right after its occupation of Nanjing." The state argued that "as the research on the incident now stands, such a conclusion cannot be made." In his testimony, Tokinoya especially reiterated those reasons, and referred to several works as the basis of the state's argument. One of those works was *Nankin Daigyakusatsu no Maboroshi* (The Illusion of the Nanjing Massacre), which denied the alleged size of the Massacre and the involvement of the Japanese forces as a military unit. Though he avoided refuting other works that had been seen as reliable studies on the topic, Tokinoya stated that the MOE's stance was to request that textbook writers avoid "conclusive descriptions."[18]

Concerning the point of the rape of Chinese women, Ienaga had originally written in a footnote of his 1983 text: "When occupying Nanjing, . . . not a few of the Japanese officers and men raped Chinese women." Another footnote also had read:

> Because of this [meeting with fierce resistance from Chinese guerrillas in Northern China], the Japanese forces almost everywhere caused immeasurable damage to lives, chastity, and the property of Chinese people, including the killing of the local residents, ... and the raping of Chinese women.

The MOE had ordered that Ienaga eliminate the mention of rape in both footnotes because, it had argued, rape in times of war by military officers and soldiers is "a common, customary practice all over the world since ancient times," so that "it is inappropriate to refer only to the rape committed by the Japanese forces, because to do so gives too much emphasis to a specific matter."[19]

In his testimony, Tokinoya stated that the reason for rejecting Ienaga's reference to the frequent rapes in Nanjing was that, while the screening authority had recognized that the Japanese Army raped Chinese women, it had taken the position that the data determining whether the frequency of that rape was extreme was inconclusive. "A lack of sufficient research" seems to be the first, last, and only explanation Tokinoya was able to give. For example, when asked if, at the time of the screening, there were academic grounds to state that "exceptionally frequent violence against Chinese women" in the war, in comparison with other wars, Tokinoya stated: "I don't think there was research from which to conclude it firmly."[20]

Ienaga's lawyer, by citing Hata Ikuhiko, who was scheduled to be another witness for the state, and who, in his volume *Nankin Incident*, wrote "the Japanese Army in the Showa period (1926–1989) was even more wicked" than the notorious old Mongolian force of the thirteenth century, which "made its men advance by enticing them into plunder and rape," pointed out that Hata for the most part based his assessment on the materials made public before the time of the screening, and asked, "Thus there was, I suppose, an academic ground for making an assessment like this at the time of screening. Wasn't there?" Tokinoya answered,

> However that may be, the book was one that was published later, long after [the screening], last year or so, and I am saying here that at the time [of the screening] there was no historical data/source that [was] put together, processed in a good academic manner, and reported such things.[21]

The Dispute over Unit 731

Similarly, Ienaga's description of Unit 731 was problematic to the MOE. Ienaga's 1983 manuscript read:

In the suburb of Harbin, [the Japanese forces] established a bio-warfare unit called Unit 731 and continued to commit atrocities such as capturing non-Japanese, for the most part several thousand Chinese, and killing them in live experiments conducted over a period of several years, until the Soviet Union's declaration of war.

In its screening of that passage, the MOE ordered that Ienaga remove the entire portion describing the Unit because, it had argued, "it is premature to include the reference to Unit 731 in school textbooks, since there has not been credible research." Ienaga had thus been forced to eliminate the entire passage.[22]

During the trial, Tokinoya again defended the MOE's decision in empiricist terms, pointing out the lack of sufficient research on the topic:

Concerning Unit 731, at the present stage, [the research] is, so to speak, still in the process of data collection. Scholarly works that capture a full and certain picture of the facts and their relationships have not yet been presented, so that [the MOE's] request was to eliminate [the description] on the grounds that it was premature [to write about it].[23]

However, what counts as "scholarly work" was a moving target. In a statement filed before the court, the state argued that in the case of Unit 731, there was a lack of "scholarly books, or academic articles published in scholarly journals, sufficiently examining the reliability of sources." Ienaga's legal team argued that this was a slightly elevated position from the one actually taken by the MOE at the time of the textbook screening and during the subsequent negotiations between the MOE and Ienaga, during which time the MOE argued that there was a lack of "trustworthy scholarly works, articles, and books."[24]

Ienaga's legal team began its cross-examination by asking Tokinoya if the textbook screening authorities at that time, including the screening committee and the textbook examiners, acknowledged the fact that Unit 731 had existed, and conducted experiments using live humans. Tokinoya answered yes. Then one of Ienaga's lawyers asked if the problem was the phrasing, which specifically mentioned *who* ("non-Japanese") and *how many* ("several thousand") were killed in the experiment. Tokinoya responded by saying that the problem was "not phrases, but as a whole." According to him, several studies had been done and several facts were known, but "there was yet no study summing [them] up as a whole." Because of this, he argued, there was not sufficient scholarly achievement on the topic to determine the significance of the event in history, so writing about the event "requires a discreet consideration."[25]

For example, while Tokinoya admitted that some work on the topic had been published by the time of the screening (and that he had read these works only after the MOE's rejection of Ienaga's manuscript), a book such as *Kieta Saikin Jikken Butai* (The Germ Experiment Unit that Disappeared), written by Tsuneishi Keiichi, was not a study that presented the full picture (even though Tokinoya regarded it as a scholarly work), and it did not, therefore, provide a sufficient basis for textbook history writing. Tsuneishi's book, he argued, was "a scholarly book for the time being," implying that the study did not definitively establish the historical facts. Tokinoya further stated that it was written "during the stage of data [collection]," and therefore it constituted nothing but "a little study" (as opposed to a full study) on the subject. In short, Tokinoya's epistemology allowed him to dismiss the fruits of some good empirical research on Unit 731, suggesting that the state's version of objectivity is, in fact, a cover for its refusal of knowledge rather than a measure of its actual interest in research.[26]

The Dispute over the Battle of Okinawa

The disagreement between Ienaga and the MOE constituted another point of dispute. In a footnote of his 1980 *Shin Nihonshi*, Ienaga had written: "Okinawa Prefecture became the battlefield of ground-level fighting, and numerous Okinawan residents, approximately as many as 160,000—young, old, men, and women—were compelled to die tragic deaths in the war." In his 1983 revision, he added a line at the end of the sentence that read, "Among these [Okinawans who died], not a few were killed by the Japanese Army."[27] The MOE rejected this addition, and after a series of negotiations between the MOE and Ienaga (along with his publisher), the final text read:

> Numerous Okinawan residents, approximately as many as 160,000—young, old, men, and women—were compelled to die tragic deaths in the war, including being killed in the shell bombing and being driven to mass suicide, and among these not a few were killed by Japanese forces.[28]

According to Tokinoya, the line Ienaga added was problematic because it could be read as saying that "Japanese forces directly killed many Okinawans," despite the fact that Okinawans were also killed by other causes. In his explanation, "the numbers" needed to be compared.

> [Which cause of death was the largest] is relative. That is, it was a fact that Okinawan residents were shot to death by Japanese forces on suspicion that they were spies, but if [Ienaga] takes up the [subject of Okinawa's] loss in terms other than those resulting directly from the United States military force, that [subject] should be taken up more broadly. Otherwise, [the description] could distort the full picture by stressing a partial, specific fact. [The request of the MOE] meant that if [you] were to write about [the killing of Okinawans by Japanese forces],

please also write about the mass suicide, in which the numbers who died were larger.[29]

The problem with Tokinoya's position was that the question of whether mass suicide caused the larger number of Okinawan deaths depended on the criteria used in the assessment, and research on the topic has indeed pointed out that the largest number of deaths among Okinawans was the result of the Japanese forces taking over the trenches in which Okinawans had hidden, forcing them out or taking their food, and so leading to their subsequent death, either from the shooting and shelling by U.S. forces or starvation. When Ienaga's legal team questioned this point, showing the statistical chart presented by Ota Masahide in his *Soshi Okinawasen* (A Complete History of the Battle of Okinawa), a source that was used by the MOE in its own argument, Tokinoya attempted to evade the issue by stating that he was not prepared to make a critique: "It's so sudden to read it just now [and respond] ... I have read the book, but in order to make a critique of it, I have to think and deliberate properly, and articulate. I cannot criticize before [I do] that."[30]

Ienaga's lawyer asked a further pointed question, referring to *Taiheiyo Senso* (The Pacific War), another source that was used by the MOE in its own argument. That book, in fact, includes the number of deaths resulting from the mass suicides that occurred in the Tokashiki and Zamami villages under the category of "the number of Okinawan residents killed at the hands of the Japanese Army." Tokinoya again evoked the importance of looking at the "historical data/source." When asked if he recognizes cases in which the number of deaths counted as the mass suicide might include those killed by the Japanese Army, he answered: "I cannot put it simply. I cannot say anything without looking at historical data/sources. That is, I refer to "direct" killing. Please consider carefully what "direct" means."[31]

Throughout his testimony, Tokinoya defended the MOE's position in terms of empiricism (of a kind) as well as on the grounds of "academic" and "scholarly" attitudes. It appears that any facts about a historical event that the MOE did not want to be included in school textbooks were seen as still being in an "inconclusive" state, or as being good only "for the time being." The passages of Ienaga's text that the MOE rejected as a whole clearly indicate its ideological and political orientation, which many critics would see as nationalist and imperialist. Perhaps, ironically, Tokinoya's testimony suggests that the MOE, including Tokinoya himself, used the empiricist-relativist logic as a cover for its ideology, and that the question of method is political in its nature.

The Alternative Views of History: Yuge Toru's Testimony

In refuting the state's view on history and history writing, Ienaga and his legal team advanced their own, more nuanced views of history. One witness on this point for Ienaga was Yuge Toru, a retired professor of the University of Tokyo, who was a specialist in ancient Roman history with experience of teaching and writing on the subject of historical research methods and methodology. Yuge was also the author of a high-school world-history textbook. Yuge first stated that historical research was conducted for the purpose of producing historical knowledge through systematic methods involving epistemology. In his view, while historical studies assume, as a premise, the existence of the past, their aim is not to restore it to its full picture, which would be impossible, but to express some kind of "truth" by looking at the past from specific positions for the social good (this he termed "history as logos"). In the production of historical knowledge, the material and raw data yielded by sources is selected and processed in order to gain ideas for the social good, and so the production of historical knowledge is based on values.

According to Yuge, the notion of "objective facts" needs to be evoked with "prudence," since historical facts are always value-laden. At one point he stated:

> [H]istorical facts all contain meanings. Historical facts without meaning— "meaning" here means meanings we attach. ... historical facts that do not contain meanings we attach do not exist. If those without meanings are referred to as "objective facts," they are not historical facts. ... Such phrases as "unbiased," or "impartial and neutral" [ways of history] writing cannot be used lightly. Such phrases cannot be used without considerable qualification.[32]

Yuge was also critical of the state's argument that historical narratives can be properly written simply by following common and established views. As he put it:

> [I]n historical research, the common/established views are highly fluid. A starting point for what is an academic view is ... the standard of what is good for society [which is based on given social values]. Thus, as that standard of the social good changes, the way of selecting historical data changes. Or, the way to interpret that selected data changes. Moreover, as new historical data is found, or unearthed, the academic view must bring itself up to date. In this way, historical studies as an academic discipline advances. ... Concerning a given theme of a given age—such themes can be big or small—the common view ... on that theme is in practice decided by the individual researcher in historical studies, who in his/her responsibility decides ... that "this is the common view," or that "this is the correct view"... That is, what is a common ... view cannot exist objectively, or independently of researchers, in historical studies.[33]

Yuge maintained that historical narratives, while often constructed by common and established views, need to be written from specific perspectives.

Those perspectives make the narratives systematic and coherent, and to develop narratives in this way, historians sometimes need to use views that are not yet established. Often, he contended, historians see that the use of unconventional views in certain narratives can serve to explicate the relations between and among contexts, and this kind of success, in turn, causes them to think that the unconventional views are, in fact, perhaps correct. For him, common/established views are not objective in and of themselves, nor are the narratives that are developed based on them.

Yuge was also critical of the position holding that historical studies must refrain from preconceptions and value judgments only to show data and sources for the purpose of revealing the past, the position held by the MOE, which Ienaga's legal team called "data-ism" (*shiryoshugi*). Yuge first affirmed that historians did indeed attach a great degree of importance to data and source, stating, "All historians give weight to historical data/sources. They cling to historical data/sources. In the end, they fight it out" in terms of historical data/sources—and in his view "this is the historians' major premise."[34]

Yuge argued, however, that there are two ways to incorporate the valuation of source. One, to which he adhered, is to attempt to represent "history as logos," by selecting and interpreting data and sources from perspectives involving specific interests and issues and by interpreting and inferring "a vacuum" (matters with no data or sources). The second, which is the MOE's position, is to consider "only what the data and source speak [as] important, that is, only [so-called] 'objective' history," and, therefore, exclude any methods undertaken to process data and source (e.g., selection and interpretation) as unscientific. The problem with the latter position is that it assumes that the characteristics of a given time exist within the data and source itself, preceding any questions or views held by those who study it.

According to Yuge, another problem with the MOE's position was that the textbook screening authorities did, indeed, have their own values, which they attempted to hide. As Yuge put it:

> In the actual screening processes, [screening officials] often tell us things such as that they do not have their own values, they make their opinions following what is written in a historical source, based on historical data/sources. Of course, however, there are sometimes cases where the screening officials impose their values with no cover [to hide them]—this, I think, has increasingly become the case lately—but in general, they place a veil of data-ism on their values and [simply] indicate the conditions [for textbook approval].[35]

Yuge asserted, "In short, data-ism has been used as a cover for their values and their ideas for social good."[36]

"If," Yuge continued, the state "really thinks that historical understanding does not presuppose any values, and really holds the position of value rejection, there is an additional problem," which might be as serious as the former. His point was that the position was outdated. As he put it:

> [The position] is one kind of methodology, but that methodology is ... probably one that prevailed up to the first half of the nineteenth century, and which in Japan lasted until the generation of our teachers. [The methodology] is one that lived on into old age. In short, I believe, it is a vulgarized nineteenth-century German historicism.[37]

The state's legal team faced considerable difficulty in the course of their cross-examination. One of the state's lawyers, Hirai Jiro, attempted to discredit Yuge's argument by asking who, if authors were free to write anything, would be responsible to guarantee the quality and content of textbooks. When Yuge responded that it would be the authors' responsibility to include what was necessary, Hirai asked Yuge if he accepted it as unavoidable that some textbooks would be produced using historical narratives based on imperialist, emperor-centered views of history. Yuge answered that, while he did not think he would like such a textbook, it would not be a problem so long as a variety of textbooks were made available, and teachers and students could choose freely from among them.

Still hoping to make Yuge admit to the necessity of state textbook screening, Hirai asked him how textbooks that violated the idea of the Fundamental Education Law would be removed. Yuge's immediate response was that he had not heard of any cases in which a textbook was disapproved because it ran counter to the Fundamental Education Law. Then he added:

> [The state] might want to say that we would get into trouble if we didn't have textbook screening, but in such cases—[if] such things were committed against the Constitution and the Fundamental Education Law—there is a court. I don't know much about law, but I think it will eventually be a matter [we] entrust to the courts for judgment.[38]

According to a spectator in the gallery, Hirai seemed not to have expected Yuge's answer, and, being somewhat flustered, was at a loss in presenting his next question.[39]

Hirai did, however, manage to continue his questioning for a while, hoping to create the impression that Yuge had insufficient knowledge of the textbook screening system, in order to discredit him. For example, Hirai pointed out that Yuge used the term "screening officials" instead of "textbook examiners" (the latter being the official name of the post).

Hirai was nevertheless unable to change the overall situation—that the state had not been able to undermine Yuge's main argument regarding the importance of epistemology and methodology in history.

The State's (Failed) Defense of its View on History

In defense of the state's views on historical research and history textbooks, Enoki Kazuo, a professor emeritus at the University of Tokyo who had also testified for the state during Ienaga's first lawsuit at the Tokyo High Court, took the stand. Enoki had previous experience authoring a history textbook, and when asked by one of the state's lawyers about his views on history education and writing, he gave the standard answer, one that basically followed the MOE's argument. He stated that the aim of history education at the elementary and secondary school levels is to give students "general, basic knowledge," and that history textbooks ought, for that reason, to include matters "centered on objective facts," to "enumerate general matters that follow the general, common view," and to avoid as much as possible "making judgments or value evaluation."[40]

When common views are not available, he explained, the proper approach, in accordance with the MOE, is to include every view available. As he put it:

> In such cases [where no common view exists], . .. [textbook authors] should write that there is this view, that view, [and so on]. I think it is wrong to pick up one view specifically and stress it in ways so as to say, "This is the truth, this is the true picture."[41]

His argument was essentially that history should hold all values, or hold none at all (i.e., an "all or nothing" argument).

During cross-examination, Enoki continued to support the MOE's empiricist views on history. When asked by Imanaga Hiroaki, one of Ienaga's lawyers, if the view that textbook authors "had best write [their textbooks] by listing things generally accepted, and should not do more than that" summed up his own position on writing history textbooks, Enoki gave a brief, definite answer: "Yes."[42] Enoki had considerable difficulty maintaining his position during subsequent questioning, however. When Imanaga questioned him about the MOE's views on history and history writing, his statements were hardly consistent, and his points sometimes made so little sense that even the lawyers of the state legal team could not hide their amusement.[43]

For example, in questioning Enoki on his views on history textbook writing, Imanaga began by attempting to clarify what Enoki meant by "generally accepted," since during the testimony Enoki had stated that "it seems wrong to write about what screening officials do not know." Enoki's clarification was that "It means those [things] generally accepted among the history experts."[44]

Imanaga attempted to align the view Enoki presented in this third lawsuit with those he had used during the first lawsuit, drawing attention to the fact that this time, Enoki more often used the term "matter" than "fact" (the former also appeared in the MOE's briefs):

> **(Q88) Imanaga:** To say historical "fact" and to say [historical] "matters" are, Sir, you stated, the same in your statements, but some hearing them would detect a difference in nuance. [I] point this out because, in your previous testimony [in Ienaga's first suit], I believe you stated that "provided that we write [history textbooks] by listing the facts generally accepted, history will be understood on its own accord." Is that correct?
> **Enoki:** Yes.[45]

Then Imanaga asked him who else among contemporary historians supported the position. "It seems," he said, "that no other person exists who holds such a view. What do you think? Is there any person who states the things [you stated]?" Enoki's answer was "I don't know any."[46] As Imanaga continued to attempt to disprove Enoki's argument, Enoki increasingly found himself at a loss for words:

> **(Q90) Imanaga:** Generally speaking, granting them to be textbooks, textbooks are still historical narratives, and, it is said historical facts are meaningful in the contexts of complicated relations of cause and effects between the facts, which may be called the "flow of history," isn't it? Sir, you too think in that way, don't you?
> **Enoki:** (No response.)
> **(Q91) Imanaga:** The question is whether it could be a book of history, if the facts were simply enumerated independently and at random, even though they are facts that are generally accepted. What do you think of this?
> **Enoki:** (After a pause) It would be determined on its own accord by what kinds of attitudes one takes in writing books, why [s/he] writes books. But, if listing [things] bit by bit, bit by bit, were to make a book, it could be said that all the things like dictionaries would be books. I think this would be incompatible with the knowledge, or the viewpoint, of those who write books.
> **(Q92) Imanaga:** From what you stated, Sir, I take it you maintain that, provided that history textbooks simply enumerated such facts [as those generally accepted], history would be understood in its own accord.
> **Enoki:** I see.
> **(Q93) Imanaga:** Is it wrong?
> **Enoki:** Yes, it is wrong. My view is that whatever it is, in enumerating [the facts], a thread of connection between them will come into being of its own accord.

(Q94) Imanaga: I think meaning is possible because of the enumeration of the facts that have connections. Is this contrary to your view, Sir?
Enoki: (No response.)[47]

Whether Imanaga's questions were deemed very articulate and precise from the viewpoint of historians, especially epistemologists in history, is perhaps beside the point. The lawyers were not specialists in the area—Ienaga's lawyers studied it only for the courtroom debate—but Enoki was from that profession. Clearly, Enoki was not fully prepared to defend the views on history advanced by the MOE. But who among contemporary historians could defend such views as "facts, facts, facts–which carry within themselves their lesson and their philosophy"?[48] It appeared that the state had been unable to find such a scholar.

In any case, Ienaga and the state clearly differed in their views of history, the nature of historical narrative, and history education. In particular, concerning the question of what historical fact is, or what counts as historical fact, the two parties were consistent in advancing different epistemologies in their courtroom disputes (though the state seemed unsuccessful in defending its position). In other words, the two parties were then obligated to produce before the court the "historical facts" consistent with their epistemologies.

Were they able to produce such facts in the subsequent courtroom arguments? Interestingly, in the disputes concerning the historical facts of specific events (i.e., the Nanjing Massacre, the murder of Okinawans by the Japanese force in the Battle of Okinawa, Unit 731, and other disputed points), there were some twists and turns. Namely, Ienaga's legal team, with the assistance of prominent figures in respective areas of study, was able to produce some historical facts, whereas the state and its witnesses often lacked the evidence to support the state's claims. In such cases, the state basically attempted to discredit the historical facts produced by the other side, while again having its witnesses testify from a position that was conveniently both "objectivist" and "relativist." To bring some focus to the essential nature of the courtroom struggle, the following section examines the testimonies given by witnesses during the course of the arguments over issues related to the description of the Nanjing Massacre.

The Dispute over the Nanjing Massacre

In Fall 1987, the Tokyo District Court heard three testimonies concerning the dispute over the use of the term "aggression" and the description of the Nanjing Massacre and the rape of Chinese women.[49] The court summoned three witnesses: Honda Katsuichi, Fujiwara Akira, and Kojima Noboru. Honda was (and is) an important journalist, one who, in the 1970s, reported on various atrocities Japan had committed in China during the Asia-Pacific

War. Fujiwara was the leading scholar in modern and contemporary military history, particularly with regard to the Asia-Pacific War, and he was, at that time, a professor at the Hitotsubashi University.[50] Kojima was a writer (and a "war historian," as he claimed) specializing in twentieth-century war history.[51] Honda and Fujiwara gave their testimonies for Ienaga; Kojima testified for the state.

The contention between Ienaga and the state over the massacre and rapes that took place in Nanjing in 1937 centered on several key questions: Who should be referred to as having committed the massacre—"the Japanese military," or individual soldiers and officers run amok? Did the Japanese forces conduct a massacre "systematically" (*soshikiteki*), or did the massacre take place in a situation of chaos? Was the MOE's request in the 1980–81 screening of Ienaga's book arbitrary, since it had passed the same passage in the 1976–77 screening and also later in the 1983–84 screening? Does Honda's work concerning the Nanjing Massacre measure up as academic work? Has rape during times of war been common to all eras and battle-fields in human history? Do the rapes committed by the Japanese forces during the Asia-Pacific War have any special characteristics in terms of number or causes? Should the rapes committed by the Japanese forces be taught in schools?[52] While these were explicit questions debated in the court, the question of the relationship between historical knowledge and the methods and methodology undertaken to acquire that knowledge was underscored in various phases.

Honda Katsuichi's Testimony and his "Oral History" Approach

Honda Katsuichi took the witness stand on September 22, 1987. In the courtroom debate, the credibility of "oral history" in general, and Honda's work in particular, became a major issue. The lawyers on both sides spent a good amount of time on the methods and methodology used in his coverage of the Nanjing Massacre. Watanabe Harumi, of Ienaga's legal team, first asked Honda about his views on the value of "testimonies" as data (i.e., data collected through interviews). In his response, Honda began by associating his work with "oral history":

> It might be easier to understand if I explain [the value] in comparison with the work of scholars. ... While, in general, [academic] historians tend [to choose] documents as their objects [of study], some of which have been printed, or some of which have been left as letters in some form, [I did] interviews when I did my report [on the Japanese war atrocities in China]. Recently the term "oral history" has been used, and [I] think [my work] falls on the [side of] oral history.[53]

Honda then pointed out that the distinction between history based on (written) documents and oral history is not absolute, since materials that now only exist in a form of print were often originally spoken by people. His example was the work of Sugae Masumi (1754–1829), a well-known travel writer and scholar of the late Tokugawa Shogunate era. Sugae collected the accounts of people residing in the places he visited and left many records, which are now used and cited as written documents. Likewise, Honda stated that the interviews he had conducted would, in the future, be available only as texts. As he put it:

> A hundred years from now, the collection of testimonies I myself compiled will only remain in the form of print. In this sense, I think that the value of documents and the testimonies would not be too different. In any case, however, [we] should make a critical examination of [the nature of] data. Concerning this point, [the two] are [also] no different.[54]

Concerning his methods in data collection and reporting, Honda, in response to Ienaga's lawyer's question, stated that two aspects were crucial: one's standpoint (*tachiba*) and rigor (*genkaku*), in terms of facts. In his view, "the complete restoration [of the past] is ... impossible," the research process "involves [a series of] selections," including "where to begin a story." In addition, "there is no standpoint that does not have a standpoint." However, a standpoint can co-exist with factual rigor. As he put it:

> Where there is a half glass of liquor, someone might view it as *still* a half, and others would see it as *only* a half. ... [H]owever, [we] have to be rigorous about the fact that there is a half. That is, [if we were to] write it down as a half when it is only one third, it would obviously be a mistake.[55]

Honda described his specific ways of conducting interviews as "landscape paintings." As he put it:

> Assume that there was a particular point where a massacre took place, and that it was on the banks of the Yangtze River outside of the Nanking Fortress, and think of the scenery. Naturally, there would be a sky, a river, and so on. If there was a sky, as a matter of course, [I would ask] if it was cloudy, clear, or raining, and without that the landscape painting would not be complete. ... I ask those details of all persons whose testimonies I hear. I listen [to them] and reconstruct the scene in a way as if I were to make it a complete picture.[56]

In the "landscape painting" process, he stated, he would, in general, disregard two kinds of information: a witness's indirect experience (e.g., hearsay) and accounts of witnesses whose "landscapes" do not match the location. Ienaga's lawyer also asked specifically about the way Honda had taken his field notes for his report on the Nanjing Massacre. Showing a sample page from his notebook, Honda explained his system of recording the data—on the left side of the notebook, he recorded everything his witness said for the first question, adding on the right side the second and third questions and responses, and noting page numbers where he recorded the additional questions and responses.

The lawyer then proceeded to ask Honda's views on the massacre and rapes in Nanjing. Concerning the Nanjing Massacre, Honda testified that, in his view, the Nanjing Massacre was the result of the conduct of the Japanese military, that numerous small-scale massacres took place before the Nanjing Massacre, and that the massacre was systematic because most of the civilians and POWs were murdered by military units such as companies and battalions, and because an order was given to them from higher-ranked military officials. He also pointed out that, in a broader sense, the Japanese military had invaded China systematically from the beginning, so it bore the responsibility for individual soldiers' conduct. Concerning the rapes, Honda testified that a great number of cases were referred to in his interviews (though it was rare for the victims themselves to speak up). He stated that in his view, invading forces tend to rape women, and that the Japanese forces were the aggressors. Even so, he added, the Japanese forces committed them "terribly frequently" in comparison to other aggressive forces.[57]

The State's Cross-examination of Honda: Discrediting "Oral History"

During the cross-examination, the state's legal team attempted to discredit Honda's work. They began by questioning Honda's background, as he was not an academic historian. They then proceeded to question his methods, and asked him if his work had been done exclusively through interviews. Honda denied that his reportorial work on the Japanese war atrocities in China was done exclusively through interviews, so the state's lawyer began to question him about the other sources he had used:

(Q 61): Besides the [interviewing], what [kinds of] investigation did [you] do?
Honda: Besides that, I looked at the literature.
(Q 62): What literature did you look at?
Honda: Is it necessary to list them one by one?
(Q 63): Was it Chinese literature? Or Japanese?
Honda: Both.
(Q 64): Can I have one or two [examples], if you remember?
Honda: I have mentioned a while ago the material Hora compiled. That is one example.
(Q 65): Only to that degree?

Honda: [Did you say] "Only to that degree"? If [I make a] list [of literature], it would consist of several pages. It was extensive.
(Q 66): Besides—what else do you have, besides Hora's volume?
Honda: Those are ... For the moment, it is impossible [for me] to declare [all of them] here.[58]

The state's lawyer continued to question Honda about his non-interview sources, and asked him to name some authors; when Honda insisted that he could not state them definitely, the lawyer asked if Honda did not have many other "sources," since there had not been many books and volumes on the topic at the time of his reporting. While Honda fought back by saying that his "sources" were not necessarily "volumes," the lawyer continued to press him on the matter, and Honda had to state that his reportorial work was "centered on oral history rather than [written] records."

The state's lawyer then proceeded to question the ways that Honda conducted his interviews. For example, Honda was asked if the interviewees were selected by the "Chinese Communist Party," the implication being that Honda's work was "biased." Honda answered that a Chinese journalist association hosted him and that the interviews were granted by the Chinese government. He stated, however, that the actual interviewees were selected by people responsible for the local communities, since it was impossible for him to know who the victims were. Honda was also asked if he "only interviewed ten people" for *Chugoku no Tabi*—a smaller number of interviewees, when compared to the other books he wrote later about the Nanjing Massacre. The reference to "only ... ten people" was used perhaps to create an impression that too few people were interviewed. Honda answered that *Chugoku no Tabi* reported on the war atrocities Japan had committed in the northeastern part of China, and that the "ten people" he referred to were those specifically interviewed for the chapter(s) on the Nanjing Massacre.

The state lawyer proceeded to question the legitimacy of "oral history,"[59] by displaying an issue of a Japanese history journal featuring an article on "oral history," in which Honda appeared as a participant in a round-table discussion with several historians.[60] The state lawyer cited a passage from one of the feature articles, written by Nakamura Masanori, a known historian of modern times, which read:

> [I]n Japan, oral history methods and methodology have not been established. Each [researcher] uses the hearing and recording [methods] in his/her own way. Because of that, [oral history] cannot be said to have come to obtain "citizenship" [i.e., legitimacy] in the study of history.[61]

While Honda responded that he had not read the passage because Nakamura's article was not directly related to the round-table discussion he took part in, the lawyer continued to attack Honda on the issue of oral history methods and methodology.[62] The state legal team spent approximately half of its cross-examination on the question of oral history methods and methodology.

The state lawyer then cited a passage from *Chugoku no Tabi,* making the point that Honda had reported on the massacre from a "Chinese viewpoint," which read: "My [Honda's] aim of visiting China ... was to shed light on the conduct of the Japanese forces in China during the war from the viewpoint of the Chinese side."[63] The state lawyer then declared that he would move on to ask Honda specifically about his views on the Nanjing Massacre. The strategy of the state's legal team was to trip up Honda in the language he used in his writings. For example, the lawyer for the state cited a passage from the paperback version of *Chugoku no Tabi,* which was published in 1981:

> On page 267 [of the book] ... you wrote "this massacre was not a planned massacre following from a top directive within the military.".... Was this the witness's view on the Nanjing Massacre at that time, in 1981, when this ... paperback was published?[64]

The state lawyer's intent here seemed to suggest that the view expressed in the passage supported the state rather than Ienaga on the issue of whether there was a "systematic" nature to the massacre. In his response, Honda attempted to explain that he had included the passage for its implicit comparison with the way Nazi Germany planned and murdered the Jews. But when pressed by the state lawyer for a simple yes or no, Honda had to say "yes" (i.e., that the massacre was not "planned" by the top military leaders).

After a similar exchange took place over a passage in *Nankin heno Michi* (The Road to Nanjing), a more recent publication by Honda, the state lawyer changed the subject to the issue of the "systematic" rape of Chinese women (in Nanjing and northern China) by Japanese forces. The lawyer again attempted to discredit Honda's view on the "systematic" nature of the rape. Honda responded that, "of course, there was no case in which the military unit as a whole [was] given the order 'Now, rape [them],' [and then] charged at [the women]." He maintained, however, that the military units committed violence against the women as units, and that in the end the Japanese military was responsible.

Honda's testimony ended with a brief reexamination by Ienaga's legal team. This allowed Honda to explain that his view of the Nanjing Massacre as not being "planned" (as was the Holocaust by the Nazis) did not mean that it was not "systematic." Honda also had a chance to state that the ways he selected his interviewees (e.g., being assisted by a Chinese journalist association and some locals) is a common procedure among journalists, who cannot begin their reporting by just "walking a street, standing on a corner, and asking 'what is right' of everyone passing."[65]

Did Honda succeed in convincing the court that his "oral history" approach was valid? In the eyes of some of the public in the galley—who were more sympathetic to Ienaga—the state cross-examination to discredit Honda's work was ineffective, though the judges' views were unknown (at least at that point).[66] In any case, Honda's testimony, on the whole, made it clear that he had a system of inquiry that produced certain kinds of new knowledge(s) that had been unavailable through traditional approaches to history. While Honda's methods and methodology perhaps had some shortcomings, mainly because he seemed to operate in the framework of "journalistic" rather than "academic" work, he was able to present some "empirical" evidence to the court in support of Ienaga. His testimony suggested the importance of having perspectives and using different methods and methodologies when opening up a new area of knowledge.

Kojima Noboru's Testimony for the State: "Objectivism" to Evoke "Inconclusiveness"

Kojima Noboru testified for the state in mid-October of 1987. State lawyers began their examination by clarifying Kojima's professional background, with the lawyers making sure that he was known as a "war historian" outside of Japan, even though he was considered a "writer" in Japan. Then the lawyers proceeded to question his approaches to history. Kojima described his methods and methodology as "generalist" and "objectivist." As he put it:

> In short, in my case ... [I] always make it central to look at [history] from a general perspective. At the same time, the most important point is to take a position from which [I] confront the facts as calmly and objectively as possible. In particular, [I] take a position not to judge the past based on contemporary views, but to understand as much as possible the situations, ways of thinking, and social contexts of those days.[67]

In Kojima's view, the recognition of historical facts and the evaluation of those facts were two different things: the phrase "Japan's aggression into China" is evaluative (and therefore not sufficiently objective), but "Japan's military advancement into China" is objective. Kojima also expressed his doubts about "truthful education" (*shinri kyoiku*), the idea promoted by progressive educators attempting to teach about Japan's past wrongdoings in the war. He stated that he did not "understand well [the concept of] truthful education," but that "to love peace" did not mean merely "to teach the misery of war." He suggested that educators teach about a "great number of factors" involved in a war.[68] The point sounded specious, but the problem was that Kojima's idea of peace (and war) education, which would teach about various aspects of war, only included the "objective" facts— from his viewpoint, of course.

For example, he was against the view that history textbooks should include descriptions of the Nanjing Massacre. He noted that few sources concerning the massacre had existed in 1980 when he conducted his research on the event. (Note that in 1980, Ienaga was in the process of writing his description of the event.) Kojima's specific methods and methodology had been to reconstruct the event based on "primary" sources (e.g., military documents issued at the time) and to disregard as "secondary" the stories of the massacre told later by those involved. Given the methods and methodology, he stated, he had experienced the scarcity of sources and, thus, the inconclusiveness of the facts. In his view, researchers in the area were faced, by-and-large, with the same situation then and now.[69]

When asked if there had been a "united view, or academic theory, at all" concerning the Nanjing Massacre around the time of the 1980–81 textbook screening, Kojima answered as follows: "No, looking back [at the situation] around those days, well, [I should say that] some saw [it] as 'the great massacre,' and others called [it] an 'illusion.' In a word, I think it was like hundreds of [heated] disputes."[70] He also added his view that the situation remained unchanged, stating, "Even now, I think, no united view based on things verified can be readily found, which [definitely] says this was this."[71] Kojima stated that the inclusion of the description of the Nanjing Massacre in history textbooks should be "circumspect," meaning that he was against it.

Curiously, it seems that Kojima's research was not geared toward verifying facts and drawing conclusions; rather, his approach was to raise questions about almost everything and to suggest that the real historical situations are unknowable. For one thing, on the issue of Chinese POWs (i. e., whether or not they were slaughtered by the Japanese military under orders), Kojima admitted that a detailed combat report (*sento shoho*) written by the military at the time suggested that such an order had been issued (though, according to Kojima, the author of the report and the regiment to which he belonged was unknown).[72] He insisted, however, that the report could not determine whether or not the order had actually been carried out. As he put it:

> I inferred ... [in my study] that [the order] had been sent widely from the superior headquarters. However, it is very doubtful that the order, in practice, had definitely been carried out and that [the slaughter of POWs was] systematically done. ... [We] cannot know whether the [real] content of the order was ... "to kill [POWs]." Or [that it was] "to deal with [them], and that some [regiments] understood it as "to kill" and did it. On this point, [we] cannot know [the facts] because the sources are really insufficient. Moreover, [the order was] sent to regiments. But [it is not known whether] the order was [then] given to battalions from the regimental commander. ... It would be good if [we] could trace and investigate the processes of actual steps to carry it out. But [we] cannot know how it was in practice.[73]

Concerning the massacre of Chinese civilians, the state's legal team again had Kojima explain the inconclusiveness of the facts. Kojima admitted that some Japanese soldiers had behaved wrongly; however, he suggested that it would be problematic to refer to those wrongdoings as having been committed by the Japanese forces, since it would give an impression that all Japanese officers and soldiers had been wrongdoers. Interestingly, he referred to the instruction given by Matsui Iwane, commander of the Middle China Quarter Force (the name given to all the Japanese forces deployed for the purpose of capturing Nanjing and its surrounding areas), which prohibited wrongdoings such as rape and robbery. He also mentioned that when Matsui had heard of the wrongdoings, he had cried and expressed his regrets and disappointments. "Thus," Kojima stated, "it is very inadvisable" to represent the event as being committed systematically by the Japanese forces.[74] (Note that here Kojima appears to assume that the instruction was clearly communicated to the Japanese officers and soldiers.)

On the issue of the rapes committed by the Japanese forces, Kojima again suggested that the true facts were unknown, or unknowable. When asked about Ienaga's view, which proclaimed that a "great amount of violent conduct" (an euphemism for rape) was one of the characteristics of Japanese aggression against China, Kojima first noted his disagreement with Ienaga's view, saying "On that [point], I do not understand well" why the plaintiff Ienaga would say that, and continued:

> With regard to this kind of violence against women, it is common that any case has no historical sources based on which [we] can truly grasp the actual situations. It is [always] only [known by hearsay that] passes along things. ... Therefore, the actual situation cannot easily be grasped. Therefore, it is very difficult to conclude.[75]

Ienaga's Legal Team's Cross-examination of Kojima: The Will Not to Know

Ienaga's legal team began its cross-examination by asking Kojima about his interpretation of the term "aggression," in particular, whether he considered *Nicchu Senso* (the Sino-Japanese War, 1937–45) a war of aggression.[76] In response, Kojima defined the term—very factually—as an exercise of military force with the intent of infringing on the land and/or the sovereignty of another country, and stated that *Nicchu Senso* was not a war of aggression because it was not intended as such.[77] Ienaga's legal team produced a copy of a book chapter written by Kojima, entitled "A Contribution to Peace,"[78] and pointed out that Kojima wrote "[F]or China [the war] was aggression by the Japanese side."[79] Before the lawyer posed any question, Kojima quickly responded, "[A]s ... written there, 'From the Chinese side, [it] can be seen as aggression.'"[80] Ienaga's lawyer immediately asked, "What do you mean by 'for the Chinese side'? Does it mean 'viewing from the Chinese side'?" Kojima answered, "Yes." "Then," Ienega's lawyer asked, "[the war] was not an aggression as viewed from the Japanese side?" Kojima responded, "[I] mean that [Japan] did not start the war with such an intent [aggression]."

In subsequent arguments, Kojima appeared to depart from his "generalist," "objectivist" position to assume a "relativist" position. Kojima's "objectivist" and "relativist" positions were not in direct opposition, as one might think. In his arguments, the two positions could coexist without much conflict. One such case involved the dispute over the specific facts of the Nanjing Massacre. While admitting that some facts were indeed facts, Kojima refused to accept certain interpretations on either ground. For example, Kojima admitted—or had to admit—that the Tokyo war tribunal had sentenced Matsui Iwane to death for being responsible for the massacre and rapes that took place in Nanjing in 1937, and that Japan accepted the judgments in the 1952 Peace Treaty. However, when Ienaga's legal team asked if the judgment and Japan's acceptance amounted to some (general) recognition that Matsui was responsible for the atrocities committed, as he was a chief commander of the Japanese forces in the operation, Kojima answered, "No it doesn't." Ienaga's legal team attempted to refute him, but they were rather ineffective in the face of Kojima's use of the "inconclusiveness" defense:

> **(Q 136)** [I] think there might be your own view(s) too, but at least in these objective documents it means that [Matsui was recognized as responsible], doesn't it?
> **Kojima:** No, it is very difficult to conclude that.
> **(Q 137)** Based on the process [of the war tribunal and the Peace Treaty], that way of thinking can stand, can't it?
> **Kojima:** No. I think it's impossible.[81]

In a sense, Kojima's approaches to history could be seen not so much as the construction of (some) knowledge(s) but as the denial of possibilities of further research and knowledge. His statements sound as if he wished to deny one's will, including his own, to learn the facts about the Nanjing Massacre.[82] For example, Ienaga's legal team questioned him, citing some passages in the report that spoke of the POWs being stabbed to death on the order of the commander of the 114th division. Kojima insisted on his position, saying: "To me, as I wrote here [in my book], and as I have said before [in my testimony], [I was shown] this detail combat report without indicating the name of unit, so I have done [my research] with my inference, so I cannot ascertain" that the POWs were slaughtered by the order.[83]

It is not clear whether Kojima's evasions were successful, but he continued to skirt the issues throughout the trial. On the issue of the rape of Chinese women, Ienaga's legal team produced a passage from Kojima's volume, *Nicchu Senso*, as evidence, in which Kojima cited part of an instruction issued by a chief staff officer (a major general of a unit consisting of several divisions) on December 20, 1938. The notification referred to "more than a hundred cases of rape" during the battles leading to the capture of Nanjing. It described the rape of Nanjing as an "abhorrent matter," and called for "attention" to be paid to the military prohibition of rape. Ienaga's legal team asked Kojima if the notification indicated the frequency of the rapes (since otherwise, the chief staff officer would not have instructed his subordinates specifically about the prohibition of rape). Kojima refused to accept the view. He stated:

> I have not encountered the documents that verify that the chief staff officer had the view [you] just stated and that he had pointed out only "more than hundred cases" from all the cases, whose [actual] number had been larger.[84]

On some specific matters, Kojima simply repeated, "I have no knowledge." When Ienaga's legal team asked Kojima whether he knew that the Japanese Army, after considering the rape of Nanjing and other places, amended its criminal law, Kojima asked, "When did it happen? I don't remember." The lawyer answered that it was in 1942 and proceeded to ask about his knowledge:

> [It was] in 1942. That is, there were rape/murder [cases], so many cases of murdering [victims] after rape that rape/murder became a crime to be sentenced to "death, life in prison, or more than seven years of imprisonment with hard labor." The Army's criminal law itself was amended in that way. There was such a process, wasn't there?[85]

Kojima's response was very polite but somewhat brazen: "I'm afraid I have had very little stock of knowledge, so I do not remember that such a change of [military] criminal law took place in 1942."[86]

On the whole, Kojima evoked his version of "objectivist" approaches when asserting the impossibility of verification and the inconclusiveness of research results, but was conveniently "relativist" at other times. From this double position, he denied many "facts" that had (and have) been constructed, or suggested, by fairly empirical studies of history. Although he might not have been convincing—some in the galley saw him as a "barefaced [liar]"—the position provided him with the language he needed for giving evasive answers. Kojima's research on the subject, however, seemed very superficial, and in some key points, Ienaga's lawyers were more knowledgeable. Kojima's testimony demonstrated that the "objectivist" position and the "relativist" position can be the flip side of the same coin—which can be characterized as the "will not to know."

Differing views on history, historical facts, historical narrative, and history education have been identified in this chapter, especially as represented in the court documents filed by the state, and in the testimonies given by witnesses for the state and Ienaga. The MOE's textbook policy statement, as well as its court argument defending its textbook screening practices, indicates that the view held by the MOE was, as a matter of convenience, at once both empiricist and relativist. On the one hand, the MOE insisted on the view that history is a science, the purpose of which is to find objective facts, and that history education needs to convey such historical facts. On the other hand, where such empirical positions could not be sustained, it was very quick to adopt a relativist, or pluralist, position granting all views equal epistemological status. The MOE's position demonstrates that the two views are two sides of the same coin, following the logic that "true knowledge must not be contaminated by power"[87] and that, if such knowledge is not available, school curricula must not involve any selection of knowledge.

An examination of the way the MOE used empiricist and relativist views to justify its directives in the textbook-screening process reveals another, significant dimension. In many cases, a strict adherence to the objectivist, or empiricist, position was used to rationalize the deletion of descriptions the MOE did not want to be included in textbooks. That position was used to close down the possibility of alternative, or oppositional, views, interpretations, and narratives. In some cases, the relativist and pluralist position was used to insert nationalist and imperialist views of historical events (e.g., a glorification of "mass suicide" in the Battle of Okinawa) into the textbooks, so as to downplay the alternative and oppositional views. The MOE's use of empiricist-relativist logic seems, in practice, to have had less to do with the academic standard it upheld than with eliminating or changing passages and nuances it found undesirable in school textbooks.

An analysis of the views presented during the court testimonies on history and writing history textbooks urges us to direct attention more clearly to the "game of truth" engaged in by both Ienaga and the state—to direct attention to epistemology and methodology in historical studies. Ienaga, his lawyers, and their witnesses (such as Yuge and Honda) succeeded to a good degree in critiquing the state's views on history, and arguing for their own epistemological and methodological positions. They argued that historians need to recognize the importance of (critical) perspective, and, at the same time, value the empirical study of history (in its broader sense). While such a position might have needed further clarification and elaboration, the witnesses for Ienaga presented his arguments with a good deal of logical consistency, in direct contrast to the state's seeming inability to defend clearly its views on history and historical research. (Of course, the state did produce witnesses who were willing to give testimonies in defense of the state's position, which might be regarded as a success.)

Although the wins and losses in this game of truth concerning the methods and methodology of historical research and their impact upon the overall situation of the lawsuit may require a careful assessment, playing this particular game appears to have helped Ienaga in at least two ways. First, it became evident that the MOE's epistemology and methodology were neither as firm nor as rigorous as it had argued. Second, as soon as the state advanced its epistemological and methodological position (especially the empiricist position), however ill-prepared, it became obligated to defend its reasons for rejecting specific descriptions of Ienaga's texts in terms of that position. This set the stage for Ienaga and his legal team, as they were then able to push the game of truth further into the realm of historical studies.

Did the state succeed in making its case for an "objective" study of history in the subsequent courtroom arguments? On this point, in the testimonies given to the court over issues related to the Nanjing Massacre, the state basically attempted to discredit the testimonies given in support of Ienaga (and to some extent, it succeeded in doing so); however, it was more or less unable to produce its own evidence. This seemed to be one consequence of its methods and methodology, which severely limited the kinds of sources historians could use. If the state really did hold an empiricist position, it would have been obligated to prove its claims on specific points of contention on the grounds of "objectivist" research, not just to suggest "insufficiency" and "inconclusiveness." (I would suggest that it could have begun the research by declassifying some of the wartime documents.) In other words, the state's epistemological and methodological position, no matter how problematic, is a position one *can* take; however, in the end, the value of an epistemology or a methodology for historical research lies in the ways it works as a part of knowledge production and an organizational system, rather than just a philosophical argument.

Although the game of historical truth that played out during Ienaga's third textbook lawsuit seemed to favor Ienaga, it was only one of several games of truth played out in court. The court was, in the end, not to decide on the paradigm(s) of historical research and the knowledge it produced; rather, it was to deliver legal decisions, and the specificity of this legal struggle would affect the outcome, which might not be immediately in favor of Ienega. Also, while Ienega and his legal team battled in court, various kinds of struggles were carried on outside the court, including those in the processes of textbook production. The next chapter discusses the court decisions and history textbooks between the mid-1980s and 1990s.

6 Court decisions on Ienaga Saburo's lawsuits

Critical trends in history textbooks, the late 1980s–1997

[L]egal rights always exist in tension with the exercise of governmental power. Nothing guarantees that rights operate to constrain the exercise of power. It is merely that they provide a significant form of and forum for public arguments. Litigation in courts of law that invokes rights to restrain government power is but the most obvious example. The field of politics of rights also plays itself out in the wider field of public political controversies which occur in public arenas.

The state apparatuses and state law are continuously driven to pursue projects of the unification of power; the success of these projects is always partial, limited, and incomplete; . .. Law is an ever-present participant in this success and failure of governance. It appears both as the means of restraining and channeling the projects of governance, yet at the same time is one of the projects' means of existence.

Alan Hunt and Gary Wickham,
Foucault and Law: Towards a Sociology of Law as Governance

In the mid 1980s, Ienaga Saburo found himself locked in three court battles with the Japanese state and the Ministry of Education (MOE), and all three lawsuits were moving up to the Japanese Supreme Court. His three lawsuits had some differences in their nature and focus (the first was a civil suit to demand compensation, focusing on education, the second an administrative suit to revoke the MOE's decision in the textbook screening of Ienaga's text, and the third was another civil suit, focusing on history), but all challenged the legitimacy of the state's exercise of power in textbook-screening processes, invoking Ienaga's rights as a textbook author. In the course of events, the court became the site of a symposium to discuss educational freedom and state power (see Chapter 1), or, alternately, the site of debates over historical methods and methodology (see Chapter 5).

Although the struggles over history textbooks continued outside the court in these years, the court indeed functioned as a "forum" for public arguments (see the quote from Alan Hunt and Gary Wickham above), and, as the court deliberated ruled, it was the judges' turn to join the debates. So how did the judges decide on Ienaga's textbook lawsuits in the late 1980s and 1990s, including the 1997 Supreme Court decision for Ienaga's third textbook lawsuit?

In particular, what were some of the important aspects of the rulings concerning the disputes over the descriptions of events that took place during the Asia-Pacific War (e.g., the Nanjing Massacre, Unit 731, and the Battle of Okinawa)? How did history textbook content change during this period? In retrospect, in a legal sense, Ienaga did not win all of the lawsuits, or all of the points he disputed; however, it is important to closely examine the way the court responded to the arguments made by Ienega and his legal team in terms of their rulings and reasoning, especially the final ruling at the Japanese Supreme Court, since some of the Supreme Court Justices made references to the textbook struggles taking place in the larger public arena.

Ienaga Saburo's First and Second Textbook Lawsuits and Court Decisions in the Late 1980s and Early 1990s

Of the three lawsuits, the second lawsuit ended first—and it did so without a proper conclusion. After its losses at the lower courts and its appeal to the Supreme Court, the Ministry of Education (MOE) changed its strategy and argued that the case was of "no benefit," and that the lawsuit was moot because, even if Ienaga were to win, the MOE had already changed the Instruction Guidelines, which meant that Ienaga's 1965 textbook (which followed the old guidelines) would no longer be used. As the second lawsuit was an administrative suit, the argument had a point. The Supreme Court turned the case back to the Tokyo High Court, which in 1989 dismissed the case on the grounds of "no benefit," without specifying further. Ienaga decided not to appeal to the Supreme Court, since the earlier decisions, including the groundbreaking Sugimoto decision of 1970, retained their value as precedents.

The first suit, meanwhile, progressed more slowly, taking twelve years to reach a second decision. In 1986, the Tokyo High Court, with Chief Justice Suzuki presiding, overturned Ienaga's earlier partial victory at the District Court. The ruling revoked the lower court decision on eleven specific points, declaring that the MOE had not been "excessively unreasonable." The court basically ruled that the Minister of Education has the power of "discretion" in the processes of authorizing textbooks, and his/her orders and suggestions in the processes are lawful if there is a "reasonable basis" (*soo no konkyo*). This view basically rendered the almost limitless power of discretion to the MOE, which could (and would) define almost anything a reasonable basis. Indeed, the court found that all the MOE's orders and suggestions had reasonable bases. Ienaga appealed the court decision to the Supreme Court. Ienaga later described the Suzuki decision as "the most terrible, lowest, and worst ruling" in his court challenges, and it "shocked" him more than any other rulings.[1]

Seven years later, on March 16, 1993, the Supreme Court (with Judge Kabe presiding) dismissed the first suit, handing Ienaga a total defeat after twenty-eight years of effort. While mentioning that parents have freedom of education at home and teachers have the freedom in deciding the content and methods of their classes, the court ruled that the state also functions to decide the content of education in order to protect children and the common good of society. It also stated that the Minister of Education's orders or suggestions can only be unlawful if they are based on an "error that cannot be overlooked" (*kankashigatai kago*). Although this view was more restrictive of the MOE's power of discretion, the court found—blanketing all the points of contention, without examining each—that no orders and suggestions in the case were based on "error(s) that cannot be overlooked." In other words, the new language did not result in a new finding (though it opened up new ground to consider the extent and limit of the state's power).

Interestingly, the Supreme Court made the decision by a "small court" (with five judges), not a "large court" (with fifteen judges) to avoid, Ienaga's legal team suspected, making a decision on the constitutionality of the state textbook screening. In addition, the court did not notify Ienaga before handing down its ruling, a questionable legal maneuver in and of itself. Ienaga first knew the court's move by media reporters contacting him at home and asking him for comments. A lot of Ienaga's supporters knew it through television news (many of whom immediately called the court and complained).[2]

Ienaga's legal team believed that, since holding a small court trial in this particular case meant in practice that the court would dismiss the case, the court avoided making the ruling known before handing it down. Though Ienaga's legal team protested the court's procedural maneuver (since it was important to avoid the same ending in the third lawsuit) and some public opinion-makers also questioned the court's procedure and judgment, the first lawsuit was finished. Ienaga sharply criticized the way the court handled the case, including the decision, but he set his hopes on the remaining third suit. As he put it:

> [The content of the decision] is terrible—there are many points of contention, but one can doubt that the judges really checked them all one by one. This is not worth the name of a "[fair] trial." ... [However,] the third lawsuit is still continuing, so I would like to rally there, and achieve the change of the precedent [set by the Supreme Court decision].[3]

The MOE welcomed the victory, and Minister of Education Moriyama Mayumi expressed her negative view of Ienaga, stating: "the first and most important thing for him [Ienaga] was that he wanted to maintain his belief, his interpretation of the war. And his interpretation is not a popular one." She defended the MOE's history textbook policy and practices, maintaining that the MOE was "trying its best to be very fair and neutral" in its textbook screening processes, pointing at some history textbooks including descriptions "connected with the war or the colonization of neighboring

[Asian] countries."[4] What Moriyama conveniently forgot to mention was that the changes she pointed out (and other changes in the history textbooks) were brought not because of the MOE's efforts and support—but *in spite of* its hindrance. (One might wonder if Ienaga won his case in the arena of history textbooks, even though he lost his case in court—and, indeed, as discussed below, the history textbooks in these years steadily increased accounts of Japan's war(s) and colonialism in the twentieth century from critical, peace-and-justice perspectives.)

It was not quite obvious how the general public received the court ruling, though the very notion of "general public" might be problematic in these complex issues of curriculum policy closely connected to the divisive issues of war memories. Major newspapers such as *Asahi Shinbun* and *Mainichi Shinbun*, ones that were more or less Tokyo-based, did not publish sharp criticisms on the ruling (unlike their responses to the court decisions in the past); however, several local newspapers made more critical comments. For example, a newspaper based in Yamanashi Prefecture stated:

> It has been twenty-eight years since the first textbook lawsuit was filed. The trends in the world as well as the time have been changing, and at this time (of change), the Supreme Court ruling, which accepts the old, unchanged view on education that was the product of the Cold War period, is close to a dead letter.[5]

Ienaga Saburo's Third Lawsuits and Court Decisions

The third suit proceeded relatively quickly, with decisions consistently granting partial victories to Ienaga—this was not an accident. As discussed in Chapter 4, in Ienaga's third textbook lawsuit, as in his first and second suits, Ienaga's foremost desire was to demonstrate that state screening of textbooks was unconstitutional. When filing the third lawsuit, however, Ienaga's legal team was very much aware that winning such a verdict was an ideal, rather than a practically achievable goal. The third suit, therefore, focused on proving the abuse of power by the MOE in requesting specific revisions of descriptions in Ienaga's textbook.

Ienaga and his legal team further decided to limit the number of specific points to dispute, primarily because of time constraints. In the course of the courtroom debates, these points came to be called "eight points of contention."[6] Of the eight, though two were not related to the war and colonialism, six involved wartime issues: the use of the term "aggression" (*shinryaku*) to describe the Japanese invasion of China, the description of the Nanjing Massacre, the reference to Japanese soldiers' rape of Chinese women (in Nanjing as well as in northern China), the reference to Unit 731, the reference to Korean resistance against Japanese force during the Sino-Japanese War, and the description of the Battle of Okinawa.

In the Kato decision of 1989, the Tokyo District Court found the state's order to change the Troop Somo description unlawful, ruling that Ienaga had been wronged on this point, and that the government should pay him 100,000 yen in compensation. Although he won a partial victory, Ienaga appealed the decision to the higher court (as did the state), in part because he wished to debate the main point of the state textbook screening as unconstitutional, and in part because he hoped to win all the other specific points of contention, including those concerning the descriptions of the Nanjing Massacre, Unit 731, the Korean resistance, and the Battle of Okinawa.

Four years later, in the fall of 1993, the Tokyo High Court softened the district court decision slightly. The court employed "the commonly accepted academic view [of 1984]" as the basis of the decision, and found that the MOE had made "errors that cannot be overlooked" on several points. The decision adopted the language of "errors that cannot be overlooked" introduced by the Supreme Court ruling on Ienaga's first lawsuit, but it applied the concept to judge each point of contention in the third lawsuit.[7] In doing so, the court ruled in favor of both Ienaga's contention regarding the description of Troop Somo and his description of the Nanjing Massacre (including mention of the widespread rapes), stating that on these points the MOE's screening had been excessive and thus unlawful. However, it ruled against Ienaga on Unit 731 and all other points.

The loss on the point of Unit 731 puzzled Ienaga and his legal team. By this time, the existence of Unit 731 had become common knowledge, mainly because of Morimura Seiichi's bestseller *Akuma no Hoshoku* (The Devil's Gluttony). To be sure, the question with which the court was concerned was whether or not Ienaga's description, or the MOE's request, was based on scholarly work established by the time of the screening—so there could be a time lag of sorts. Ienaga, however, thought the ruling was "political," suspecting that the court "might have taken into consideration the international attention to the issues of the Nanjing Massacre and rape," but that it did not do the same for the (less watched) issues of Unit 731.[8] While appreciating his partial win, Ienaga appealed the points he lost to the Supreme Court, determined to continue his court battles (and he did so until 1997, when the Supreme Court handed down its ruling).

For its part, the state did not appeal immediately. Moreover, the state could (incidentally) appeal by May 1994, the deadline for Ienaga to file the statement for appeal, but it did not. At this point, Ienaga's legal team argued that the state's partial loss became definite (and many newspapers reported it). However, the state maintained that it did not give up the possibility of appealing, that it would decide after examining Ienaga's statement, and that it could file the appeal by the time when the court began to hear the case (the law was somewhat imprecise about the dates of appeals in cases like this). It turned out that the state did not appeal at all. When the state did not, legal experts more or less agreed that, technically speaking, Ienaga's partial victory and so the state's partial loss at the Tokyo High Court became definite, and that the remaining question would be whether Ienaga could win more points at the Supreme Court.

The reasons why the state did not appeal were not disclosed, though the state's inaction was seen as a reflection of the changing national and international politics over Japan's unresolved issues of war and war memories, in which it increasingly found its nationalist textbook policies constrained by regional East Asian oppositions. Another theory was that the state was not able to find a good argument against the ruling that recognized the state's power of discretion in authorizing and regulating school textbooks, but that simultaneously found the state guilty of the arbitrary (and convenient) use of that power.[9]

One might also speculate that the tumultuous Japanese politics of 1993 (and in the following years) made the state (the MOE, in particular) indecisive. In July 1993, the Liberal Democratic Party (LDP) lost the majority in the Lower House election. In August, a seven-party, anti-LDP coalition formed the cabinet with Hosokawa Morihiro as the Prime Minister, who plainly admitted Japan's colonialism and aggression into Asia.[10] Reportedly, Hosokawa's statements surprised the MOE officials, who "could not hide their uneasiness," as it might lead to questioning of the MOE's de facto censorship of history textbooks.[11]

In any case, Ienaga's legal challenges seemed to have gradually put the state into a tight corner—it became more difficult for the state to directly impose its right-wing nationalist views of the war, or of any subject for that matter, by way of textbook screening. This indeed meant that right-wing nationalists needed to come up with additional strategies, or find a breakthrough, if possible. Meanwhile, as discussed below, after the international and national censure in 1982 of the Japanese government's history textbook screening, history textbook authors, who were generally inclined to be critical, cosmopolitan, and in favor of peace-and-justice perspectives, labored for inclusion of a wide range of war-related topics, including Japan's war atrocities and colonial oppression.

History Textbooks in the Late 1980s and Early 1990s

Since the mid-1980s, a number of history textbooks came to include (and expand their descriptions of) wartime issues as well as issues involving the Japanese colonization of Taiwan and Korea. The social and historical circumstances presented the textbook authors with an opportunity. The MOE relaxed its textbook policies and screening practices, and the state had to maintain good diplomatic relations with its Asian neighbors; the Neighboring Countries Clause gave textbook authors a basis upon which they were able to write about Japanese war atrocities from critical perspectives; because of Ienaga's textbook lawsuits in general, and his third suit in particular, historical research produced more empirically supported knowledge on many aspects of the war and colonialism; and the court decisions, though still siding with the state in many ways, set a certain limit upon the state's power in the authorization of textbooks.

Descriptions of the Nanjing Massacre in textbooks continued to increase in these years. Textbooks referring to the number of Nanjing Massacre victims as exceeding 200,000 passed the textbook screening. All of the 1984 editions of junior-high school history textbooks, all of the 1985 editions of high school Japanese history textbooks, and six out of seven of the 1986 editions of elementary school social studies textbooks included some description of the Nanjing Massacre (though the MOE did not allow elementary school texts to refer to the number of victims as discussed below).[12]

Some of the textbooks also expanded their descriptions of Japanese tyranny in the occupied territories in Asia. For example, the 1984 edition of one junior-high school history textbook included the following paragraphs:

> In [the parts of] Southeast Asia that Japan occupied, independent governments were established, but Japan held the reins. In the occupied territories, ordinary people's lives became very hard, as materials and rice needed for the pursuit of war were collected by force. On top of that, the Japanese military ruled highhandedly, taking the lives of more than 6,000 resident Chinese in occupied Singapore and severely punishing people who opposed its policies in the Philippines and other regions. As a result of this kind of occupation policy, resistance to Japan spread to various regions.[13]

Some textbooks also came to include—though not entirely without restriction—descriptions of the massacre of Okinawans by Japanese forces. For example, the 1985 edition of Ienaga's text added a reference to this event (though he had to change his original phrasing in order to pass the screening).[14] In another example, one of the 1987 edition junior-high school texts stated:

> In April [1945] U.S. forces landed on Okinawa, intense battles unfolded ... and Okinawa residents were dragged into battle. In that situation, some lost their lives because of the forced group suicides and massacres of residents [by the Japanese forces]. In June, after more than 120,000 of [the total population of] 570,000 Okinawans had become the victims, Okinawa was conquered [by U.S. forces].[15]

The proliferation of critical perspectives and materials in history textbooks did not mean, however, that the MOE halted all censorship, or that it abandoned its nationalist orientation. For example, a reference to the number of victims was removed from an elementary school text at the MOE's request. According to the MOE, reference to the number of victims did not meet the specific needs of the elementary school children's developmental stage, when, the MOE maintained, students did not need to know specific numbers. For another, the MOE strongly pressed local schools to implement its nationalist policies such as hoisting the Hinomaru flag and singing the Kimigayo anthem at school ceremonies. In other words, the improvements to textbooks were possible because historians endeavored to examine the history of the war from the viewpoints of Asian and Okinawan victims, and because textbook authors made efforts to incorporate new, critical knowledge, even though the MOE was not supportive.

The early 1990s saw the continuation of the trend and some history textbooks began to include more details in their description of the Nanjing Massacre. Because of the dispute over the facts (and interpretations) of the massacre in Ienaga's third lawsuit, historical research significantly advanced the knowledge on the massacre. Among Japanese, some consensus on the subject was forming, and a number of textbook authors were interested in learning the research findings and including some of these findings in their texts. Such texts did not escape the screening processes without suffering some changes and deletions; nonetheless, the texts generally incorporated the updated achievements of scholarly research.

Some texts included direct quotations from historical data and sources, which in a sense took advantage of the MOE's insistence on "data-ism" (see Chapter 5). One text read:

> The supplies were insufficient for the troops of the Japanese Army heading toward Nanjing, and so many troops acquired their food on the spot. Because of this, the Japanese soldiers took produce from the fields, attacked farmhouses to find food, looted various goods from the shops, and took from private houses pieces of furniture such as tables and chairs to use as firewood for cooking meals. Moreover, Japanese soldiers, looking for goods to pillage, frequently entered the back rooms of private houses to find and assault women who were hiding there. These acts of pillage drew the antipathy and resistance of the farmers and peasants, some of whom the Japanese Army viewed as [organized] anti-Japanese resistance and killed on the spot. The Japanese Army captured Nanjing on December 13, and then began a clean-up operation, during which time it massmurdered huge numbers of Chinese prisoners of war. One of the division commanders wrote in his diary: "In general, the line was not to have prisoners of war, so that [the division] decided to do away with them [Chinese prisoners of war] one and all," and "the number one division did away with was approximately 15,000, and one company, garrisoned at Taiheimon, did away with approximately 1,300." The Japanese Army committed atrocities such as murdering civilians who had not been able to flee for safety, and so stayed in Nanjing, assaulting women, setting fire, and plundering.[16]

For those committed to teaching about the war from critical (and peace-and-justice) perspectives, the changes brought forth in the newer editions of history textbooks were certainly an improvement over the older editions.[17] The changes indicated that the critical views on the Asia-Pacific War—and cosmopolitan, peace-and-justice perspectives—became established and accepted generally, at least in the arenas of history research, textbooks, and education. It is perhaps important to note that these changes took place side by side with Ienaga's court battles, and before even the final Supreme Court ruling was made.

The 1997 Supreme Court Decision for Saburo Ienaga's Third Textbook Lawsuit

In May 1997, the Japanese Supreme Court notified Ienaga and his legal team that the court would hold a hearing at its third small court beginning at 1:30 pm on July 18. Holding a hearing meant that the Supreme Court would quite likely amend the previous ruling in favor of Ienaga (because the state did not appeal), and doing it at a small court meant that the court would basically hear the case to consider the specific points Ienaga continued to dispute, which for the most part consisted of the wartime issues, but that the court would not change the position(s) held by the previous rulings on the issue of constitutionality of the state's textbook screening.[18] So this was not the most perfect turn of events, but realistically the best scenario from Ienaga and his legal team's perspective. Indeed, Ienaga was pleased. As he put it, "When I received a confirmation of [the Supreme Court hearing], honestly speaking, I felt happy. ... We [Ienaga and his legal team] intend to do our best ... to convince the court."[19]

On July 18, the Supreme Court held the hearing for approximately two hours, during which time Ienaga had a chance to speak for five minutes as the plaintiff. Ienaga thought it would be uninteresting if he simply read the documents already submitted to the court, so he brought to the court *Horitsu Kaishakugaku* (Study on Interpretation of Law), a volume by Egi Makoto, and a newspaper clipping containing Minobe Tatsukichi's review on the volume. This way, when Ienaga cited Egi, he was able to use the text to demonstrate this to the court.[20] He felt that he argued fully his main points.[21]

On August 27, Ienaga's thirty-two-year challenge to the Japanese government's textbook censorship came to an end, as Japan's Supreme Court, consisting of five judges, handed down its decision on his third lawsuit. As expected, the court avoided entering arguments concerning the constitutionality of the state textbook screening—a central issue Ienaga had fought for more than three decades—but it ruled in his favor on several points, including those regarding the descriptions of Japan's wartime conduct. The exception was the contention concerning the use of the term "aggression," for which the court found no damage on the part of Ienaga, who had not altered the term because the MOE had "suggested" the change rather than ordering it. (The third suit was a damage claim suit, and where the court found no damage it did not enter arguments over the historical facts in the case.)[22]

In overall picture, the Supreme Court by and large supported the Tokyo High Court decision (a major difference being that it decided in favor of Ienaga on the point of Unit 731, as discussed below). However, on many points the judges' opinions were divided, and, therefore, the decision was accompanied by more than a few dissenting and supplemental opinions. Interestingly, the decision referred—though somewhat implicitly—to the textbook controversy of the 1990s. In particular, it included criticism of the arguments advanced by the nationalists outside the court (e.g., the liberal view of history).[23] Moreover, Presiding Judge Ono in his opinion stated particularly that Japan's school textbooks should include descriptions of the suffering Japan's past aggression had caused its neighbors, and that such inclusion would constitute a positive educational consideration. However, Ienaga's victory was partial and the ruling did not amend the previous rulings on the constitutionality of the state textbook screening.[24]

In the section that follows, I examine in some detail the Supreme Court decision, to which I refer as the "Ono decision" (after the chief justice). I discuss it along with the Tokyo High Court decision, since the integrity and propriety of the latter was at issue in the Ono decision. These decisions are no simple documents, for even on the points Ienaga lost, we often find that the Court's decisions did not entirely favor the state. In this sense, it is important to analyze the documents in their own light.[25]

The Nanjing Massacre, the Rape of Chinese Women, and Unit 731

Three specific points of contention were related to the war atrocities Japan committed in China. Regarding the points of contention concerning the Nanjing Massacre, the illegality of the state order with respect to the actual altering and removal of content was disputed on two major fronts: the cause of the massacre (whether the massacre was an organized act of the Japanese Army), and the time line (when it should be understood as having taken place). In 1993, the Tokyo High Court in essence awarded Ienaga a victory on the dispute. The decision ruled that the period in which the massacre occurred was not limited to the period "immediately after the occupation," and that, therefore, the state order was legal. The court ruled, however, that the state's order (excepting a part concerning the time line) that compelled Ienaga to change the original phrasing was illegal, since the revised phrasing representing the massacre as happening because of "rage" was a one-sided explanation. Ienaga appealed the former point.[26]

The Ono decision basically supported the Tokyo High Court decision and rejected the arguments made by the Ienaga's legal team—but perhaps it was the state that lost the point in a larger picture. The court recognized that the main point of the MOE's order had been to keep the readers from understanding the massacre as having been systematically committed by the military command,

and that the Tokyo High Court had found that order illegal. The Ono decision ruled that, "in conclusion," it approved the Tokyo High Court decision, since the issue of the time line did not constitute another separate point. That is, the Ono decision found that the main point of the MOE's order was illegal.[27]

Concerning the point of the rape of Chinese women, the Tokyo High Court stated, "it goes without saying that [raping in war] is an act of inhumanity that should be censured." The court made a distinction, however, between the rape that happened in Nanjing and the rape that happened in the northern part of China. It ruled that the research reporting the frequent rape in Nanjing had been sufficient, but that it had been insufficient with respect to the rape that had occurred in the northern part of China. Thus, the court found that the MOE's order to remove the reference in the first instance (with respect to Nanjing) was illegal, but that it was legal with regard to northern China.[28] The Ono decision basically supported that court decision, but not unanimously. Judges Ono and Ozaki, in their minority opinions, opposed making the distinction between the rape that took place in Nanjing and the rape that occurred in northern China, and stated that the MOE's order of elimination of the reference to rape should as a whole be considered illegal.[29]

While in principle supporting the Tokyo High Court decision on the above points, the Ono decision ruled in favor of Ienaga on the point concerning the reference to Unit 731. Previously, the Tokyo High Court ruling had found with the state on this point, regarding the scholarly research up to 1983 as insufficient. The court regarded *Akuma no Hoshoku*, one of the first three books written on the topic by Morimura Seiichi, as not following the form of academic writing.[30] The Ono decision, however, ruled that the MOE's order to eliminate the description of Unit 731 was illegal because no scholarly work had *denied* the existence of Unit 731 and its cruel experiments. Interestingly, in his opinion supplementing the decision, even the somewhat conservative Judge Sonobe, who voted against the rulings on the issue in the Ono decision, denied a point that school textbooks cannot include descriptions of events that have not been fully elucidated. He argued that, for a variety of reasons (e.g., the death of the persons involved), many wartime events cannot be necessarily cleared up with respect to such particulars as the cause, development, and the exact number of victims.[31]

Anti-Japanese Resistance in Korea and the Battle of Okinawa

Concerning the dispute over the description of the anti-Japanese resistance that took place in Korea around the time of Sino-Japanese War (1894–95), the Tokyo High Court ruled in favor of the state. The court saw Ienaga's use of the language "anti-Japanese resistance" as vague and as likely to create some confusion vis-à-vis more commonly used terms such as the Togakuto Rebellion or the Kogo Peasant War. Thus the court basically accepted the state's argument, ruling that the order of the MOE had not been intended to conceal Japanese aggression against Korea, but only to request a change that would make the description precise, accurate, and easy to understand.[32]

The Ono decision supported the Tokyo High Court ruling, finding the term "anti-Japanese resistance" as vague and confusing to high school teachers and students. It also stated that in 1983 when Ienaga wrote the text the research on the various Korean resistance movements of the period was still insufficient.[33] The judges seemed very divided on the issue, with a supplemental opinion written by Judge Sonobe, who voted for the ruling, and dissenting opinions from Judges Ono and Ozaki. However, on the point regarding whether school textbooks should include the Korean resistance against Japan, all the judges seemed to agree with each other (and perhaps with Ienaga). Even Judge Sonobe wrote as follows:

> I do not think that it is inadequate to write in textbooks that an event took place in which the Korean people took up arms and resisted the Japanese forces advancing into Korea after the Sino-Japanese War broke out. To the contrary, as in the dissenting opinions, [I too] think that such a description is necessary in order to allow [students] to understand correctly the nature of the Sino-Japanese War and the relation between Japan and Korea in modern times.[34]

Concerning the dispute over the death of Okinawans in the Battle of Okinawa, again, the court decisions were in favor of the state. However, a close look at the statements reveals that Ienaga's basic arguments were recognized and in some cases supported. For example, the Tokyo High Court recognized that it was the common view that the distinctive character of the Battle of Okinawa was that numerous Okinawan residents were killed not only by being dragged into the war but also by having been driven to commit suicide by the Japanese forces.[35] Furthermore, the Ono decision added that, in order to teach about the actual suffering of Okinawan residents, it was necessary to include the "mass-suicide" in textbooks, and that it was possible for textbook authors to add proper explanation to avoid students' "misunderstanding [the event] as the residents' voluntary suicide." Indeed, the ruling pointed out, Ienaga actually revised the text in that way and the MOE eventually accepted the revision. The court did not award Ienaga a win on this point because the MOE's comment actually helped Ienaga clarify the text (and so it caused no damage). Clearly, while not ruling in favor of Ienaga in the game of legal truths, the court sided with Ienaga in terms of the game of historical truths and in terms of educational truths.[36]

The Supreme Court's Response to the Textbook Controversy of the 1980s and 1990s

Ienaga's third lawsuit focused more on the issue of the depiction of "history" than had the first and second. Though some may feel that Japan's judicial system had been attempting to determine what the historical facts were, and what the correct textbook descriptions were, this is not really the case. In most cases, the courts considered whether the requests made by the MOE in the process of Ienaga's textbook screening were "reasonable" (the criteria used by the Tokyo High Court), or "unerring" (that of the Supreme Court), in light of commonly accepted academic views.

For the most part the courts avoided entering the historians' debate; rather, they seem to have built rules of textbook writing and authorization. By and large, the courts took the position that the MOE's requests should be based on facts verified by the academic research of the time. In that sense, the decisions, especially that of the Supreme Court, would apply pressure to the state, since, strictly speaking, the state could no longer ignore "commonly accepted views" and "verified facts" in history studies when it imposed its views on textbook authors. However, as pointed out by Judge Sonobe's opinion above, the loss or destruction of record, or the death of all the victims (as in the case of Unit 731), often makes it impossible to verify every particular of wartime events. The judges' opinions show that they debated this point and did not come to a unanimous conclusion.

Another interesting feature of the Ono decision is its implicit reference to Japan's right-wing history revision movement in the 1990s, led by Fujioka Nobukatsu of the University of Tokyo. Fujioka's movement was outside the lawsuit, so the Supreme Court judges did not directly refer to the movement or its argument, but several of the judges in their opinions made implicit references to it. Judge Sonobe stated: "It is undeniable that the actual situation of wartime events such as the Nanjing incident ... has in part been unknown to this date; however, that does not mean that the Nanjing incident ... did not happen."[37] This clearly refutes the logic used in the right-wing revisionist discourse that represents the "Nanjing Massacre as an illusion." Even Judge Chikusa, who opposed the decision finding that the MOE's request concerning Unit 731 was illegal, admitted a need to let the younger generation understand accurately Japan's past acts, even if those were disgraceful to Japan.[38]

Presiding Judge Ono's opinion is especially notable. First of all, he argued for further limitation of occasions upon which the MOE would be allowed to request revisions. He then directly quoted the words of Shiba Ryotaro: "A nation telling lies in its textbooks ... will eventually be ruined." Shiba is a popular historical fiction writer who died several years earlier and whose work has been appropriated by the history revision movement to justify its position and appeal to the public. Thus, the quote speaks directly against that movement. In the same opinion, Judge Ono also argued strongly in favor of writing about Japan's wrongdoings during the war and during its colonial rule in Asia.[39]

The game of historical truth was one of the multiple games of truth played out in court, in which Ienaga and his legal team, calling notable historians and journalists as expert witnesses, had a slight upper hand;

however, it seems to me, the game of educational truth was essentially left in a state of deadlock, particularly regarding the question concerning who has the right to decide the content of school textbooks specifically, or of education in general. Ienaga did not win his arguments for the unconstitutionality of state textbook screening in general (even the Sugimoto decision of 1970 in the second suit found that the state's textbook screening as applied to Ienaga's text was unconstitutional). I would argue that Ienaga and his legal team faced difficulty because of the complexity of and tension concerning curriculum making. Society has a certain responsibility for school curricula, and the government is, for good or ill, a part of society.

The question here, perhaps, is one of restraining the state's power, not denying it. In this regard, Ienaga and his legal team moved—out of necessity and somewhat reluctantly—in the right direction, making it central to question the government's abuse of its power: questioning such abuse is one way—and maybe the only practical way—to define and limit the state's power(s). However, since such a view recognizes the state's partial and qualified authority over school textbooks, Ienaga's team, including his lawyers and supporters, were, in essence, divided on that point. Also it would be necessary to rethink the kinds of roles the government should play to make the best textbooks available to the younger generations. For example, it can function to ensure the fairness and transparency of the entire system of school textbooks from the production and adoption to the use of them in schools, rather than utilizing direct censorship.[40]

Reflecting on his thirty-two years of court battles, Ienaga stated that "the textbook lawsuits were not only battles to win or lose inside the court, but also the movements of citizens developed with the court at the core."[41] Indeed, outside the court, the struggles over history textbooks and war memories continued—and intensified occasionally—in the late 1980s and indeed intensified in the early 1990s. As discussed above, in the late 1980s and early 1990s, most history textbook authors labored for inclusion of wartime issues from critical, peace-and-justice perspectives, and so history textbooks continued to expand their content of the war atrocities committed by Japan during the years of the Asia-Pacific War. Textbook authors were willing to take advantage of advances in historical research achieved by of Ienaga's court challenges and the court rulings (which did not award Ienaga a total victory, but which began to suggest a limit to state power) to incorporate new findings and topics. One of the topics they began to include at the beginning of the 1990s was the issue of "comfort women," which became the central issue of the struggle over the national narratives in the 1990s, following a fierce backlash from the right-wing nationalists when Japanese politics was increasingly in flux.

7 Nationalism, democracy, and the textbook market

Right-wing nationalist history textbook projects, 1982–2007

> If the meanings of concepts are taken to be unstable, open to contest and redefinition, then they require vigilant repetition, reassertion, and implementation by those who have endorsed one or another definition. Instead of attributing a transparent and shared meaning to cultural concepts, post-structuralists insist that meanings are not fixed in a culture's lexicon but are rather dynamic, always potentially in flux. Their study therefore calls for attention to the conflictual processes that establish meanings, to the ways in which such concepts as gender acquire the appearance of fixity, to the challenges posed for normative social definitions, and to the ways these challenges are met—in other words, to the play of force involved in any society's construction and implementation of meanings: to politics.
>
> Joan Wallach Scott, *Gender and the Politics of History*

The 1982 international and national censure against the Japanese state's textbook screening, along with other events such as Ienaga's third lawsuit, brought a momentum for textbook authors to include more critical, cosmopolitan, and peace-and-justice perspectives into their texts. However, since the censure, the nation has also witnessed recurrent flare-ups and eruptions in the Japanese history textbook controversy. At the same time, the cultural and political landscape has also undergone substantive changes both inside and outside Japan in the late 1980s, 1990s, and the beginning of the twenty-first century: Emperor Hirohito died in January 1989, signaling the possibility of a shift in Japan's cultural politics; South Korea became more democratic; the Berlin Wall came down; the Gulf War broke out, raising questions over the future of Japan's 1946 Constitution (and specifically Article 9 which declared the renunciation of war); the Soviet Union collapsed; supported by women's movements in Korea, Japan, and across the world, some of the so-called "comfort women" broke their half-century of silence; Japan's economic recession and structural adjustments occurred; and the Iraqi War commenced.[1]

The changing landscape, in essence, heralded the end of the Cold War era and its geo-political (and military) dispensation in East Asia. The Cold War, having been the world order of the post-World War II period, had effectively kept the lid on discussions between Japan and its Asian neighbors of divisive issues relating to Japan's wartime record of atrocities. With that world order clearly becoming a thing of the past, one might have expected, or hoped, that Japan would finally be ready to address unresolved issues of the Asia-Pacific War, including issues concerning teaching about the Japanese war atrocities as a critical part of its remembrance. This did not happen. As discussed below, instead, the Japanese history textbook controversy has gone through its most conflictive and openly contested processes in recent years,[2] which leads to questions concerning the features of recent developments, the ways major groups, individuals, and stakeholders fought the textbook struggles, and the nature of new strategies and tactics, if any, in terms of both the challenges posed for the dominant and official interpretations of Japan's wartime conduct and the counter-offensives with which these challenges are met.

Any society's construction and implementation of meanings of concepts such as gender involves politics, or the play of social force(s), and requires vigilant repetition, reassertion, and implementation, as Joan Scott argues.[3] I would further argue that the meanings that a nation establishes for its past (and so its identity) are always among the most contested, politically charged, and ideologically complex. It is, therefore, interesting to examine the ways in which a gender dimension comes into play in the Japanese struggles over history textbooks, as "nation" is clearly a gendered project. So too is it interesting to examine the ways in which various social forces fought to construct and implement different versions of the nation's history (and history textbooks) in a capitalist democracy such as Japan's,[4] where the battleground has never been level, politically or otherwise, but where citizens, individually or collectively, can express their opinions and take action.

Right-wing Nationalist Offensives and their History Textbook Project

The right-wing nationalists responded to the history textbook controversy of 1982 (and the relaxation of textbook policy by the Ministry of Education (MOE)) by launching several offensives. In their view, the modification of history textbooks represented a change for the worse. First, they attacked the media as having falsely reported the MOE's order to amend the term "aggression" to "advance" in lines referring to the Japanese invasion of northern China in the 1981–82 round of textbook screening. It was true that no such exact orders were made in that round (because the term had been altered previously), but similar changes in terminology in sections referring to the Japanese invasion of Southeast Asia and southern China were indeed the result of the MOE's direct and indirect pressure.[5] Despite the general accuracy of media portrayals of MOE policies, the nationalists attempted to use this minor inaccuracy to discredit all the media reports concerning this issue. (Since the 1970s, right-wing nationalists have often used this kind of tactic to discredit their opponents and confuse the public.)

The nationalists also criticized the government's handling of the international aspects of the controversy. In their view, each nation is entitled to decide the content of its own school curriculum, and it was humiliating from a diplomatic perspective that Japan had to apologize for its textbooks to countries such as China and South Korea. In the fall of 1982, one of the major right-wing organizations, the National Conference to Defend Japan (*Nihon o Mamoru Kokumin Kaigi*, established in 1981), therefore announced that it would develop its own Japanese history textbook for high schools. This organization had as its main goal the revision of Japan's 1946 Constitution, which pledged Japan to a pacifist role in international affairs and forbade her to maintain her own armed forces. The organization's chair was a former Japanese ambassador to the United Nations and a member of Nakasone's informal "brain trust." (Its membership to date has consisted of some affiliated religious organizations, business leaders such as the former CEOs of Sony and Sankei Shinbunsha [publisher of the right-wing daily newspaper *Sankei Shinbun*], and several prominent right-wing scholars.)

The right-wing nationalist history textbook project began in the spring of 1984, with Hara Shobo selected as the publisher, and the draft was submitted to the MOE in the summer of 1985. However, the MOE was not able to easily authorize the text because it contained numerous factual errors as well as misprints, in part because the authors had rushed to complete it in time for the 1985 celebration of Emperor Hirohito's sixtieth year on the throne. It also clearly challenged the spirit of the 1946 (Peace) Constitution. Although the MOE's Textbook Screening Council approved the text conditionally in January 1986, it had to convene an extra session in May, because some council members felt the revised manuscript was still "distasteful," "biased," and "lacking in consideration for neighboring countries." Nonetheless, the council passed it, essentially because of political pressure (Prime Minister Nakasone was in favor of the text, though he did not back it publicly). At this point, it became clear that *Shinpen Nihonshi*, the first nationalist school textbook in postwar Japan, would be published in 1987.[6]

What followed was extraordinary—and was dubbed by some observers as "measures beyond laws and rules." Soon after approval of the text, the MOE requested further revisions (an extensive revision after approval had no precedence). Some speculated that the MOE was attempting to avoid media criticism about careless mistakes that the text still contained or that it needed to appease some Textbook Screening Council members. However, soon the South Korean media and the Chinese government voiced criticism of the new book, and the MOE decided to request another revision (for example recommending the use of the term "massacre" instead of "incident" to refer to the Nanjing Massacre). One of the MOE's high-ranking officials, knowing it was against MOE's own regulations, even asked the publisher to backdate the request so that it would appear to have been received before the approval of the text.[7]

Eventually, because diplomatic tensions did not abate, some cabinet members asked the MOE to withdraw its approval of the text, but the MOE (under Education Minister Kaifu Toshiki) rejected this, choosing instead to request a third revision at the end of June, this time with the informal involvement of the Ministry of Foreign Affairs. Nevertheless, a fourth revision was requested before the MOE went to a press conference, at which the MOE official(s) announced the results of the textbook screening. The MOE maintained that in order to have good textbooks, it was within the Education Minister's authority and responsibility to take extraordinary measures.[8]

The text's authors (and the right-wingers behind them) publicly criticized the government for ignoring its own laws and rules, but they had achieved their primary goal. The leftists and moderates concerned with the issues of school textbooks felt that the extraordinary measures would create a bad precedent and that the MOE should not have approved the textbook in the first place. Partly in order to address these criticisms, the Ad Hoc Council on Education deliberated on the textbook screening system and decided to enable the Education Minister to order revisions even after approval of a textbook (the change was announced in 1988 and brought into effect in 1990). In other words, the government changed its rules *ex post facto*.[9]

However, *Shinpen Nihonshi* did not sell well (approximately 8,000 copies sold in the first year), in part because textbooks at the high school level were (and still are, as of July 2007) adopted by each school. At the high-school level teachers had a say in the textbook adoption choices and, by and large, they did not support *Shinpen Nihonshi*. The text's failure on the market continued in the following years and indeed decades: 9,357 copies were sold in 1989, but the text's market share declined steadily thereafter. Eventually, in 1993, Hara Shobo discontinued publication, and another publisher, Kokusho Kankokai, published the book under the new title *Saishin Nihonshi* [The most recent edition: Japanese history]. However, the new publisher also stopped publication after a short time, as the book did not sell well (only 2,682 copies sold in 2001). Yet another company, Mei-seisha, run by a right-wing organization, took over the publication rights in 2001 and, with the MOE's approval, the company published the text under the same title (*Saishin Nihonshi*). Its latest market share was 0.9 percent (5,017 copies sold) as of Spring 2005—and this market share would not change until the next round of textbook screening and adoption. Some critics argue that the market share of the text indicates the limited extent of the right-wing nationalist influence over history teachers in high schools in particular, and history teachers in general.[10]

In any case, in the late 1980s and early 1990s, it appeared that the right-wing nationalists were not significantly increasing in strength, nor very successful in enlarging the scope of their influence. They could no longer expect the MOE to impose nationalist views on history through its text-book-screening processes as freely as it had before, since the MOE had to be cautious because of the international and national attention it would draw and because of the court rulings (as discussed in Chapter 6); and their own history textbook project, while it (relatively easily) overcame the MOE's reluctance by mobilizing their political capital, ran into the problem of market shares (or lack thereof).

Japanese politics also showed signs of disarray during these years. In November 1987, Takeshita Noboru succeeded Nakasone to become Prime Minister. (Takeshita had been a ranking member of Tanaka Kakuei's largest LDP faction, which Takeshita had left with others to form his own in 1985, which caused a damage within this largest LDP faction.) The new administration was short-lived, with Takeshita resigning in January 1989 because of a corruption scandal, and, for various similar reasons, none of his LDP successors managed more than a brief tenure in office.[11] There was, however, no doubt that the struggle over history textbooks and war memories would continue throughout the 1990s (and indeed beyond). It did, and, in fact, it entered a new phase with a new issue—that of "comfort women."

The Emergence of the Comfort Women Issue in the Early 1990s

To many Japanese the existence of wartime "comfort facilities" (*ianjo*) and "comfort women" (*ianfu*) was not exactly a secret. A number of wartime reports, diaries, and memoirs published after the Asia-Pacific War referred to these women and facilities.[12] For example, in his memoirs published in the late 1970s, Nakasone Yasuhiro, who would serve as Japan's Prime Minister from 1982 to 1987, mentioned his involvement in building comfort facilities on the island of Borneo when he was a young naval officer. After the occupation of the island, he stated, "There were some [men] who raped the native women and some who indulged in gambling. In some cases I built comfort facilities for these men, with considerable effort."[13] Nakasone wrote about it rather proudly (and casually) without any noticeable feeling of guilt or shame—in part because the contemporary meaning of (military) comfort women as victims and survivors of Japan's war crime was not yet constructed.[14]

In the 1970s and 1980s, in both Japan and South Korea, several seminal works, including feminist journalist Matsui Yayori's article published in *Asahi Shinbun*, examined the issue of comfort women from critical and feminist perspectives; however, the Japanese public, while feeling pity for the women, by and large remained unaware of the event as a war crime. Besides, very few former comfort women broke their silence.[15] It was only after the successes of the South Korean democratic and feminist movements in the late 1980s and the growing international cry, feminist or otherwise, in the early 1990s for the prosecution of rapes in military conflicts (such as those that took place in the former Yugoslavia and in Rwanda) that the postwar Japanese normative meaning of comfort women faced a fundamental challenge.[16]

When the issue of comfort women first surfaced in the Japanese Diet in 1990, the Japanese government (under Prime Minister Kaifu) flatly denied a request for an investigation, maintaining that the wartime state and its military had had no involvement in this matter. However, in 1991 the first former Korean comfort woman came out in public, followed by others in various Asian countries, and they spoke openly of their terrible experiences. At the same time, research by Japanese historians such as Yoshimi Yoshiaki demonstrated that the military had in fact been intimately involved.

In 1993, the Japanese government (under Prime Minister Miyazawa) heard the testimonies of fifteen former comfort women in Seoul, and on August 4, Chief Cabinet Secretary Kono Yohei stated that the Imperial Japanese Forces were directly and indirectly involved in the establishment and administration of comfort facilities. Although the Kono statement remained somewhat ambiguous—perhaps deliberately—on several key points such as legal responsibility and compensation, it expressed "a firm determination" to remember the historical facts "through historical research and education."[17]

These developments, particularly Kono's statement, gave textbook authors the justification they needed for including the topic in their textbooks. In all, twenty-two Japanese history textbooks for high school students referred to "comfort women" and passed the MOE's 1992–93 and 1993–94 textbook screenings (in fact, the only textbook containing no reference was the right-wing nationalist textbook discussed above). All seven of the social studies history textbooks for junior high school students that included a reference to "comfort women" also passed the 1995–96 screening. By 1997, many textbooks in other social studies-related areas (e.g., geography, world history, contemporary society) also included the topic. A paragraph in the 1997 edition of one junior high textbook of the period read as follows:

> In colonized Taiwan and Korea, the compulsory draft was implemented. There were also women who were forced to accompany the military to the front as comfort women. Because the labor force inside the country [Japan] was limited, approximately 700,000 people from Korea and 40,000 from China were taken by force and made to work in places such as coal mines.[18]

It appeared that the new significance of comfort women would take hold in the nation, and that it would usher in the gradual demise of the right-wing nationalist influence on history textbooks that had begun in the mid-1980s. In retrospect, however, this was only the beginning of the struggle over the meaning of comfort women, with right-wing nationalists in the mid 1990s launching a fierce campaign against the inclusion of the issue in history textbooks. In 1993, when Kono made the above statement, almost forty years of LDP single-party rule also came to an end. As discussed below, the right-wing nationalists were able to exploit the turbulence and uncertainty of Japanese politics in the following years, and the ways in which they influenced the LDP, Diet members, MOE officials, and public discourse more generally indeed contained new elements and strategies.

Fluctuations of Japanese Politics and Neo-Nationalist Movements

The LDP lost its majority in the Lower House election in July 1993, because of a split in which some factions and influential politicians broke away and established new parties. On August 6, only a few days after the Kono statement, a seven-party coalition government was formed under an anti-LDP banner. Upon taking office, Morihiro Hosokawa of the Japan New Party, the new Prime Minister, made several remarks on key aspects of Japan's wartime conduct. He said of the Asia-Pacific War: "I personally recognize it as a *shinryaku senso* (war of aggression), an *ayamatta senso* (wrong war)."[19] In a subsequent speech, he called the colonization of Korea "colonial rule" (*shokuminchi shihai*) instead of using the conventional euphemism "annexation" (*heigo*).[20] These were the first such clear-cut admissions by a postwar Japanese prime minister.

Hosokawa's statements were regarded as threatening by the right. In the autumn, a group of right-wing LDP politicians established the (LDP) Committee for the Examination of History. Approximately 100 LDP Diet members joined, including the future prime ministers Hashimoto Ryutaro, Mori Yoshiro, and Abe Shinzo. They agreed to launch a campaign promoting views of history that held the Asia-Pacific War to be justifiable and denied the existence of the Nanjing Massacre and comfort women.[21]

Although Hosokawa was popular with the electorate, he resigned in April 1994 after being accused of corruption, and was succeeded by Hata Tsutomu (of the *Shinseito*, a new party established by former LDP members). The political scene became increasingly tumultuous and uncertain, and right-wing politicians became ever more vocal. For example, in May 1994, Justice Minister Nagano Shigeto denied the factuality of the Nanjing Massacre and Japanese aggression. The Hata administration fired him almost immediately, only to collapse in on itself soon afterwards when the Japan Socialist Party (JSP) left the coalition.

In June, the LDP returned to power by forming a three-party coalition government with the Socialist Party (SP) and the *Sakigake* (another small new party). The new coalition was a compromise for both the SP and the LDP, with both moving towards the center ground. Murayama Tomiichi of the SP became Prime Minister, but real power lay with the LDP (with Kono as its party president). While Murayama soon announced the SP's abandonment of many of its long-held leftist positions on major postwar political issues (e.g., its opposition to the U.S.–Japan Security Treaty, to the SDF, and to the Hinomaru flag and the Kimigayo anthem), the LDP agreed to issue a Diet resolution apologizing to Asian victims of Japan's past aggression (a general apology, not specifically to the comfort women).[22]

However, the right wing of the LDP, including some cabinet members, openly dissented from this move. In the following months of 1994 and 1995, several cabinet members and influential politicians made remarks denying

Japanese wartime aggression. Some were dismissed, while others apologized in order to keep their posts. Also during these months, the right-wing politicians of the LDP (along with some opposition party members such as Nagano) worked hard to block the resolution of apology that was to be issued on the fiftieth anniversary of Japan's surrender. They strongly opposed the inclusion of key terms such as "Japan's war of aggression" and "Japan's colonial rule of Korea." The LDP leadership was not really able to control them, but nonetheless decided to allow the terms to be included in somewhat indirect ways. The Lower House passed the resolution in June 1995, to the anger of the LDP right-wingers, and the LDP leadership then decided not to lay the resolution before the Upper House. This situation left both the left and the right extremely dissatisfied.[23]

After the event, right-wing politicians and organizations began to focus their attacks on history textbooks. In January 1996, Murayama resigned, and Hashimoto of the LDP became the Prime Minister, with the SP remaining in the coalition but no longer holding any cabinet positions. The LDP thus returned to power in name and reality, and the history textbook issue was one of the few issues that united a majority of LDP Diet members, who held differing views on other policy areas from structural reform to gender equality. The textbook issue was also an avenue through which LDP hawks could work with hawks of other parties. Subsequently, right-wing elements repeatedly demanded the removal of textbook references to "comfort women" (which, under its regulations and rules, the MOE could not do).[24]

In the public arena, new faces joined the nationalist cause and energized its activities by attracting media interest. One such face was Fujioka Nobukatsu, a professor of education at the University of Tokyo. He had originally been a leftist scholar (and had his name and followers among teachers); however, after taking a year's leave of study in the United States around the time of the Gulf War, he converted to the right, and in early 1995, he started a group called the "Liberal-View-of-History Study Group" (*Jiyushugi Shikan Kenkyukai*).

Fujioka published many articles in journals for teachers such as *Shakaika Kyoiku* (Social Studies Education) and *Gendai Kyoiku Kagaku* (Contemporary Education Science), as well as in the right-wing media, including *Sankei Shinbun*, criticizing history education in postwar Japan and current history textbooks as "masochistic" (*jigyakuteki*) and lacking "pride in the history of our nation."[25] He also argued for a pedagogy called the "debate" approach, in which students would be encouraged to debate by taking opposing positions on controversial issues such as the Nanjing Massacre. The debate approach (as a form of instructional method) drew some (positive) attention from teachers (and parents) discontented with the prevailing teacher- and textbook-centered pedagogy in history classrooms in which students often ended up only memorizing key dates and names (for exams), rather than thinking about and discussing topics.

In late 1996, he and others such as Nishio Kanji, a scholar of German literature and philosophy, established the Japanese Society for History Textbook Reform (*Atarashii Rekishi Kyokasho o Tsukurukai,* hereafter the JSHTR), declaring that they would publish "a new history textbook" to be used in junior high schools in 2002.[26] Later, Fusosha (a subsidiary company of Sankei Shinbunsha) was chosen to be the publisher, which began a process of textbook development.

The State's New Approach: Guided "Self-Censorship"

The new right-wing nationalist movement had two closely related agendas: one to develop their text and have it adopted by school districts, and the other to attack the existing texts to make the publishers (and authors) revise their texts. They were able to seize the political opportunity. Although Prime Minster Hashimoto's main political agendas were the reform of the state's administrative system (*gyosei kaikaku*) as well as the economic and banking-system reforms, he was a leader of right-wing LDP members (and had been president of the Nihon Izokukai, a nationwide association of the war bereaved, from 1993 to 1995). The issues of history textbooks, including the references to comfort women in these texts, were a frequent topic of debates in the Diet sessions in his tenure. The LDP hawks worked with the hawks of opposition parties to counter the critical trends in history textbooks, and Hashimoto also expressed his intention to consider a reform of the textbook screening system as a part of his education reform agenda.[27]

In June 1998, Education Minister Machimura Nobutaka of the Hashimoto cabinet, responding to a question raised by Diet member Nagano Shigeto (the Justice Minister fired in 1994 for denying the existence of the Nanjing Massacre and Japanese aggression) in a special committee session in the Upper House, stated that history textbooks "lacked balance" and that the MOE was deliberating on ways to improve the situation. In particular, Machimura referred to three possible means of improvement: first, through textbook screening; second, by "ensuring a good balance ... at the stage of authoring" (i.e., before the submission of textbook drafts to the MOE); and third, through improvements at the stage of textbook adoption.[28] The MOE's censorship role in the textbook screening process was nothing new, but Machimura's response was novel in making explicit reference to the textbook authoring and adoption stages, and in his implication that the MOE would seek ways to intervene at those stages.

In January 1999, the MOE asked publishers to make their textbook content more "balanced" and to reconsider their choice of authors. In the summer, although a few publishers made minor textbook corrections and replaced some authors in charge of writing sections that included the issue of comfort women, overall it appeared that they did not intend to significantly alter sections related to Japanese wartime atrocities. The content of the earlier drafts of the textbook editions prepared for publication in

2002 were little changed from previous editions. However, when the final drafts of the same books were actually submitted to the MOE in the spring of 2000, many descriptions concerning Japanese wartime atrocities had been cut back or removed altogether, the publishers having exercised "self-censorship" of the texts.[29]

The most striking development was the almost total erasure of the comfort women issue from the textbooks. In the previous editions of 1997, all seven junior high history textbooks on the market had made some reference to this issue. In the new drafts for 2002 textbooks, three of the seven textbooks completely removed all such references. Among the four texts that contained references to the issue of comfort women, one draft text included only the sentence "many Korean and other women were sent to the front," whereas the previous edition referred to the issue in three different sections and included a photo of former Korean comfort women requesting compensation and Japanese supporters.[30] Another two texts referred to it only briefly, using the phrase "comfort facilities."[31] Only the last text used the phrase "comfort women," and this was the only text that expanded its discussion from the previous edition.[32]

While the treatment of the comfort women issue best illustrates the degree of self-censorship exercised by the publishers, the draft texts also altered or cut descriptions of other Japanese wartime atrocities. For example, in the 2002 editions, only one text referred to the "Three-Lightenings Strategy" (*sanko sakusen*, the Japanese wartime military strategy "kill all, burn all, and loot all"), whereas in the old editions five out of seven textbooks referred to it.[33] Other examples of self-censorship included: the removal of the term "aggression" (by two draft texts);[34] the omission of any mention of Unit 731 (a biowarfare unit which conducted a series of experiments upon live people and POWs) by all of the 2002 editions, whereas one 1997 edition textbook had referred to it;[35] and fewer references to resistance to Japanese rule in Korea and other Asian countries (with two draft texts removing the lines referring to the Korean independence movement and anti-Japanese movements).[36] These revisions constituted a sea change in the realm of history textbook content (and to date this sea change has remained intact, as of July 2007, as 2006 editions of history textbooks for junior high school students avoid containing controversial terms such as "comfort women").[37]

Publishers did not disclose what happened between the summer of 1999 and spring of 2000 to cause them to make these revisions in such a short period of time. Some Japanese experts such as Tawara Yoshifumi alleged, however, that political pressure had been applied by high government officials. According to Tawara, in December 1999, as the deadline for the submission of textbook drafts neared, CEOs of the publishing houses received telephone calls from "a source in the Prime Minister's office" asking them to "use discretion" in dealing with the textbook reference to "war comfort women" (*jugun ianfu*).[38]

Tawara speculated that Machimura (the former Education Minister who spoke of "three ways to improve textbooks" in 1998) might have been involved because at that time he was working in the Prime Minister's office to develop an agenda for educational reform.[39] Another theory was that publishers were extremely nervous about a potential loss of market share because of right-wing attacks on their textbooks as "masochistic." The truth has not yet emerged (and perhaps never will, given the general reluctance in Japanese business circles to openly criticize the government). From the very beginning of the MOE's textbook screening process, however, it was clear that the 2002 edition of history textbooks would include fewer discussions of Japanese war atrocities. This was, of course, very much what the MOE desired, because it would forestall the sorts of diplomatic problems that tended to arise as a result of direct censorship. Indeed, this seems to be what Machimura suggested in his pronouncement a few years ago, indicating that what occurred subsequently might more accurately be described not simply as "self-censorship," but as *guided* self-censorship."

The *"New History Textbook"*

Meanwhile a draft history textbook authored by members of the JSHTR was also submitted for screening in April 2000.[40] Soon after submission, Nishio Kanji, the lead author, appeared on a TV program to promote it. The publisher, Fusosha, also distributed promotional leaflets and some photocopies of the text to schools and teachers, while the authors undertook a series of lectures and study meetings to inform politicians and local community leaders about the text. As the content of the new book became public knowledge, more and more people, including many historians and history teachers, began to express their dismay and concern both at the chauvinism and basic inaccuracy of the text. In addition, there were protests and criticism from South Korea, China, and other Asian countries.[41]

However, right-wing forces within Japan were determined not to give way. In the autumn of 2000, when a member of the Textbook Screening Council (Noda Eijiro, a former ambassador to India) raised a serious question about the text and began to discuss rejecting it with other members (something that he was within his rights to do in his role as a council member), right-wing newspapers such as *Sankei Shinbun* reported that he was "engineering" disapproval of the text. LDP hawks demanded that the MOE remove him from his position, and after some hesitation the MOE eventually transferred him to another section. Similarly, when the LDP Secretary General, Nonaka Hiromu, responded to Chinese protests by implying that the government would correct the text through the screening process, young LDP hawks and JSHTR members made him retract his statement, indicating the strength of nationalist power in the LDP.[42]

In the spring of 2001, after the authors of the text had made 137 corrections, the newly constituted Ministry of Education and Science (hereafter MOES)[43] approved the text and declared that it would request no further revisions.[44] The South Korean and Chinese governments requested a further revision, but the

MOES refused (even though technically it could still advise revisions because of the changes to textbook screening procedures introduced in 1990). Instead, the MOES argued that the local education boards, rather than the MOES itself, would be responsible for textbook adoption. The MOES's neutrality here was questionable at best, since its statement meant that the education boards could disregard teachers' opinions about the textbooks (teachers had tended to prefer textbooks with critical, peace-and-justice perspectives). In fact, right-wing forces had been working steadily to exclude teachers from the textbook adoption processes, with some local education boards having already changed their adoption procedures to lessen teacher influence.

Continuing Struggles over Textbook Adoption: The Textbook Market as an Arena

The situation was hardly auspicious for those opposing the adoption of the *New History Textbook*. Concerned citizens and groups, including a variety of people such as seasoned leftists and concerned parents, exchanged information through the Internet, organized study meetings, and initiated local petitions. Many appeals—some reported by the media, and others posted on websites— were issued by different groups and individuals, including the novelist and Nobel Laureate Oe Kenzaburo and renowned historians inside and outside Japan. Labor unions, including the Japan Teachers Union, found common ground, despite the fact that they had disagreements on other matters. International pressure was also stepped up, most notably with a petition signed by 400,000 South Koreans opposing the adoption of the text. In mid-July and August, as the deadline neared for the education boards to make their final decisions, grassroots activists redoubled their efforts. Even so, it seemed the activists were fighting an uphill battle.[45]

Among the public schools, the textbook adoption council of Shimotsuga District, a consolidated district of two cities and eight towns located in Shimotsuga County, Tochigi Prefecture, was the first body to decide to adopt the new right-wing text. Although each city or town in Shimotsuga had its own local education board, decisions on textbook adoptions were to be made at the level of the (consolidated) Shimotsuga District. However, shortly after the media reported their decision to adopt the *New History Textbook*, the council began to receive strong criticism from both inside and outside the region. For example, the mayor of a local town wrote to a newspaper:

> What I witnessed there on the Chinese front where I joined [to fight during the war] was nothing but aggression. Who made the rule that imposes a textbook which is so internationally problematic ... on towns and cities by a majority decision, and when? ... The education board members of our town will not agree to vote [for it] since they understand well

enough the will of the people in our town. I urge the [textbook adoption] council of the Shimotsuga District to reflect [on this matter] seriously.[46]

In another case, a group of homemakers collected more than 1,500 signatures against the text within five days. By the end of July, all the education boards in Shimotsuga had reversed the decision. In a sense, therefore, the MOES's designation of local education boards as responsible for textbook adoption (which was also the position of JSHTR in the debate over the textbook adoption) could be said to have backfired.[47]

The events in Shimotsuga marked a turning point. The local education boards reported to have been in favor of the text did not win enough votes to adopt it after all. The only exceptions were the Tokyo Metropolitan Education Board, which selected the text for a few schools and classes for mentally and physically handicapped children, and the Ehime Prefectual Education Board, which chose it for its schools for handicapped and deaf children. In both cases, the board members were appointees owing their positions to governors strongly supportive of the text. Because several private schools adopted the text, the market share of the *New History Textbook* was approximately 0.039percent (amounting to 543 copies used in schools as textbooks) in the spring of 2002.[48] As the JSHTR's goal was to gain 10 percent of market share, this was regarded as failure by the group as well as by the oppositional groups.[49]

In the following years, the JSHTR strengthened its ties with other right-wing political and religious organizations (in part because its membership was in decline in the early part of the twenty-first century).[50] It also kept a close relationship with the hawks in the LDP, who often held important posts either in the party or in the Koizumi administration. Indeed, Koizumi Jun'ichiro, an "eccentric" (*henjin*) among LDP politicians,[51] became Prime Minister in April 2001, and, as a hawk, he supported the JSHTR throughout his tenure. Perhaps importantly, Koizumi also promoted young conservative/nationalist Abe Shinzo to positions with ever-increasing responsibility. LDP's platform at the party convention in January 2005 included making an amendment of the Fundamental Law of Education and the correction of bias in textbooks was among its goals for the year. Abe Shinzo, after becoming the Prime Minister in September 2006, succeeded in amending the law.

Meanwhile, a revised edition of the *New History Textbook* passed the MOES's 2004–2005 textbook screening, and again throughout the country the struggles of social forces for and against the *New History Textbook* ensued. On the one hand, the JSHTR had favorable momentum—because the MOES amended some textbook adoption policies and nationalistic sentiment was on the rise because of the cases of abduction of Japanese citizens by North Korea. On the other hand, the opposition forces, with their experience in the previous round, also mounted their protests swiftly. After several months of hard-fought, emotionally charged battles, the text did not sell well. Most of the local education boards made efforts to remain neutral and decided on the less controversial, "safe" texts. With only a few education boards such as Tokyo's Suginami Ward Board of Education and the Otawarashi Board of Education in Tochigi Prefecture adopting it, the text's market share again turned out to be small—0.39 percent (4,912 copies adopted in total).[52]

The defeat spurred on the JSHTR's internal power struggles, resulting in some core members forming another group with the intention of writing another textbook. Fusosha decided to work with the new group, and so, in May 2007, the JSHTR, with Fujioka Nubukatsu as the new chair, announced that it would seek another publisher. The text needs to go through another round of textbook screening, which is slated to begin in the fall of 2009 (currently the MOES conducts textbook screenings every four years). One can speculate that it could be difficult to find a publisher for a book so deficit-ridden. As of July 2007, the future of the *New History Textbook*—or the JSHTR itself for that matter—is uncertain.

For all its attempts, the JSHTR has so far gained very little ground in spreading the *New History Textbook* through schools and classrooms; however, we have to note that its movement has served extremely well in producing the outcome desired by Japan's right-wing nationalism: Japan's history textbooks currently (in 2007) in use in junior high schools include fewer materials that discuss Japan's war atrocities than those used in 1997. Among the eight text-books on the market, none refer to comfort women in the main text; only two include the term "taken-by-force" (*kyosei renko*, forced labor of Korean and Chinese men); and almost none of the texts refer to the number of victims killed in the Nanjing Massacre. Because the local education boards prefer to adopt "safe" texts, the market has become more oligopolistic.[53] Publishers continue to subscribe to guided self-censorship and the MOES continues to strengthen its nationalist orientation in textbook screening processes.

For more than several decades, the Japanese history textbook controversy has been a persistent cultural and political struggle at home, and since 1982 the controversy has increasingly been set in the context of Japan's international relations. At the end of Cold War the nation definitely needed to develop new history textbook perspectives and policies both with respect to its relations with its Asian neighbors and with respect to the education of its own youth. Japanese politics, however, became uncertain (and very confusing at times), as the political system established in 1955—the LDP rule opposed by several parties, including the SP—became dysfunctional (and there was a prolonged economic recession). In a sense, right-wing nationalism has taken greater advantage of the national feeling of uncertainty and stagnation than its opponents, by selling old (nationalist) texts in a new package, that of the *New History Textbook*.

The controversy has been a symbolic battle with implications for the real world, as it has also been a war by proxy, the target of struggle being not merely textbooks *per se* but the founding principles of postwar pacifist Japan as embodied in documents such as the 1946 Constitution. History lessons "[instruct] people how to think and act as national subjects and how to view relations with outsiders."[54] In the final analysis, therefore, the history textbook controversy can be seen as a part of a larger struggle over Japan's national identity and security policy fought by leftists, moderates, conservatives and right-wing nationalists, with the last group forming the (ideological) core of the dominant power bloc, and thereby having significant influence over state policy and practice.[55]

The political struggles at home have also strongly influenced (and been influenced by) the history textbook controversy, as the struggle has been constant between the leftist and the nationalist camps. We should note, however, that the elements of the dominant bloc—different factions of the LDP, other political parties, and bureaucracies such as the MOE—have differences. In particular, the LDP has always had factional conflicts: in the late 1970s, the LDP was rife with internal power struggles; and in the mid and late 1980s the party was corrupt and its internal struggles irreconcilable. Further, since the early 1990s, the LDP has been unable to maintain its single-party rule. In this context, the attacks on textbooks, particularly history textbooks, served as an anchoring point around which to unite the various LDP factions and through which its young politicians have sought to gain more influence. It was also a tool through which the LDP could forge alliances with right-wing elements of other parties. Right-wing nationalism, in other words, has served the LDP well as a kind of ideological glue.

The recent "politically neutral" role the Japanese state played in the controversy offers an empirical insight into the nature of the modern state and its ways of wielding power—its governmentality. Michel Foucault states that "it is not through law that the aims of government are to be reached" but by "multiform tactic[al]" devices which are in essence regulatory, of non-legal character.[56] The MOE (which became the MOES in 2001) has built up its control over textbooks and schools by accumulating ministerial regulations, rules, and customs over several decades. It has gradually developed "the complex and multiple practices of a 'governmentality' which presupposes ... rational forms, technical procedures, instrumentations through which to operate."[57]

It should be noted here, however, that the MOE has developed these practices by maintaining close ties with right-wing nationalists. In this case, the administrative power of the state has a link to the existing discourse of right-wing nationalism and its power over the nation. Although the MOE has claimed that its regulations and procedures are neutral, and that they are applied to everyone evenhandedly, it has clearly exercised discretion with regard to how those regulations are applied. It has often helped nationalists achieve their major goals by bending regulations (in some cases by introducing a new regulation to justify a fait accompli), while generally rejecting—in the name of the same regulations—most requests from textbook authors taking cosmopolitan, peace-and-justice perspectives, or from Japan's Asian neighbors.

The recent developments in the Japanese history textbook controversy vis-à-vis textbook adoption battles also reveal an interesting point regarding the politics surrounding history textbooks in a capitalist democracy. The ways in which Japanese citizens (from the center to the left on the political spectrum) have united and fought against the *New History Textbook* shows that citizens have the power to resist the combined forces of the state and right-wing nationalists. At this point, new technologies such as the Internet seem to have helped these citizens more than they did the nationalists. The decisions made by the school districts in terms of their choice of textbook show that, if there is a market, "consumers" can also have the power to oppose, or not to buy, a certain product. However, this resulted in the districts adopting a "safe," less controversial text, rather than a critical, peace-and-justice oriented text among the available texts. Of course, we should not forget that their choices are already limited, since the right-wing nationalists, along with the quiet cooperation of the state, have effectively removed a great number of critical descriptions of the war in the past decade.[58]

Epilogue

The Japanese history textbook controversy and the significance of Ienaga Saburo's textbook lawsuits

> You can observe, in so far as the multiple games of truth are concerned, that what has always characterized our society, since the time of the Greeks, is the fact that we do not have a complete and peremptory definition of the game of truth which would be allowed, to the exclusion of all others. There is always a possibility, in a given game of truth, to discover something else and to more or less change such and such a rule and sometimes even the totality of the game of truth.
>
> Michel Foucault,
> "The Ethic of Care for the Self as a Practice of Freedom"

Ienaga Saburo's court challenges to the state textbook screening processes have played a central role in the struggle over the national narrative and identity of postwar Japan. His concern with historical truth, including the teaching of history and the production of history textbooks, should be seen as a concern for the present and future as much as the past. Narratives of the past construct (and reconstruct) the identities of persons, and as such "persuade [them] to act in ways they might not otherwise act."[1] As George Orwell put it in *Nineteen Eighty-Four*, "Who controls the past controls the future,"[2] and such a phrase helps to explain the intent and efforts of Japanese nationalist attempts to revise history through the state's de facto censorship of history textbooks. Narratives that speak of "nation" and a nation's past are powerful tools that invite people to share a common sense of identity by supplying definite meanings that inform individuals of who "we" are and where "we" come from. Of course, narratives of this kind are pretense at best, since a question of identity is essentially forever unsettled and puzzling, but the maintenance of a given hegemony in part depends upon such commonsensical views and the feelings people hold about themselves.[3]

Postwar Japanese historical and political conditions provided a specific set of circumstances in which the struggle over national narrative and identity took place, and out of which Ienaga's court challenges were conceived and developed. August 15, 1945—the "end" of the war, as most Japanese have called it instead of Japan's defeat in the war—was not really the end of the war. In many countries neighboring Japan, the actual war situation continued.[4] As the situation shifted to the Cold War (though in Asia it was not always "cold"), the U.S. policy on the Tokyo war tribunal exempted from prosecution a large number of those responsible for Japan's war crimes, including Emperor Hirohito. Japan's acceptance of the tribunal court judgments meant that the pursuit of war crime issues by the external forces ended there, and, simultaneously, that pursuing such matters by the Japanese themselves became "taboo."

Since then, the Japanese government, controlled by the LDP, has not really come to terms with either the question of war responsibility, including that of accountability for colonial rule, or the voices of people in Asia who suffered both physically and mentally because of Japanese conduct during the war.[5] Japanese citizens—including those who played a part in Japan's postwar oppositional and alternative political forces—might not have been perfectly "innocent" in this matter, and may well have "collaborated" in Japan's ignorance of war responsibility. In particular, at certain moments in its postwar history Japan has seen insurgencies of grassroots nationalism. One such moment occurred in the 1950s, when the Allied occupation ended, and another in the 1990s, when the Cold War framework collapsed. While a critical examination through a complex lens may be necessary to understand these nationalist phenomena,[6] it is nonetheless significant to point out here that it was between these two moments when Ienaga's textbook lawsuits were fought.

To be sure, for those Japanese truly committed to forming alternative narratives and identities centered on terms such as "democracy," "rights of citizens," and "freedom," the year 1945 did not mark the end in terms of their struggles within Japan (just as it did not for many throughout Asia). The "liberation" brought about by the occupation forces might have provided some illusion of such an "end," but it soon became clear that the powers responsible for the years of reckless war had escaped the question of war responsibility, and were prepared to repress the emergence of Japanese voices that had begun to address the issue from critical, cosmopolitan, peace-and-justice perspectives. Here we have to note that the "freedom" which people in Japan had come to enjoy was (and still is) a "practice" rather than a goal or an achievement: without practice—or I would argue struggle—"freedom" would not have had the meanings that they desired.[7] It follows that the meaning of "freedom" depends on the practices that people carry out in the name of that term, and the significance of Ienaga's court challenges, in my view, rests first and last on this point.

Ienaga was one of very few scholars who recognized in the 1960s two aspects of the ordinary Japanese war experience—that is, that of offenders (externally) and that of victims (internally). He unequivocally argued the need to pursue, by the Japanese themselves through their own judiciary, the issue of war crimes and responsibility.[8] His uniqueness was that he was not just arguing the position, but was himself pursuing the question of war responsibility in his own way, along with his scholarly work. He filed the textbook lawsuits, an approach totally unfamiliar to many Japanese, and fought his battle in the name of the 1946 Constitution, which takes a pacitist position and which contains phrases such as "freedom and the sovereign rights of the people." His was a practice of that freedom and those rights, and constituted perhaps the only way to construct, hold, and pin down, however momentarily, the fragile and certainly fluid meanings of those terms.

Ienaga's textbook lawsuits constituted, in effect, the Japanese judicial pursuit of Japanese war crimes and responsibility (however extraordinary a form it took for such a matter).[9] Of course, the trial was not to pass judgment on individuals who had committed the war crimes, but to try the power that had committed the crime and then attempted to conceal it. It is no coincidence that Ienaga took a position that gave resonance to the voices of war victims in China, Korea, and other Asian countries. The immediate impact of Ienaga's 1970 victory (the Sugimoto Decision) was that other textbook authors began presenting more information concerning Japan's war atrocities. While the partial victories in Ienaga's third lawsuit may have reflected a change in the international situation, a situation in which Japan was compelled to listen to the victims' voices, his lawsuits as a whole actually stimulated both research and public interest in the wartime conduct of the Japanese military. Ienaga also succeeded to some extent in mobilizing international support for his cause. These developments, in fact, prepared the (ordinary) Japanese for accepting, or at least understanding, those voices as "truths."[10]

In the context of contemporary educational thought, Ienaga's thirty-year challenge to the state raised, fairly directly, the question of whose knowledge ought to be taught in schools and thus represented in school textbooks.[11] This is, in part, a question of process and authority: who should decide the content of education and how should they proceed? No democratic nation has resolved this question, and the tendency seems to be to ignore it.[12] In my view, it is important to develop a democratic process by which educational content can be debated, negotiated, and selected. Because we cannot teach everything, we need to make selections, and in this sense textbooks need to be produced through a "free, contributive and common process of participation in the creation of meanings and values."[13]

The state in all likelihood has a role, or perhaps multiple roles, to play in ensuring the fairness and transparency of such a process. No one in the field of curriculum studies, I would say, could possibly argue that society has nothing to do with school curricula. We all recognize that the state is a part of society (for good or bad), as are many other organizations and groups. The real issue seems, to me, to be how to define the kinds of roles the state as well as other social agencies need to play in the process of curriculum-making, including textbook production and distribution. The current Japanese system, which has allowed the state and the Ministry of Education to advance the nationalist agenda incrementally by way of *faits accomplis*, without a proper legal basis and transparent procedures, is very problematic, to say the least; however, the alternative should not be a "free market" system in which the socially dominant, powerful groups decide the kinds of knowledge(s) that will be represented in the school curriculum and exercise their power, political, economic, or otherwise, to implement it.

In a society that provides a universal education, school textbooks offer teachers and students "symbols to start with," "signs that some larger community exists," and as such "the possibility—indeed, the actuality—of a shared collective identity."[14] A selection of knowledge is always involved, however. When such selective knowledge represents a collective identity—be it national, regional, or international—such an identity is inherently problematic, since it includes some people and excludes others. It is little wonder, therefore, that divergent social forces compete for influence over the symbols that textbooks present. Textbooks for this reason tend to be controversial, and, ironically or not, need to be so as long as a society wishes to be democratic. Critics who view the problem as already resolved in their society may be too optimistic, and certainly naive, just as those who give up, thinking the problem will never be settled, are too pessimistic (and nihilistic). Ienaga's series of lawsuits clearly suggests a possible third option, one that might actually change the way people see the world and themselves—by playing "the multiple games of truth," as Foucault argues. In this third option, we can work at forming an oppositional narrative and identity and, simultaneously, building consensus for such a formation. To represent a new articulation of diverse, often antagonistic discourses in a text is "the equivalent of alliance building in the social."[15]

The question of what counts as historical truth was another issue keenly contested in the course of Ienaga's court battles. Popular audiences, including some critics, discussing Ienaga's case may often frame the issues in simple terms, speaking, for example, of the knowledge held by the "Japanese" versus that held by the "Chinese" on the question of the war atrocities committed by the Japanese forces during the years of Asia-Pacific War. However, the question involves complex epistemological issues, for which recent scholarship provides no easy solutions.[16] While the traditional notion of "objective" knowledge that assumes that knowledge existing outside of the relationships of power is in need of critical reworking, the problem is not solved by simply assuming that everyone's knowledge is as good as everyone else's. In fact, the state's arguments before the court revealed that the "objectivist" position can go hand-in-hand with the "relativist" position; or, more precisely, that the two positions can be two sides of the same coin. Scholars and teachers, therefore, need to advance a more nuanced view of knowledge.

In this regard, I would argue that we should begin by abandoning the logic that holds that true (scientific) knowledge must be free of power. This is not to say that the power-knowledge nexus makes all true knowledge impossible.[17] Rather, it is to suggest that any construction of knowledge requires both a perspective, or perspectives, and sound methods and methodologies that are more or less systematic in their respective ways. It is also to suggest that we should remain open to new "ways of distinguishing true and false," as they are closely linked to the ways we govern others, our social relations, and ourselves.[18] New perspectives often require new methods and methodologies as was the case in the use of oral history methods for approaching the facts of the Nanjing Massacre. Still, there will always be tensions, dilemmas, and struggles involved in the production and organization of any knowledge—and this might well be intrinsic to (true) knowledge. If this is the case, we had better not try to avoid, or eliminate, such tensions, dilemmas, and struggles. Instead, we need to examine them carefully and find a way to work through them, and to move with them.

One of the important conclusions that we can draw from the study of the postwar Japanese textbook controversy, including Ienaga's court battles, is that the maintenance of a given hegemony involves multiple games of truths and complex cultural practices. It follows that a counter-hegemonic project, if it wishes to be effective, needs to play multiple games of truth simultaneously, developing and using a set of flexible and diverse strategies and discourses. For example, Ienaga's textbook lawsuits involved at least three games of truth—legal, educational, and historical—and discovering how to link these together to his (and oppositional and alternative forces') advantage was a constant, important strategic consideration. Ienaga, his legal team, and his supporters, including historians and teachers, confronted with the tensions, dilemmas, and struggles involved in these games of truths, made specific choices. While losing on some fronts, they won some important court decisions and brought about critical changes in school textbooks, although these gains are not permanent, as the recent success of the right-wing nationalist backlash has shown. It seems to me that the question of whether Ienaga's court challenges have lasting effects, or any significance at all, both inside and outside Japan, depends in part on us—on how we build on the legacy of his struggle.

Notes

Introduction

1 The name of the war and the years included have also been a part of ongoing controversy, which is discussed in Chapter 3.

2 A case in point is the unanimous passage of a resolution by the U.S. Congress (House Resolution 121) in July 2007. The resolution was sponsored by Japanese American congressman Mike Honda and garnered 168 bipartisan cosponsors.

3 This study employs an adjective "right-wing" for the Japanese nationalism and nationalists of the right with particular reference to their revisionist approaches to historical memory and textbook controversies, although their ideological positions taken by political parties, groups, and figures discussed under the rubric have varied from moderate conservatism to something akin to fascism. Nationalism of the left has also existed in Japan; however, it is beyond the scope of this study to examine it. As I see it, a recent volume by Oguma Eiji may be considered to be a seminal study on Japanese left-wing nationalism. See Oguma Eiji, "*Minshu*" to "aikoku": Sengo nihon no nashonarizumu to kokyosei ["Democracy" and "patriotism": Nationalism and the sense of public in postwar Japan] (Tokyo: Shinyosha, 2002).

4 Joan Wallach Scott, *Gender and the Politics of History* (New York: Columbia University Press, 1988).

5 This study occasionally employs the term "progressive" to refer to groups and individuals more or less associated with oppositional and alternative forces in the moderate and left camps, although diversities and complexities have existed among them. For further discussion, see Carol Gluck, "The Past in the Present," in *Postwar Japan as History*, ed., Andrew Gordon (Berkeley: University of California Press, 1993), 70–79; and Takashi Yoshida, *The Making of the "Rape of Nanking": History and Memory in Japan, China, and the United States* (New York: Oxford University Press, 2006), 7.

6 This is primarily because a war divides the world into two binary categories: "our nation" and "the enemy." This "us" and "them" dichotomy constitutes a solid basis to construct and maintain a normative national narrative and identity. See, for example, Yoshiko Nozaki and Hiromitsu Inokuchi, "What U.S. Middle Schoolers Bring to the Classroom: Student Writing on the Pacific War," *Education About Asia* 3, no. 3 (1998): 30–34.

7 For further discussion on the controversy over U.S. atomic bombings in Hiroshima and Nagasaki, see, for example, Laura Hein and Mark Selden, ed., *Living with the Bomb: American and Japanese Cultural Conflicts in the Nuclear Age* (Armonk: M.E. Sharpe, 1996); and Edward Linenthal and Thomas Engelhardt, ed., *History Wars: The Enola Gay Controversy and Other Battles for the American Past* (New York: Metropolitan Books, 1996). Note that the memory and interpretation of these U.S. atomic bombings continue to be controversial in

Japan. As recently as July 2007, Japan's Minister of Defense Kyuma Fumio spoke of these events as "having been inevitable" (*shoganakkata*), which triggered a nationwide protest, resulting in his resignation.

8 Daniel Jonah Goldhagen, *Hitler's Willing Executioners: Ordinary Germans and the Holocaust* (New York: Vintage Books, 1997). For further discussion on the Goldhagen debate, see, for example, Robert Shandley, ed., *Unwilling Germans? The Goldhagen Debate* (Minneapolis: University of Minnesota Press, 1998); and Colin Hay, "Willing Executors of Hitler's Will? The Goldhagen Controversy, Political Analysis and the Holocaust," *Politics* 20, no. 3 (2000): 119–128.

9 For the notion of "theory as a relay," see Michel Foucault, "Intellectuals and Power: A Conversation between Michel Foucault and Gilles Deleuze," in *Language, Counter-memory, Practice: Selected Essays and Interviews by Michel Foucault,* ed. Donald F. Bouchard (New York: Cornel University Press, 1977), 205–206.

10 By "game," Foucault means, "an ensemble of rules for the production of the truth … not a game in the sense of imitating or entertaining." See Michel Foucault, "The Ethic of Care for the Self as a Practice of Freedom," trans. J. D. Gauthier, S. J., in *The Final Foucault,* ed. James Bernauer and David Rasmussen (Cambridge, MA: The MIT Press, 1991), 16.

11 For the notion of "official knowledge," see Michael W. Apple, *Official Knowledge: Democratic Education in a Conservative Age,* second edition (New York: Routledge, 2000).

12 Richard Shaull, "Preface," in *Pedagogy of the Oppressed,* Paulo Freire, trans. Myra Bergman Ramos (New York: Continuum, 1970), 15. The emphasis is original.

13 Michel Foucault, "Questions of Method," in *The Foucault Effects: Studies in Governmentality,* ed., Graham Burchell, Colin Gordon, and Peter Miller (Chicago: University of Chicago Press, 1991), 82.

14 See Chapter 2 for further discussion on the contexts in which Ienaga hit on the idea of bringing court challenges.

15 Alan Hunt and Gary Wickham, *Foucault and Law: Towards a Sociology of Law as Governance* (London: Pluto Press, 1994).

16 For example, Christopher P. Hood refers to a pseudonymous criticism that "Ienaga appears to be 'a neo-Stalinist' who attempts to 'glorify the Red Army' in Manchuria in his book *Taiheiyo senso* [The Pacific War]." In this view, Ienaga "has been more concerned with avoiding the issue of war responsibility than with addressing it," and his "quest for 'responsibility' is superficial at best and diversionary at worst." Christopher P. Hood, *Japanese Education Reform: Nakasone's Legacy* (New York: Routledge, 2001), 96–97.

17 Norma Field, *In the Realm of a Dying Emperor: Japan at Century's End* (New York: Vintage Books, 1993).

18 Herbert M. Kliebard, "Curriculum Theory: Give Me a 'For Instance,'" in *Forging American Curriculum: Essays in Curriculum History and Theory* (New York: Routledge, 1990), 181.

1 Japan's Defeat, Educational Reform, And The Struggle Over The Japanese National Narrative And Identity In The Early Postwar Years, 1945–1965

1 Yamazumi Masami, *Nihon kyoiku shoshi* [A Concise History of Japanese Education] (Tokyo: Iwanami Shoten, 1987), 143. The term *kokutai* is often translated as national polity, but the exact translation of the term is difficult. For further discussion, see Richard Minear, *Japanese Tradition and Western Law: Emperor, State, and Law in the Thought of Hozumi Yatsuka* (Cambridge: Harvard University Press, 1970), 56–83.

2 At the point of defeat, many school officials, teachers, and parents at grassroots levels also expressed their unwavering loyalty to the emperor. See Yoshiko

Nozaki, "Educational Reform and History Textbooks in Occupied Japan," in *Democracy in Occupied Japan: The U.S. Occupation and Japanese Politics and Society*, ed. Mark E. Caprio and Yoneyuki Sugita, (London: Routledge, 2007), 121–122.

3 The actual processes of identity formation through education need to be understood as being complex and flexible. See in particular Raymond Williams, "Base and Superstructure in Marxist Cultural Theory," in *Problems in Materialism and Culture* (London: Verso, 1980), 38–40.

4 Michael Omi and Howard Winant, *Racial Formation in the United States* (New York: Routledge, 1986), 68.

5 For presurrender textbook contents, see Nakamura Kikuji, *Kyokasho no shakaishi: Meiji ishin kara haisen made* [A Social History of Textbooks: From the Meiji Restoration to the Defeat in the War] (Tokyo: Iwanami Shoten, 1992); Nakauchi Toshio, *Gunkoku bidan to kyokasho* [Fine Militarist Stories and Textbooks] (Tokyo: Iwanami Shoten, 1988); and Saburo Ienaga, "The Glorification of War in Japanese Education," *International Security* 18, no. 3 (1993/94): 113–122. For the Imperial Rescript on Education, see footnote 9.

6 For more details, see John Caiger, "Ienaga Saburo and the First Postwar Japanese History Textbook," *Modern Asian Studies* 3, no. 1 (1969): 1–17.

7 See, for example, Nakamura, *Kyokasho no shakaishi*, 220–221; and Yoko H. Thakur, "History Textbook Reform in Allied Occupied Japan, 1945–52," *History of Education Quarterly* 35, no. 3 (1995): 261–278.

8 See Yamazumi, *Nihon kyoiku shoshi*.

9 The Imperial Rescript on Education was in essence the narrative of Japan's nationhood in terms of Imperial sovereignty. The Rescript was read by principals or teachers at the school ceremonies during the presurrender period. For more discussion, see, for example, Byron K. Marshall, *Learning to be Modern: Japanese Political Discourse on Education* (Boulder: Westview Press, 1994), 58–62; and Teruhisa Horio, *Educational Thought and Ideology in Modern Japan* (Tokyo: University of Tokyo Press, 1988), 65–72.

10 The October 22 directive also ordered that those teachers who had been removed from their positions because of their opposition to the war and wartime education be reinstated (i.e., it ordered the de-purging of liberal and anti-militarist teachers). On October 30, SCAP, giving more specific instructions for the purge of militarist teachers, also ordered that all present and prospective teachers be evaluated in terms of their wartime deeds (and current beliefs) to be qualified as adequate for postwar education. The Japanese government, after issuing an imperial edict and a series of ordinances, began the process of teacher evaluation and purging in May 1946. For further discussion, see Nagahama Isao, *Kyoiku no senso sekinin: Kyoikugakusha no shiso to kodo, zoho* [Education's War Responsibility: Educational Researchers' Thoughts and Deeds, Enlarged Edition] (Tokyo: Akashi Shoten, 1992), 268–309.

11 See Nakamura, *Kyokasho no shakaishi*, 220–238.

12 The stopgap textbooks were distributed in the 1947 school year also. For further discussion of the stopgap textbooks, see Tokutake Toshiko, *Kyokasho no sengoshi* [The Postwar History of Textbooks] (Tokyo: Shin Nihon Shuppansha, 1995), 44–45; and Kyoiku no Sengoshi Henshu Iinkai, ed., *Sengo kyoiku kaikaku to sono hokai heno michi* [Postwar Educational Reform and the Course of its Collapse] (Tokyo: San'ichi Shobo, 1986), 131–132.

13 Ienaga Saburo, "Kongo no kokushi kyoiku" [Future Education of National History], *Shocho* (October 1946): 14. Ienaga also stressed the importance of empirical studies of history, and criticized not only studies conducted by imperialist historians of the presurrender period but also the arguments made by Marxist historians who revived the tradition immediately after Japan's defeat.

14 Ienaga Saburo, *"Kunino Ayumi" hensan shimatsu* [The Circumstances of Writing *Kunino Ayumi* from the Beginning to the End] (Tokyo: Minshusha, 2001), 52; and Ienaga Saburo, "Sengo no rekishi kyoiku" [Postwar History Education], in Iwanami Koza Nihon Rekishi 22, Bekkan no. 1 (Tokyo: Iwanami Shoten, 1968), 319.

15 Ienaga, "Sengo no rekishi kyoiku," 316.

16 Toyoda's text indeed contained a number of passages that were modeled after, or revised from, the textbook previously used. The last version of Toyoda's text was a ministerial document entitled "Zentei shotoka kokushi jo an" [Provisional Textbook on National History for Elementary Course, The First Volume: Draft]. Toyoda passed a copy to Ienega, which is reprinted in Ienaga *"Kunino Ayumi" hensan shimatsu*, 9-49. See also Ienaga, "Sengo no rekishi kyoiku," 314–317; and Thakur, "History Textbook Reform," 267–268.

17 Another project, this one for normal schools, was also in progress under the leadership of Maruyama Kunio, who remained as an author for the new project.

18 The Japanese government had developed the system of teacher training schools since 1872, but, in 1947, it was reorganized into the postwar university system.

19 Although the periodization here roughly corresponds to the division of history into four periods—*kodai, chusei, kinsei*, and *kindai*—that are commonly used in postwar scholarship on Japanese history, the MOE did not employ these terms at this point.

20 In this chapter, I refer to these commissioned to write the texts as "authors"; however, the texts were published by the state as the author. The names of actual authors were disclosed, but not listed as such in the volumes.

21 Ienaga *"Kunino Ayumi" hensan shimatsu*, 54-56. See also Ienaga, "Sengo no rekishi kyoiku," 318–319; and Yamazumi Masami, *Shakaika kyoiku no shuppatsu* [The Start of Social Studies Education] (Tokyo: Nihon Tosho Senta, 1981), 16–18.

22 Ienaga's specialty was in the area of ancient Japanese history. His Ph.D. dissertation was on eighth- to twelfth-century Japanese cultural history. According to Ienaga, most of the members were empiricist historians who were rather apolitical around that time and who had had little experience of teaching history in grade schools. See Ienaga, "Sengo no rekishi kyoiku," 319.

23 See Caiger, "Ienaga Saburo," 12–13, for the actual citation of the opening paragraphs of the textbook.

24 Ienaga *"Kunino Ayumi" hensan shimatsu*, 59–64. The chronological table aimed at showing the regime changes in the past, and Joseph C. Trainor, a CIE officer in charge of the textbook project, insisted that it should indicate the emperor's real power as weak from 1868 to 1931 and in name only from 1931 to 1945. Although Ienega agreed with Trainor at that point, he later suspected that Trainor intended to justify the U.S. policy that did not prosecute the emperor for war crimes.

25 "Zadankai sengo kokushi kyoiku no saikai o megutte: Arimitsu Jiro sensei ni kiku" [A Round Table Discussion with Arimatsu Jiro: On Resuming National History Education in the Postwar Era], *Rekishi to Chiri* 316 (1981): 87.

26 "Zadankai shusengo juichinen o kaerimite: Sengo no gakkai o kaikosuru, rekishi kyokasho no tadotta michi" [A Round Table Discussion to Reflect on Eleven Years since the End of the War: Memories on the Postwar Academy and the Path of History Education], *Nihon Rekishi* 100 (1956): 19.

27 The term is still popular. See Yoshida Yutaka, *Nihonjin no sensokan: Sengo-shi no nakano henyo* [Japanese Views on the War: Changes in the Postwar History] (Tokyo: Iwanami Shoten, 1995), 26–34.

28 Before the verdict, the United States had officially decided (in October 1948) to prioritize Japan's economic recovery over its democratization in order to counter the Eastern bloc, and for this reason to terminate the war tribunal earlier than it had planned. In fact, several A-class war crime suspects detained and waiting for another round(s) of prosecution had been released before the decision. The day

after the execution (December 24, 1948), all of the rest were set free, including Kishi Nobusuke, who later became Prime Minister, and the planned second and third rounds of prosecutions were canceled. The early release did not apply to B- and C-class war crime suspects.

29 See Richard H. Minear, *Victors' Justice: The Tokyo War Crime Trial* (Princeton: Princeton University Press, 1971).

30 For more on the emergence of the issues of comfort women as a Japanese war crime, see Chapter 7. For further discussion, see Tanaka Toshiyuki, "Naze beigun wa jugun ianfu mondai o mushishitanoka: Jo" [Why Did the U.S. Forces Ignore the Issue of War Comfort Women? Part 1], *Sekai* 627 (1996): 174–183 and "Naze beigun wa jugun ianfu mondai o mushishitanoka: Ge" [Why Did the U.S. Forces Ignore the Issue of War Comfort Women? Part 2], *Sekai* 628 (1996): 270–279. See also, Yuki Tanaka, *Japan's Comfort Women: Sexual Slavery and Prostitution during World War II and the US Occupation* (New York: Routledge, 2002).

31 Monbusho, *Shotoka kokushi ge* [Primary School National History, Volume 2] (Tokyo: Tokyo Shoseki, 1943), 174.

32 Monbusho, *Kuni no ayumi ge* [The Course of the Nation, Volume 2] (Tokyo: Nihon Shoseki, 1946), 49.

33 Monbusho, *Nihon no rekishi ge* [History of Japan, Volume 2] (Tokyo: Chutogakko Kyokasho Kabushikigaisha, 1946), 104.

34 Monbusho, *Nihon rekishi ge* [Japanese History, Volume 2] (Tokyo: Shihangakko Kyokasho Kabushikigaisha, 1947), 204.

35 See also Tawara Yoshifumi, "Nankin daigyakusatsu jiken to rekishi kyokasho mondai" [The Nanjing Massacre and the History Textbook Controversy], in *Nankin jiken o do miruka: Nichi, chu, bei kenkyusha niyoru kensho*, ed. Fujiwara Akira (Tokyo: Aoki Shoten, 1998), 118.

36 Monbusho, *Kuni no ayumi ge*, 48.

37 Monbusho, *Kuni no ayumi ge*, 51.

38 The critics consisted mainly of Marxist historians but included some ethno-historians such as Wakamori Taro, who advocated research on and the teaching of a history of ordinary people.

39 The reason *Kunino ayumi* was most criticized was in part because it was the first text to appear and in part because it still frequently—and unnecessarily in my view—referred to acts of successive emperors. See also Thakur, "History Textbook Reform," 270–271; Yamazumi, *Shakaika kyoiku no shuppatsu*, 18–19; and Kimijima Kazuhiko, *Kyokasho no shiso* [Thoughts on Textbooks] (Tokyo: Suzusawa Shoten, 1996), 274–278.

40 After the first postwar election, Katayama Tetsu, chair of the Socialist Party (Shakaito), formed a coalition cabinet in June 1947, which supported the educational reform, but was not able to finance basic matters such as school house reconstruction. See Kyoiku no Sengoshi Henshu Iinkai, *Sengo kyoiku kaikaku*, 115–129.

41 Horio, *Educational Thought and Ideology*, 121.

42 See Horio, *Educational Thought and Ideology*, 108–129. In fact, the Edict lost its effect because of the Diet resolution in 1948.

43 For more about the 1946 U.S. Education Mission, see Gary H. Tsuchimochi, *Education Reform in Postwar Japan: The 1946 U.S. Education Mission* (Tokyo: University of Tokyo Press, 1993).

44 This situation, which was in the MOE's words to be the case for the time being, in fact, became permanent.

45 Monbusho, *Gakushushido yoryo: Ippanhen, shian* [Instructional Guidelines: General guide, A Tentative Plan] (Tokyo: Monbusho, 1947), 2. The quote is the author's translation. SCAP requested the MOE to translate the guidelines into English,

and the translation of the *1947 General Guide*, entitled *A Tentative Suggested Course of Study: General*, lingers today, which is reprinted in Kokuritsu Kyoiku Kenkyujo-nai Sengo Kyoiku Kaikaku Shiryo Kenkyukai, ed., *Monbusho gakushushido yoryo 1* (Tokyo: Nihontosho Senta, 1980). There are slight differences between the Japanese and English versions.

46 For further discussion of the *1947 Instruction Guide*, see Nagao Akio, *Shin karikyuramuron* [New Curriculum Theory] (Tokyo: Yuhikaku, 1989), 14-17; and Yokoyama Yoshinori, "Kyokasho saiban to gakushushido yoryo" [The Textbook Lawsuits and the Instructional Guidelines], in *Rekishi no hotei: Ienaga kyokasho saiban to rekishigaku*, ed. Kyokasho Kentei Sosho o Shiensuru Rekishigaku Kankeisha no Kai (Association of People Involved in Historical Studies and Supporting the Textbook Screening Lawsuit, hereafter APIHS) (Tokyo: Otsuki Shoten, 1998), 109–110.

47 The system, instituted in 1947, consists of six years of elementary school education (compulsory) and three years of junior high school education (compulsory) for all children. It is a single track co-education system.

48 See Kimijima, *Kyokasho no shiso*, 280; and Usui Kaichi et al., *Atarashi chuto shakaika heno izanai* [An Invitation to New Secondary Social Studies] (Tokyo: Chirekisha, 1992), 155–162.

49 In practice, schools ended up with using *Kuni no ayumi*, since *Nihon no rekishi* turned out to be rather difficult for junior-high students. See Kimijima, *Kyokasho no shiso*, 281.

50 See Kimijima, *Kyokasho no shiso*.

51 Kanazawa Kaichi, *Aru shogakkocho no kaiso* [A Memoir of a School Principal] (Tokyo: Iwanami Shoten, 1967), 61.

52 For the curriculum developed at Sakurada, see Furukawa Masayoshi and Murai Mitsuyoshi, *Sakurada karikyuramu* [Sakurada Curriculum] (Tokyo: Gakugeisha, 1947).

53 There were many street urchins in Tokyo in these years because the air raid carried out by the Allied powers near the end of the war left a huge number of children orphaned and homeless. It is estimated that the air raid over Tokyo on March 10, 1945 killed approximately 80,000 civilians. For a discussion on these street children, see John W. Dower, *Embracing Defeat: Japan in the Wake of World War II* (New York: Norton & Company, 1999), 62–64.

54 Kanazawa, *Aru shogakkocho no kaiso*, 60.

55 Readers may detect a form of nationalism in Kanazawa's words. The late occupation years saw signs of postwar grass-roots nationalism(s) among the Japanese in both left and right spectra of politics. Such nationalism(s) were not expressed overtly during the occupation, but after Japan's independence there was a surge of grass-roots nationalism(s). See also Yoshida, *Nihonjin no sensokan*, 38–41, 72–75.

56 The MOE even suggested that each classroom could adopt different textbooks. See Tokutake, *Kyokasho no sengoshi*, 57; and Nakauchi Toshio et al., *Nihon kyoiku no sengoshi* [The Postwar History of Japanese Education] (Tokyo: Sanseido, 1987), 105.

57 See Tokutake, *Kyokasho no sengoshi*, 59.

58 A list later compiled contains nineteen entries of junior high school Japanese history textbooks published for use in the years 1952–1954, fifteen of which are examined for the present study. In a similar vein, forty-one entries of junior high school social studies history textbooks are found in the list as being published for use of years 1952–1955. Among them, twelve are examined for the present study: six of these use the term aggression in describing the Manchurian Incident and Japanese military activities leading up to it. See Hirotake Nagayoshi, Nakamura Kikuji, and Kato Saneharu, *Kyokasho kentei soran: Chugakkohen* [A General List of Screened Textbooks: Junior High] (Tokyo: Komiyayama Shoten, 1969), 104–109.

59 Wakamori Taro, *Gendai nihon no naritachi: Ge* [The Formation of Contemporary Japan, Volume 2] (Tokyo: Jitsugyo no Nihonsha, 1952), 105.
60 Nakaya Kenichi and Onabe Teruhiko, *Gendai sekai no naritachi: Ge* [The Formation of the Contemporary World, Volume 2] (Tokyo: Jitsugyo no Nihonsha, 1952), 94.
61 Mutai Risaku, *Chugaku shakai ge* [Junior High School Social Studies, Volume 2] (Tokyo: Kairyudo, 1954), 105.
62 Mutai, *Chugaku shakai ge*, 108.
63 See also Tawara, "Nankin daigyakusatsu jiken," 118–119.
64 Atarashii Shakai Henshu Iinkai, ed., *Atarashii shakai 3: Nihon no shakai no hatten* [New Social Studies, Volume 3: The Development of Japanese Society] (Tokyo: Tokyo Shoseki, 1955), 170.
65 Atarashii Shakai Henshu Iinkai, *Atarashii shakai 3*, 173.
66 See Ienaga Saburo, *Kyokasho kentei* [Textbook Screening] (Tokyo: Nihon Hyoronsha, 1965), 79–81. Also see Benjamin C. Duke, "The Textbook Controversy," *Japan Quarterly* 19, no.3 (1972).
67 The "red purge" not only ousted members of the Japan Communist Party but also their "sympathizers" (who were not clearly defined). Recent research shows that the process of the "red purge" began in 1949 with a Japanese government ordinance to regulate political organizations and ended in 1951, and that more than 27,300 people were purged. See Hirata Tetsuo, *Redd page no shiteki kyumei* [A Historical Examination of the Red Purge] (Tokyo: Shinnihon Shuppansha, 2002).
68 The Liberal Party in the Fall of 1955 merged with the Democratic Party and formed the Liberal Democratic Party. Ikeda became Prime Minister in 1960.
69 The MOE was also constantly attempting to revise the social studies curriculum.
70 The Socialist Party had been divided. The number here is the total of the two, with its left faction winning 89 seats and its right faction 67 seats. Eventually, in October, the party was reunited.
71 Ishii was once a music teacher in Ehime prefecture and an influential member of the JTU in charge of the JTU's textbook-related matters. He was then employed by the JTU as a public relations officer, but was dismissed in disgrace in 1954 because of his corrupt relationships with some textbook companies.
72 For further discussion regarding Ishii's testimony, *The Deplorable Problems of Textbooks*, and the 1955 formation of the conservative bloc, see Kyoiku no Sengoshi Henshu Iinkai, ed., *Minshukyoiku heno kogeki to teiko* [The Attack on the Democratic Education and the Resistance] (Tokyo: San'ichi Shobo, 1986), 14-22.
73 This was unprecedented in the whole history of the Japanese Diet.
74 See Tokutake, *Kyokasho no sengoshi*, 100.
75 The MOE replaced committee members such as Nakajima Kenzo, a scholar in French literature and pacifist, with right-wing nationalist scholars such as Koyama Iwao. Koyama was a philosopher in the Nishida Kitaro's Kyoto school, was purged because of his collaboration in the war (and later depurged), and, after becoming the committee member, played the key part in rejecting many history textbooks in the late 1950s. Interestingly, Koyama helped Ienaga publish his first single authored volume *Nihon shisoshi niokeru hitei no ronri no hattatsu* (The Development of Logic of Negation in History of Japanese Thought), as Ienaga was strongly influenced by Tanabe Hajime, the successor of Nishida, who was also Koyama's mentor. See also *Ienaga Saburo, Ichi rekishi gakusha no ayumi: Shinban* [One Historian's Odyssey: New Edition] (Tokyo: Sanseido, 1977), 116–118.
76 In 1955, Tokutake Toshio, inspired by Ienaga's talk, explored the possibility of bringing a court case against textbook screening, but gave up the idea. See *Ienaga kyokasho saiban junenshi* [The Ten-Year History of Ienaga's Textbook Screening Suit], ed. NLSTS (Tokyo: Sodo Bunka, 1977), 255.

77 Two prominent academics and textbook authors, Hidaka Rokuro and Nagasu Kazuji, publicly denounced the screening and withdrew their contributions to *Akarui shakai*, a popular social studies textbook for junior high schools published by Chukyo Shuppan.

78 The full time textbook examiners included Murao Jiro, who specialized in ancient Japanese history at the University of Tokyo and who would play the central role in censoring history textbooks until his retirement in 1975. The emperor-centered view of history (*kokoku shikan*) involves right-wing nationalism—or ultranationalism—and chauvinism. It conflates history and mythology, justifies the absolute power and sovereignty of successive emperors (and the family line), and supports military expansion of the empire (imperialism). Although the exact phrase *kokoku shikan* was coined in the early 1940s, the thought originated in the late Edo period. Hiraizumi Kiyoshi, a historian known for his strong view of emperor-centered history, taught at Tokyo Imperial University between 1923 and 1945. Many of his advisees, including Murao Jiro and Tokinoya Shigeru, worked for the MOE as textbook examiners in postwar years.

79 When the book was disapproved, the MOE informed the authors of only some of the reasons for rejection, upon the authors' request. This, in practice, made publishers and authors self-disciplined; it forced them, when resubmitting their texts, to alter them even more than the MOE would request.

80 The provision had originally read: "The [MOE's] Division of Elementary and Secondary Education, for the time being, draws up the *Instruction Guidelines*. This, however, does not mean to stand in the way of [local] school boards making their own instructional guidelines." The statement was modified by the elimination of the second sentence.

81 For further discussion of the MOE's ordinance and the 1958 *Instruction Guidelines*, see Nagao, *Shin karikyuramuron*, 19–22; and Yokoyama, "Kyokasho saiban," 107–122. See also Nagai Kenichi, "Gakushushido yoryo no hotekikosokusei" [The Legal Force of the *Instruction Guidelines*], in *Shin gakushushido yoryo to kyoshi*, ed. Nagai Kenichi (Tokyo: Eideru Kenkyujo, 1991), 160–179; and Ogawa Masato, "Gakushushido yoryo wa donoyoni hensenshitekitaka" [How the *Instructional Guidelines* Have Changed], in *Shin gakushushido yoryo*, ed. Nagai, 33–44.

82 Ienaga's textbook was one of those rejected. See Chapter 2 for further discussion of the screening results of Ienaga's book. Shuppan Rôren (the publishing industry workers' union) decided to make the rejection reasons public, publishing a periodical *Kyokasho Repoto* (Annual Report on Textbooks). See, for example, Tokutake, *Kyokasho no sengoshi*, 103–114.

83 Hirotake Nagayoshi, Nakamura Kikuji, and Kato Saneharu, *Kyokasho kentei soran: Chugakkohen* [A General List of Screened Textbooks: Junior High] (Tokyo: Komiyayama Shoten, 1969), 74–103.

84 Twenty-three high school Japanese history textbooks were on the market in 1957, twenty in 1966, and twenty-six in 1969. Nakamura Kikuji, Kato Saneharu, and Hirotake Nagayoshi, *Kyokasho kentei soran: Kotogakkohen jokan* [A General List of Screened Textbooks: High School, Volume 1] (Tokyo: Komiyayama Shoten, 1970), 132–145. To date, many high school textbooks whose market share was small, including Ienaga's *Shin nihonshi*, have been able to survive.

85 Their comments on history textbooks were compiled and recorded by the publishing industry workers' associations, which later became a union. See note no. 82.

86 Tawara, "Nankin daigyakusatsu jiken," 120.

87 Tawara, "Nankin daigyakusatsu jiken," 120.

88 Excerpts are from Tawara, "Nankin daigyakusatsu jiken," 120. It is said that Koyama Iwao for the most part made these comments.

89 The comment meant that the term was not the one actually used during the war.

90 The examiner meant that the author(s) should mention that other countries, mostly Western countries, colonized Asian countries.
91 Tokutake, *Kyokasho no sengoshi,* 102–104.
92 Tawara, "Nankin daigyakusatsu jiken," 120.
93 In fact, to date the series remains one of the most popular junior high school social studies textbook series that have ever published. The other series was *Chugakusei no Shakaika,* published by Chukyo Shuppan, whose market share declined in the late 1970s.
94 Atarashii Shakai Henshu Iinkai, *Atarashii shakai 3,* 170–171.
95 Nishioka Toranosuke, *Atarashii shakai 2* [New Social Studies, Volume 2] (Tokyo: Tokyo Shoseki, 1962), 291–292.
96 Atarashii Shakai Henshu Iinkai, *Atarashii shakai 3,* 173–174.
97 Atarashii Shakai Henshu Iinkai, *Atarashii shakai 3,* 173.
98 Nishioka, *Atarashii shakai 2,* 298.
99 Nishioka, *Atarashii shakai 2,* 298.
100 As discussed above, some textbooks in the 1950s had included lines on the topic of the emperor's role in stopping the war, but the 1952 edition of *Atarashii shakai* had not.
101 Nishioka, *Atarashii shakai 2,* 298.
102 Nishioka Toranosuke et al., *Shintei atarashii shakai 2* [New Impression Social Studies, Volume 2] (Tokyo: Tokyo Shoseki, 1969), 294.
103 Atarashii Shakai Henshu Iinkai, *Atarashii shakai 3,* 171.
104 Nishioka, *Atarashii shakai 2,* 292. Of the other two illustrations, the first was a photo entitled "The Beginning of the Japan–China Incident in 1937," captioned "On July 7, 1937, the Japanese and Chinese Armies clashed at the Marco Polo Bridge in the suburb of Beijing." The photo shows a combat scene that took place in Shanghai. The second illustration was a map showing Japan's expansion of the war; it was captioned "Prime Minister Konoe pronounced no expansion of the war, but the battle line expanded day by day."
105 Nishioka, *Atarashii shakai 2,* 292.
106 Nishioka Toranosuke et al., *Atarashii shakai 2* [New Social Studies, Volume 2] (Tokyo: Tokyo Shoseki, 1966), 291.

2 The politics over education

1 Ienaga Saburo, "Kyokuto saiban ni tsuiteno shiron" [An Essay on the Tokyo War Tribunal], *Shiso* (August 1968), as cited in Yoshida Yutaka, *Nihonjin no senso-kan: Sengoshi no nakano henyo* [Japanese Views on the War] (Tokyo: Iwanami Shoten, 1995), 160–161. For a translation of Ienaga's autobiography, see Saburo Ienaga, *Japan's Past, Japan's Future: One Historian's Odyssey,* trans. Richard Minear (Lanham: Rowman & Littlefield, 2001).
2 See Ienaga Saburo, *Senso sekinin* [War Responsibility] (Tokyo: Iwanami Shoten, 1985), i–iii. To be sure, he was a high school teacher during the wartime years. He was, however, not able to teach his students what he learned from his research because of the police informant system that was widespread throughout the country.
3 Ienaga Saburo, "Gakumon o surumono no yorokobi to kurushimi" [The Pleasure and Distress of Those Who Pursue Scholarship], *Keisei* (July 1953), as cited in Ienaga, *Senso sekinin,* iii.
4 Later research strongly suggests that the case was plotted by the occupation force, led by the United States, which was in the process of red-purging and looking for reasons to ban the JCP.
5 Kyokasho Sosho o Shiensuru Zenkokurenrakukai [The National League for Support of the School Textbook Screening Suit, hereafter NLSTS], ed., *Ienaga kyokasho saiban no subete: 32-nen no undo to korekara* [All the Aspects of Ienaga

Textbook Lawsuits: Thirty-Two Years of its Activities and its Future] (Tokyo: Minshusha, 1998), 44–45. For Ienaga's argument for "the freedom of critique of trials," see Ienaga Saburo, *Saiban hihan* [Critique of Trials] (Tokyo: Nihon Hyoronsha, 1959). Ienaga also supported another similar case called Hakkai Incident Case.

6 NLSTS, ed., *Ienaga kyokasho saiban ju-nenshi* [A Ten Year History of Ienaga's Textbook Lawsuit] (Tokyo: Sodo Bunka, 1977), 253.

7 As discussed in the previous chapter, the appointed school boards members replaced the elected members in 1957, because of the passage of the bill in 1956.

8 The JTU, however, because of its fractional strife, was somewhat weak in providing consistent leadership for the struggle around that time. See Yamazumi Masami, *Nihon kyoiku shoshi* [A Concise History of Japanese Education] (Tokyo: Iwanami Shoten, 1987), 214–215.

9 The kinpyo trials gradually focused more on labor issues rather than education issues.

10 Approximately 30,000 union member teachers in Tokyo took a one-day leave in opposing the kinpyo, and the union leaders were arrested and prosecuted. The latter were found not guilty by the Supreme Court later.

11 As discussed in the previous chapter, this was the same year that the MOE asserted that its *Instruction Guidelines* would gain legal force.

12 The Supreme Court decision of 1976, which was the final decision on the cases, held that, while the state power could constitute "the improper control," the [exercise of] state power that was needed and reasonable for acceptable purposes could interfere in curriculum content and instructional approaches. The decision was deliberately ambiguous, but researchers interpreted it as basically calling for the limitation of state power in education.

13 A passage cited in Kyoiku no Sengoshi Hensan Iinkai, ed., *Kodo keizai seichoka no kyoiku* [Education under High Economic Growth] (Tokyo: San'ichi Shobo, 1986), 71–72.

14 During that period, either an overall or a partial revision and screening of textbooks usually took place every three years. In addition, textbooks needed to be revised as the *Instruction Guidelines* were revised. Textbook manuscripts are for the most part conditionally approved. Ienaga published his critique of the textbook screening of 1955 in *Rekishi chiri kyoiku* (History and Geography Education). The Publishing Industry Workers' Union also published its critique in the brochures *Genko kyokashoseido no shomondai* (The Problems of the Current Textbook Production System) and *Kyokasho wa dareno monoka* (Who Owns Textbooks?).

15 For example, Ienaga Saburo, *Kyokasho kentei: Kyoiku o yugameru kyoiku-gyosei* [The Textbook Screening: The Educational Administration that Distorts Education] (Tokyo: Nihon Hyoronsha, 1965).

16 NLSTS, *Ienaga kyokasho saiban ju-nenshi*, 34–36.

17 "Kyokasho saiban teiso niju-shunen: Ienaga-san oini kataru" [20th Anniversary of Textbook Lawsuits: Ienaga Talks A Great Deal], in *Kyokasho saiban nyusu: Shukusatsuban 3*, ed. NLSTS (Tokyo: NLSTS, 1985), 369. The original was published in *Kyokasho Saiban Nyusu* 208 (June 20, 1985): 3. *Kyokasho saiban Nyusu* (Textbook Lawsuit News) was a monthly newsletter of the NLSTS, a nationwide support group for Ienaga's court challenges. The newsletters were later compiled and made into five volumes of *Kyokasho saiban nyusu: Shukusatsuban* (The Textbook Lawsuit News: Reduced-Size Edition).

18 All of the lawyers working for numerous JTU education trials co-signed on his complaint along with his four lawyers. See Ienaga Kyokasho Sosho Bengodan, ed., *Ienaga kyokasho saiban: Sanjuni-nen ni wataru bengodan katsudo no sokatsu* [The Ienaga Textbook Lawsuits: A Summary of the Legal Team's Actions over

Thirty-two Years] (Tokyo: Nihon Hyoronsha, 1998), 36–37. His legal team grew as Ienaga's lawsuits progressed, consisting of more than twenty lawyers.

19 Ienaga's statement on June 12, 1965, cited in Tokutake Toshiko, *Kyokasho no sengo-shi* [The Postwar History of Textbooks] (Tokyo: Shin Nihon Shuppansha, 1995), 141–142.

20 NLSTS, *Ienaga kyokasho saiban ju-nenshi*, 44–46. Only *Yomiuri News* ran articles written by right-wing intellectuals campaigning against Ienaga's suit.

21 The Japanese civil procedure has no pretrial stage. It consists of preliminary hearings and trial hearings.

22 The weakness of the legal grounds of the state textbook screening is still the case today.

23 Kimijima Kazuhiko, "Ienaga kyokasho saiban sanjuni-nen: Sono hanketsu o do hyoka suruka" [Thirty-Three Years of Ienaga's Textbook Lawsuit: How to Evaluate the Decisions], *Senso Sekinin Kenkyu* 19 (1998): 59. See the previous chapter for further discussion of the 1947 Constitution and the laws referred to here.

24 For further discussion of these three legal arguments, see Kimijima, "Ienaga kyokasho saiban sanjuni-nen," 58–59.

25 Ienaga Kyokasho Sosho Bengodan, *Ienaga kyokasho saiban*, 62.

26 Textbooks were, and still largely are, the "curriculum" in the daily practice of many Japanese classrooms.

27 NLSTS, *Ienaga kyokasho saiban ju-nenshi*, 51–54.

28 Ienaga was a professor at Tokyo University of Education, an institution that specialized in educational research and that later became University of Tsukuba.

29 Ienaga Kyokasho Sosho Bengodan, *Ienaga kyokasho saiban*, 62.

30 Ienaga Kyokasho Sosho Bengodan, *Ienaga kyokasho saiban*, 66. The only points not contested were those requesting the correction of simple mistakes, such as typos.

31 For details in English, see Saburo Ienaga, "The Historical Significance of the Japanese Textbook Lawsuit," *Bulletin of Concerned Asian Scholars* 2, no. 4 (1970): 8–10; Saburo Ienaga, "The Glorification of War in Japanese Education," *International Security* 18, no. 3 (1993–94): 124–126.

32 The MOE's argument was not exactly correct. The 1952 Security Treaty between the United States and Japan did not include the terms "facility" and "area" (though the 1960 Treaty of Mutual Cooperation and Security between United States and Japan did). Since Ienaga included the passage in his section of the 1952 San Francisco Peace Treaty, the MOE's argument was not, in a literal sense, accurate.

33 Ienaga Kyokasho Sosho Bengodan, *Ienaga kyokasho saiban*, 64–65.

34 Ienaga Kyokasho Sosho Bengodan, *Ienaga kyokasho saiban*, 122–123.

35 For more detail, see NLSTS, *Ienaga kyokasho saiban ju-nenshi*, 103–106.

36 For further discussion, see, for example, Ronald. P. Dore, "Textbook Censorship in Japan: The Ienaga Case," *Pacific Affairs* 43 (1970–71): 548–556.

37 NLSTS, ed., *Shorishita kyokasho saiban: Kyoshi to kokumin niyoru kyoikusozo o mezashite* [The Textbook Lawsuit Won: Toward the Creation of Education by Teachers and Parents] (Tokyo: Rodojunposha, 1970), 64–69. The book contains the entire decision.

38 NLSTS, *Shorishita kyokasho saiban*, 91–94.

39 NLSTS, *Shorishita kyokasho saiban*, 74.

40 NLSTS, *Shorishita kyokasho saiban*, 74.

41 NLSTS, *Shorishita kyokasho saiban*, 75–79. For further discussion of the Sugimoto decision, see Teruhisa Horio, *Educational Thought and Ideology in Modern Japan* (Tokyo: University of Tokyo Press, 1988), 189–196; Kimijima, "Ienaga kyokasho saiban sanjuni-nen," 60–61; and Yokoyama Yoshinori, "Kyokasho saiban to gakushushido yoryo" [The Textbook Lawsuits and the Instructional

Guidelines], in *Rekishi no hotei: Ienaga kyokasho saiban to rekishigaku,* ed. Kyokasho Kentei-sosho o Shiensuru Rekishigaku Kankeisha-no-kai (Association of People Involved in Historical Studies and Supporting the Textbook Screening Lawsuits, APIHS) (Tokyo: Otsuki Shoten, 1998), 119–120.

42 Hayashi Kentaro, Mori Katsumi, and Enoki Kazuo wrote the documents.

43 One result of these efforts was volumes such as Rekishigaku Kenkyukai, ed., *Gendai rekishigaku to kyokasho saiban* [Contemporary Historical Studies and the Textbook Lawsuits] (Tokyo: Aoki Shoten, 1973).

44 The documents were also published as Toyama Shigeki and Oe Shinobu, ed., *Ienaga nihonshi no kentei* [The Screening of Ienaga's Japanese History] (Tokyo: Sanseido, 1976).

45 Judge Hosui's words at a meeting to make arrangements with Ienega's legal team for the first hearing, as cited in Ienaga Kyokasho Sosho Bengodan, ed. *Ienaga kyokasho saiban,* 136.

46 NLSTS, *Ienaga kyokasho saiban ju-nenshi,* 139.

47 NLSTS, ed., *Ienaga kyokasho saiban no subete: Sanjuni-nen no undo to korekara* [All the Facts about Ienaga's Textbook Lawsuit: The Thirty-Two Years of the Movement and Thereafter] (Tokyo: Minshusha, 1998), 305.

48 For further discussion of the impact of the Sugimoto decision upon the larger cultural and educational politics, see Mainichi Shinbunsha Kyoiku Shuzaihan, *Kyokasho senso* [Textbook War] (Tokyo: San'ichi Shobo, 1981), 148–160; Tokutake, *Kyokasho no sengoshi,* 186; and Tokutake Toshio, *Kyokasho saiban wa ima* [The Current State of Textbook Screening] (Tokyo: Azumino Shobo, 1991), 155–170.

49 Yamamoto Aya, "Miraini hana hirakaserutameni" [For Blossoms in the Future], in *Kyokasho saiban nyusu: Shukusatsuban,* ed. NLSTS (Tokyo: NLSTS, 1975), 484. The original was published in *Kyokasho Saiban Nyusu* 87 (May 15, 1974): 2.

3 Counter-memories of the Asia-Pacific war

1 Yoshiko Nozaki and Hiromitsu Inokuchi, "Student Writing on the Pacific War: What U.S. Middle Schoolers Bring to the Classroom," *Education About Asia* 3, no. 3 (1998): 33.

2 The official term for the war announced by the Japanese government on December 12, 1941. Though the government defined the war as an outgrowth of the military conflicts with China since 1937, it avoided defining these conflicts as wars. Had it declared war, the government would have been obligated to follow international conventions.

3 It is no coincidence that the Tokyo war tribunal, led by the United States, by and large ignored the sufferings of Asian people and countries. For further discussion of the use of two terms (*daitoa senso* and *taiheiyo senso*) during and after the war, see Ienaga Saburo, *Taiheyo senso* [The Pacific War] (Tokyo: Iwanami Shoten, 1968), 1–13.

4 In the late 1960s, for example, when Ienaga was publishing a volume entitled *Taiheiyo senso,* a ground-breaking book on the war, he was compelled to explain his choice of title, in the first sentence of the preface. In his view, while the term "Fifteen-Year War" (15-nen senso) might be precise, its usage has not yet been accepted by the Japanese public. However, he could not use "World War II" because the book covered only "Japan's direct involvement" in that war. Nor could he use "Great East Asian War," which was "utterly unacceptable" to him. He chose *Taiheiyo senso* as a "second-best policy." See Saburo Ienaga, *The Pacific War, 1931–1945: A Critical Perspective on Japan's Role in World War II,* trans. Frank Baldwin (New York: Pantheon Books, 1978), vii. For further discussion of the term "Fifteen-Year War" and its significance (and problematics) in history education, see Kimijima Kazuhiko, "Continuing Legacy of Japanese Colonialism: The Japan-South Korea Joint Study Group on History Textbooks," in *Censoring*

History: Citizenship and Memory in Japan, Germany, and the United States, ed. Laura Hein and Mark Selden (Armonk: M. E. Sharp, 2000), 208–210.

5 After all, many Japanese, even through their tears, felt the collapse of the Japanese imperial state with some relief (and found it encouraging), at least as historian Yoshimi Yoshiaki later recalls. The phrase *taiheiyo senso,* which came with that relief, is therefore of some significance for Japanese. For further discussion, see Yoshimi Yoshiaki, "'Ianfu' mondai to kingendaishi no shiten" [The Issue of "Comfort" Women and the Perspective of Modern/Contemporary History], in *Simpozium nashonarizumu to "ianfu" mondai,* ed. Nihon no Senso Sekinin Shiryo Senta (Tokyo: Aoki Shoten, 1998), 35–36.

6 Yoshida Yutaka, *Nihonjin no sensokan: Sengo-shi no nakano henyo* [Japanese Views on the War: Changes in Postwar History] (Tokyo: Iwanami Shoten, 1995), 129–164.

7 Yoshida, *Nihonjin no sensokan,* 129–164.

8 Inoue Kiyoshi, *Tenno no senso sekinin* [The Emperor's War Responsibility] (Tokyo: Gendai Hyoronsha, 1975).

9 For the memory of Nanjing Massacre, see Yoshida Takashi, *The Making of the "Rape of Nanking": History and Memory in Japan, China, and the United States* (New York: Oxford University Press, 2006).

10 Edgar Snow, *Azia no senso* [The War in Asia], trans. Moriya Iwao (Tokyo: Misuzu Shobo, 1956).

11 Edgar Snow, *The Battle for Asia* (Cleveland: The World Publishing Company, 1941), 57.

12 H. J. Timperley, *What War Means: The Japanese Terror in China* (London: Victor Gollancz., 1938). Timperley then was a China correspondent of the *Manchester Guardian.* The bibliographical information from the original Japanese translation is unavailable. The new translation is H. J. Timperley, "Senso towa nanika: Chugoku niokeru nihongun no bogyaku" [What is the War: Japanese Atrocities in China], in *Nicchu senso: Nankin daigyakusatsu jiken shiryoshu,* ed. Hora Tomio (Tokyo: Aoki Shoten, 1985).

13 Kamiyoshi Haruo, ed., *Sanko* [Three Lightnings] (Tokyo: Kobunsha, 1957). *Sanko* was later re-published by the Chugoku Kikansha Renrakukai (The Association of Returnees from China), a group consisting of veterans who had fought and been imprisoned in China, pardoned, and returned to Japan. For a review of the research on the Nanjing Massacre, see Kasahara Tokushi, Matsumura Takao, Yoshimi Yoshiaki, Takashima Nobuyoshi, and Watanabe Harumi, ed. *Rekishi no jijitsu o do-ninteishi do-oshieruka* [How to Verify and Teach Historical Facts] (Tokyo: Kyoikushiryo Shuppankai, 1997), 76. Also see the testimony given by Fujiwara Akira at the Tokyo District Court in 1987, which is published in Kyokasho Kentei Sosho wo Shiensuru Zenkokurenrakukai (The National League for Support of the School Textbook Screening Suit, hereafter NLSTS), ed., *Nankin daigyakusatsu/731 butai: Ienaga kyokasho saiban daisanjisosho chisaihen 4* [The Nanjing Massacre and Unit 731: Ienaga Textbook Lawsuit, the Third Suit, District Court, Volume 4] (Tokyo: Rongu Shuppan, 1991), 42–115.

14 Hora Tomio, *Kindai senshi no nazo* [The Mysteries of Modern Military History] (Tokyo: Jinbutsuoraisha, 1967).

15 Honda Katsuichi, *Chugoku no tabi* [A Journey in China] (Tokyo: Asahi Shinbunsha, 1972), 4-5. Also see his statement and testimony given for Ienaga at the Tokyo district court in 1987, which is published in NLSTS, ed., *Nankin daigyakusatsu/731 butai,* 3–41.

16 For further discussion on the responses to Honda's reports, see NLSTS, *Nankin daigyakusatsu/731 butai,* 14–15, 39. Even though the negative response was limited, a senior journalist at the newspaper felt it to be greater than expected. See the preface of Honda, *Chugoku no tabi,* vii.

17 Kasahara Tokushi, *Ajia no nakano nihongun: Senso sekinin to rekishigaku/rekishi kyoiku* [The Japanese Military in Asia: War Responsibility and History Studies/History Education] (Tokyo: Otsuki Shoten, 1994), 22-23, 27–28.

18 Izaya Pendasan, *Nihonjin to yudayajin* [The Japanese and the Jews] (Tokyo: Yamamoto Shoten, 1970). The 1970s saw a blooming of *Nihonjinron* (the theory of Japanese "uniqueness"), and Pendasan's book was one of the first. Numerous articles and books in Japanese as well as English have also been published criticizing the theory of Japanese uniqueness. See, for example, Peter Dale, *The Myths of Japanese Uniqueness* (London: Croom Helm, 1986); Ross Mouer and Yoshio Sugimoto, *The Images of Japanese Society* (London: Kegan Paul International, 1986); Aoki Tamotsu, *"Nihon bunkaron" no henyo: Sengo nihon no bunka to aidentiti* [The Change of the Theory of Japanese Culture: Culture and Identity in Postwar Japan] (Tokyo: Chuo Koronsha, 1990); and Harumi Befu, *Ideorogi toshiteno nihon bunkaron* [The Theory of Japanese Culture as Ideology] (Tokyo: Shiso no Kagakusha, 1987). I have discussed the theory of Japanese uniqueness, orientalism, and the issue of curriculum, in Yoshiko Nozaki and Hiromitsu Inokuchi, "On Critical Asian Literacy," *Curriculum Perspectives* 16, no. 3 (1996): 72–76.

19 Asami Sadao, *Nise yudayajin to nihonjin* [A Bogus Jew and the Japanese] (Tokyo: Asahi Shinbunsha, 1983).

20 Izaya Bendasan, *Nihonkyo nitsuite* [On Japanism] (Tokyo: Bungei Shunju, 1972), and Izaya Pendasan, *Watashi no nakano nihongun* [The Japanese Military Within Myself] (Tokyo: Bungei Shunju, 1975).

21 Some American-owned newspapers around the time also published the story. See Timperley, *What War Means*, 284–285.

22 For further discussion on Suzuki's work, see Kasahara, *Ajia no nakano nihongun*, 21–22.

23 For example, Honda Katsuichi, ed., *Pen no inbo* [The Conspiracy by Pen] (Tokyo: Ushio Shuppansha, 1977).

24 Hora Tomio, *Nankin jiken* [The Nanjing Incident] (Tokyo: Shin Jinbutsuoraisha, 1973); *Nicchu sensoshi shiryo 8: Nankin jiken I* [The Data of the China-Japan War, Volume 8: Nanjing Incident I] (Tokyo: Kawaideshobo Shinsha, 1973); and *Nicchu sensoshi shiryo 9: Nankin jiken II* [The Data of the China-Japan War, Volume 9: Nanjing Incident II] (Tokyo: Kawaideshobo Shinsha, 1973).

25 For example, Hora Tomio, *"Maboroshi"ka kosaku hihan: Nankin daigyakusatsu* [A Critique on Illusionization: The Nanjing Massacre] (Tokyo: Gendaishi Shuppankai, 1975), and Hora Tomio, *Ketteiban: Nankin gaigyakusatsu* [Definitive Edition: The Nanjing Massacre] (Tokyo: Aoki Shoten, 1982).

26 See Chapters 4 and 7 for discussion of the continuing use of this strategy in the history controversy of the 1980s and 1990s.

27 Hosokawa Morisada, *Hosokawa nikki: Ge* [Hosokawa Diary: The Second Volume] (Tokyo: Chuokoronsha, 1979), 56-57. In his diary, Hosokawa refers to the name of the commander whose troops conducted the atrocities as having been "Cho." According to recent research, Cho was one of the staff officers responsible for the mass-murder of prisoners of war in the Nanjing Massacre. See Fujiwara Akira, "Tenno to okinawasen" [The Emperor and the Battle of Okinawa], in *Okinawasen to tennosei*, ed. Fujiwara Akira (Tokyo: Rippushobo, 1987), 38. See also Fujiwara Akira, *Nankin daigyakusatsu* [The Nanjing Massacre] (Tokyo: Iwanami Shoten, 1985), 20; and "Shogen niyoru nankin senshi: Saishukai" [The War History of Nanjing by Testimonies: The Last Episode], *Kaigyo*, March 1986.

28 The writings were mostly in the form of novels. For one such novel, see Furukawa Shigemi, *Okinawa no saigo* [The Postwar Okinawa] (Tokyo: Chuosha, 1947). For further discussion of postwar writings and records on the Battle of Okinawa, see, for example, Nakahodo Shotoku, *Okinawa no senki* [The War Records of Okinawa] (Tokyo: Asahi Shinbunsha, 1982).

29 Okinawa Taimuzusha, ed., *Tetsu no bofu* [The Typhoon of Iron] (Naha: Okinawa Taimuzusha, 1950). In 1949, the newspaper company launched a project to interview survivors. Three journalists, including Ota Yoshihiro, worked on the project.

30 I translate the term as "mass suicide," but the original Japanese term has a stronger tone of self-determination (which *jiketsu* generally means). When used in the military context, *jiketsu* means "servicemen's own choice of suicide," usually because of defeat. Ota extended that meaning to describe the Okinawan civilians' deaths in Gyokusai.

31 Two decades later, Ota, the man who coined the term, expressed regret for this creation. He felt it would "lead to a misinterpretation of the event," since it "gives an impression that [people killed themselves] of their own free will." Ota Yoshihiro, "Dohyo o machigaetahito: Sono Ayako-shi eno hanron" [A Person Who Went to the Wrong Ground: A Refutation to Ms. Sono Ayako], *Okinawa Times* (Okinawa, Japan), May 11, 1985, as cited in Ishihara Masaie's statement filed at the Tokyo High Court, and published in *Okinawasen, somotai, kyoiku genba: Ienaga kyokasho saiban daisanji sosho kosaihen 3*, ed. NLSTS (Tokyo: Minshusha, 1996), 70.

32 This was an amendment to the law defining the conditions of pensions for the servicemen's survivors: the amendment stated that Okinawans who had lost their family members in the Battle could receive a pension if they claimed it. The Japanese government position was (and is) to provide no survivors' pension for *civilian* deaths in World War II, but it made an exception for the Battle of Okinawa.

33 Nakasone Masayoshi, ed., *Okinawa no higeki* [The Tragedy of Okinawa] (Naha: Kachoshobo, 1951). Nakasone, a teacher at the Okinawa Shihan Gakko (teacher training school) during the war, was a survivor himself. He chronologically rearranged the notes of survivors of the Star Lilies (*Himeyuri Butai*), a group of teenage female students of his school who had "volunteered" to serve as war nurses. See Ota Masahide and Sotoma Moriyoshi, ed., *Okinawa kenjitai* [Okinawan Healthy Boys Troop] (Tokyo: Nihon Shuppankyodo, 1953). The book is a collection of notes of survivors of the Tekketsu Kin'notai, a group of teenage male students of the Okinawa Shihan Gakko who "volunteered" to serve in the Battle of Okinawa. The two editors were survivors of the group, which had lost more than 300 of its 480 members in the battle.

34 Kinjo Kazuhiko and Obara Nasao, ed., *Minnamino iwao no hateni: Okinawa no isho* [The End of the Southern Steep Mountains: Notes of the Deceased in Okinawa] (Tokyo: Kobunsha, 1959). Kinjo's two sisters were in the Star Lilies.

35 Boeicho Boeikenshujo Senshibu, *Okinawahomen rikugun sakusen* [The Army Strategy in the Battle of Okinawa] (Tokyo: Asagumo Shinbunsha, 1968), 252.

36 Boeicho Boeikenshujo Senshibu, *Okinawahomen rikugun sakusen*, 253.

37 Sono began her data collection for the first book in the summer of 1968. The book, which was written in documentary style (e.g., it did not use pseudonyms) dealt with the deaths of young Okinawan girls who had been dragged into the war, including members of the Star Lilies. The *Shukan Gendai*, a weekly magazine for news and amusement, first ran her stories, which were eventually published as a book, *Ikenie no shima* [The Island of Sacrifice] (Tokyo: Kodansha, 1970). The second was *Kiritorareta jikan* [The Time Cut Off] (Tokyo: Chuokoronsha, 1971), which dealt with the issue of the "mass suicide" in a more abstract fictional manner (e.g., the main three characters were not given names but were referred to merely as an angler, a woman, and a priest).

38 Sono Ayako, *Aru shinwa no haikei: Okinawa tokashiki no shudan jiketsu* [The Background of a Certain Myth: The Mass Suicide of Tokashiki, Okinawa] (Tokyo: Bungei Shunju, 1973). The volume is the third and last of her Okinawa

series. Sono's main sources were survivors from the Japanese Army, though she used some Okinawan "voices" to confirm her point.

39 Ienaga, *The Pacific War*, 185.

40 Ienaga, *Taiheyo senso*, 213–214. The translation is from Ienaga, *The Pacific War*, 185.

41 Although by this time more than sixty books had already been written and published about the Battle of Okinawa, both as historical records and personal accounts, the beginning of the 1970s saw a remarkable increase in publications on the topic in Japan. See the testimony given by Aniya Masaaki in 1985 at Tokyo District Court, in NLSTS, ed. *Okinawasen no jisso: Ienaga kyokasho saiban daisanjisosho chisaihen* [The Real Situation of the Battle of Okinawa: Ienaga Textbook Lawsuit, Third Suit, at the District Court] (Tokyo: Rongu Shuppan, 1990), 180.

42 Okinawaken Kyoshokuin Kumiai Senso Hanzai Tsuikyu Iinkai, ed., *Korega nihongun da: Okinawasen niokeru zangyaku koi* [This was the Japanese Military: War Atrocities in the Battle of Okinawa] (Naha: Okinawaken Kyoshokuin Kumiai, 1972).

43 Arasaki, "Okinawa nitotte sengo toha nanika," 230. Also see Gibe Kagetoshi, "Okinawa-sen no mikata kangaekata" [How to View and Think of the Battle of Okinawa], *Rekishi Chiri Kyoiku* 198 (1972): 62.

44 Taminato Tomoaki, "Okinawa to kyokasho saiban," 107.

45 For a general discussion of Okinawa and the textbook lawsuit, see Taminato Tomoaki, "Kyokasho saiban to watashi: Okinawa karano hatsugen" [The Textbook Lawsuit and Me: A Voice from Okinawa], in *Kyokasho saiban kara kyoiku o kangaeru: "Saikosai hanketsu o toshite*, ed. Umehara Toshio and Kyoiku-kagaku Kenkyu-kai (Tokyo: Kokudosha, 1993), 134–136.

46 "Kyokasho haiken: Okinawa" [A Look at Textbooks: Okinawa], in *Kyokasho saiban nyusu: Shukusatsuban,* ed. NLSTS, 39. The original was published in *Zenkoku Renrakukai Nyusu* [The NLSTS News] 7 (February 27, 1967): 7. *Zenkoku Renrakukai Nyusu* soon changed its name to *Kyokasho Saiban Nyusu* [The Textbook Lawsuit News].

47 A rejected geography textbook (published by Sanseido), cited in "Kyokasho haiken: Okinawa," 7.

48 "Kyokasho haiken: Okinawa," 7.

49 This remained the case to the end of Ienaga's three lawsuits in August 1997, at which point the Okinawan newspapers gave more space to the decision and covered its matter in more detail than did any newspaper on the main islands of Japan.

50 Another point in Ienaga's lawsuit with which Okinawans were deeply concerned dealt with Ienaga's reference to the Pacific War as a "reckless war."

51 The group was formed by taking advantage of a gathering opposing to the (re) institutionalization of Japan's National Foundation Day as a national holiday. The holiday was in place in the presurrender period, celebrating the founding of the country by the emperor's ancestors.

52 The Tokyo metropolitan area had 1965 (1,577 individuals and 388 organizations), Aichi Prefecture 1184 (1,089 individuals and 95 organizations), Osaka Prefecture 904 (816 individuals and 88 organizations), Fukuoka Prefecture 899 (535 individuals and 364 organizations). See "Kaiin nonyusha ichiran" [The List of Paid Membership Numbers], in *Kyokasho saiban nyusu: shukusatsuban*, ed. NLSTS, 282. The original was published in *Kyokasho Saiban Nyusu* 52 (July 15, 1971): 4.

53 Being caught between a tiger and a wolf is the Chinese equivalent of "between Scylla and Charybdis." See Ishido Tokuichi, "Watashitachi no kaeru 'sokoku' ni tatakai wa aru" [There Would Be Struggles in the Homeland to Which We Will Return], in *Kyokasho saiban nyusu: Shukusatsuban*, ed. NLSTS, 266. The original was published in *Kyokasho Saiban Nyusu* 50 (May 15, 1971): 4.

54 Miyayoshi Chiyo, "Shiawase tsukuru hahaoyani" [To Be a Mother Who Makes Happiness], *Kyokasho Saibain Nyusu* 66 (1972): 5.

55 Ienaga Saburo and Takashima Nobuyoshi, *Kyokasho saiban wa tsuzuku* [Building on the Textbook Lawsuits] (Tokyo: Iwanami Shoten, 1998), 24.

56 Takeuchi Rizo, Tanaka Takeo, and Konishi Shiro, *Shin Nihonshi* [New Japanese History] (Tokyo: Jiyushobo, 1974), 285.

57 The word *jihen* instead of *senso* was used during the war to avoid a declaration of war against China.

58 Kodama Kota et al., *Chugaku shakai: Rekishiteki bunya* [Junior High Social Studies: Historical Area] (Tokyo: Nihon Shoseki, 1975) and Kawasaki Tsuneyuki et al., *(Kaitei) hyojun shakai: Rekishi* [(Revised) Standard Social Studies: History] (Tokyo: Kyoiku Shuppan, 1975).

59 Kodama et al., *Chugaku shakai* (1975), 309.

60 Tawara, "Nankin daigyakusatsu jiken," 121. The same number appears in the other textbook. Kawasaki et al., *(Kaitei) hyojun shakai,* 300.

61 Ukai Nobushige et al., *(Shintei) atarashii shakai* [(New Impression) New Social Studies] (Tokyo: Tokyo Shoseki, 1975), 283.

62 Ukai Nobushige et al., *(Shinpen) atarashii shakai* [(New Edition) New Social Studies] (Tokyo: Tokyo Shoseki, 1978), 272. The 1969 and 1971 editions of the same book contained only the passage "[The Japanese Army] captured Nanjing." For further discussion of the previous editions of the textbook, see Chapter 1.

63 *Shosetsu Nihonshi,* a high school Japanese history textbook published by Yamakawa Shuppan, was the last to add a description of the massacre. The book had the largest share of its market. See Tawara, "Nankin daigyakusatsu jiken," 122.

64 Kodama Kota et al., *Chugaku shakai: Rekishiteki bunya* [Junior High Social Studies: Historical Area] (Tokyo: Nihon Shoseki, 1969), 299. Kodama Kota et al., *Chugaku shakai: Rekishiteki bunya* [Junior High Social Studies: Historical Area] (Tokyo: Nihon Shoseki, 1972), 315. The 1966 edition of the same book also contained a similar passage, which was one of the earliest appearances of the issue in the textbooks of Japanese history.

65 Kodama Kota et al., *Chugaku shakai: Rekishiteki bunya* [Junior High Social Studies: Historical area] (Tokyo: Nihon Shoseki, 1975), 315.

66 Kodama Kota et al., *Chugaku shakai: Rekishiteki bunya* [Junior High Social Studies: Historical Area] (Tokyo: Nihon Shoseki, 1978), 294.

67 Kodama Kota et al., *Chugaku shakai: Rekishiteki bunya* [Junior High Social Studies: Historical Area] (Tokyo: Nihon Shoseki, 1981), 256.

68 Ukai et al., *(Shintei) atarashii shakai,* 288.

69 Kawasaki et al., *(Kaitei) hyojun shakai: Rekishi,* 309.

70 This continued to be the general trend. According to a survey conducted by Nakamura Fumio, all but one of the high school Japanese history books published for use in the 1987 school year included some reference to Korean forced laborers. The one textbook that did not include the reference was *Shinpen Nihonshi* [New Edition Japanese History], which was written by a group of right-wing intellectuals in the late 1980s, and published by Hara Shobo in 1987. See Nakamura Fumio, *Koko nihonshi kyokasho: Kentei kyokasho juhachi-satsu o hikaku kentosuru* [High School Japanese History Textbooks: A Comparative Examination of Eighteen High School Japanese History Textbooks that Passed the Screening] (Tokyo: Sanichi Shobo, 1987), 305–306.

71 Ukai et al., *(Shintei) atarashii shakai,* 290.

72 The Great Tokyo Air Raid was part of an air attack on Japanese cities by U.S. bombers. At the beginning, the raid was aimed at the military facilities and factories, but it soon attacked the civilian population as well. On March 10, 1945, the air attack killed approximately 80,000 civilians within two and a half hours of bombing, in what is now called the Tokyo Daikushu. Thereafter, the bombers

attacked other large cities such as Nagoya, Osaka, and Kobe, and after these cities were turned to rubble, they attacked other local medium-sized and small cities. It is estimated that at least 256,000 civilians were killed in that series of air raids, that 2,210,000 houses were entirely destroyed, and that approximately 9,200,000 civilians were wounded. These numbers do not include the damage caused by the two atomic bombs.

73 For further discussion of Emperor Hirohito's war responsibility, see, for example, Ienaga, *Senso sekinin*, 257–267. Even in 1987, only one high school Japanese history textbook referred to the question of the emperor's war responsibility, and this occurred in connection to the Tokyo war tribunal. See Nakamura, *Koko nihonshi kyokasho*, 331.

74 See Ienaga, *The Pacific War*, 232–233. For an analysis of the description of Japan's surrender in the history textbooks (though it focuses on the textbooks of the 1990s), see Christopher Barnard, *Ideology in Japanese High School History Textbooks: A Functional Grammar Approach*, Ph.D. Dissertation, Temple University, 1998; Christopher Barnard, *Nankin gyakusatsu wa "okotta" noka: Koko rekishi kyokasho heno gengogakuteki hihan* [Did the Nanjing Massacre "Occur"? A Linguistic Critique of High School Textbooks] (Tokyo: Chikuma Shobo, 1998).

75 Kawasaki et al., *(Shinpan) hyojun chugaku shakai*, 306.

76 Kawasaki et al, *(Kaitei) hyojun chugaku shakai*, 312.

77 Kodama et al., *Chugaku shakai: Rekishiteki bunya* (1972), 317. The 1969 edition of the same book did not refer to the event.

78 Kodama et al., *Chugaku shakai: Rekishiteki bunya* (1975), 317. The same passage appeared in the 1978 edition of the same book, and the passage in the 1981 edition differed only slightly.

79 Ukai et al., *(Shintei) atarashii shakai*, 291.

80 See "Kyokasho kijutsu to kentei nimiru tennosei no kage" [The Shadow of the Emperor-Centered System in the Textbook Description and Screening], in Shuppan Roren Kyokasho Taisaku Iinkai, ed., *Kyokasho Repoto* 33 (1989): 126–128. According to the report, three out of six elementary school social studies textbooks (which cover Japanese history) and all the junior high social studies history textbooks referred to the event. Most of the high school Japanese history textbooks referred to the event, while they also began to include the emperor's role in the opening of the war against the United States (and other Allied countries).

81 Ukai et al., *(Shintei) atarashii shakai*, 282.

82 Ukai et al., *(Shintei) atarashii shakai*, 284.

83 Ukai et al., *(Shintei) atarashii shakai*, 289.

84 Ukai et al., *(Shintei) atarashii shakai*, 289.

85 Chantal Mouffe, "Radical Democracy: Modern or Postmodern?" in *Universal Abandon: The Politics of Postmodernism*, ed. Andrew Ross (Minneapolis: University of Minnesota Press, 1988), 38.

4 Ienaga Saburo's third lawsuit and strategic conjectures

1 The *Elementary Instruction Guidelines* were revised and announced in 1977 and implemented in 1980, the *Junior High School Instruction Guidelines* in 1977 and 1981, and the *High School Instruction Guidelines* in 1978 and 1982. New features of the guidelines were intended to create more spare time by selecting content carefully, a stress on moral education through extra-curricular activities, and the strong suggestion that the "national flag" be hoisted and the "national anthem" be sung at school events. See Ogawa Masahito, "Gakushu shido yoryo wa do hensenshitekitaka" [How the Instruction Guidelines Have Changed], in *Shin*

gakushu-shidoyoryo to kyoshi, ed. Nagai Kenichi (Tokyo: Eideru Kenkyujo, 1991), 33–44.

2 As a result of the election, in the Upper House, the LDP, combined with the non-LDP conservatives who would vote with it, barely had the majority. Tanaka's political ally U.S. President Richard Nixon had resigned several months earlier.

3 In the Lower House, the LDP barely had the majority by having non-LDP conservatives join the party. For further discussion of the LDP's factional strife, see Ishikawa Masumi, *Sengo seijishi* [The Postwar Political History] (Tokyo: Iwanami Shoten, 1995), 129–140.

4 The LDP again barely maintained the majority of the Lower House by having non-LDP conservatives join the party. One of the reasons for the LDP's defeat was Ohira's idea to introduce the comprehensive consumption (sales) tax.

5 Ishikawa, *Sengo seijishi*, 140–152.

6 It was translated by Saigo Takehiko, a scholar of language education. A different version was also written by Leo Tolstoy and translated by Uchida Risako. The story has also been popular in some parts of the United States. The English translation currently available is *Turnip: An Old Russian Folktale* (New York: Philomel Books, 1990).

7 For details of the Minshato's deceptive, dubious attack on textbooks, see Usui Kaichi et al., *Atarashii chûtô shakaika heno izanai* [An Invitation to New Secondary Social Studies] (Tokyo: Chirekisha, 1992), 172–175.

8 The textbook had been written by Ienaga alone and so had listed Ienaga as the sole author. The 1980 manuscript, however, was written with a greater degree of collaboration with several associate writers.

9 The record was later published as Ienaga Saburo, *"Misshitsu" kentei no kiroku* [The Record of Textbook Screening Behind "Closed Doors"] (Tokyo: Kyokasho Kentei Sosho o Shiensuru Zenkokurenrakukai [The National League for Support of the School Textbook Screening Suit, hereafter NLSTS], 1983). For more details of the 1981–82 screening process of Ienaga's description of the Nanjing Massacre, see Ienaga, *"Misshitsu" kentei*, 60–64.

10 Ienaga, *"Misshitsu" kentei*, 60.

11 Ienaga, *"Misshitsu" kentei*, 60.

12 Ienaga, *"Misshitsu" kentei*, 60–61.

13 Suzuki Akira, *"Nanjing daigyakusatsu" no maboroshi* [The Illusion of the "Nanjing Massacre"] (Tokyo: Bungei Shunjyu, 1973).

14 Ienaga, *"Misshitsu" kentei*, 61.

15 Ienaga, *"Misshitsu" kentei*, 65.

16 Ienaga, *"Misshitsu" kentei*, 5.

17 For further details of Eguchi's textbook screening experience, see, for example, Eguchi Keiichi, "Kyokasho mondai to okinawasen: Nihongun niyoru kenmin satsugai o chushin ni" [The Textbook Controversy and the Battle of Okinawa: On the Description of the Murder of Okinawans by the Japanese Army], in *Okinawasen to tennosei*, ed. Fujiwara Akira (Tokyo: Rippushobo, 1987), 223–254; and Eguchi Keiichi, "'Nihonshi' kingendaishi: Okinawa kankei" [The Modern and Contemporary Japanese History: Okinawa-Related Items], in *Kyokasho mondai towa nanika*, ed., Shakaika Kyokasho Shippitsusha Kondankai (Tokyo: Miraisha, 1984), 204–207.

18 Eguchi, "Kyokasho mondai," 225–226.

19 Eguchi, "Kyokasho mondai," 227.

20 Eguchi, "Kyokasho mondai," 227.

21 Eguchi, "Kyokasho mondai," 229. "Yugun" was the term Okinawans used for the Japanese Imperial Forces.

22 Eguchi, "Kyokasho mondai," 230.

23 Eguchi, "Kyokasho mondai," 224–230. Later Ienaga's legal team approached and asked Eguchi if he was willing to bring a textbook lawsuit against the government. Eguchi was almost persuaded but did not proceed. Instead, he was called to testify for Ienaga in Ienaga's first and third suits. See Ienaga Saburo and Takashima Nobuyoshi, *Kyokasho saiban wa tsuzuku* [Building on the Textbook Lawsuits] (Tokyo: Iwanami Shoten, 1998), 50.

24 Eguchi, "Kyokasho mondai," 233.

25 In a sense, the concern of the Chinese government was not unreasonable, since, according to its own regulations, the Japanese government did not (and does not) possess the power to dictate across the board what textbook authors should or should not include in their textbooks.

26 Ienaga, *"Misshitsu" kentei*, 123.

27 Ienaga, *"Misshitsu" kentei*, 123.

28 For example, the Informal Gathering of Social Studies Textbook Authors was established.

29 The phrase "by Japanese forces" in Japanese was "Nihongun no tameni," which can also be translated as either "for the Japanese forces" or "because of the Japanese forces."

30 Ienaga Saburo, *Zoku "misshitsu" kentei no kiroku* [Textbook Screening Behind "Closed Doors," Second Volume] (Tokyo: NLSTS, 1991).

31 Ienaga, *Zoku "misshitsu" kentei*, 52.

32 Ienaga, *Zoku "misshitsu" kentei*, 52–53.

33 The passage cited by the examiner was from Ienaga Saburo, *Taiheiyo senso* [The Pacific War] (Tokyo: Iwanami Shoten, 1968), 215. The English translation of the passage is available in Saburo Ienaga, *The Pacific War, 1931–1945* (New York: Pantheon, 1978), 187, which reads:

> Armies from time immemorial "have had a permissive policy toward sex as a means of keeping the soldiers contented and obedient." The Imperial Army with its "comfort stations" was no exception. The military commanders cannot evade ultimate responsibility for the atrocities (especially those related to sexual conduct) at Nanking and in other battle areas.

34 Ienaga, *Zoku "misshitsu" kentei*, 38.

35 Ienaga, *Zoku "misshitsu" kentei*, 53.

36 Ienaga, *Zoku "misshitsu" kentei*, 53.

37 For details of the circumstances of the decision to include (and exclude) specific points of contention in Ienaga's third suit, see Kyokasho Kentei-sosho o Shiensuru Rekishigaku Kankeisha no Kai (Association of People Involved in Historical Studies and Supporting the Textbook Screening Lawsuit, hereafter APIHS), ed., *Rekishi no hotei: Ienaga kyokasho saiban to rekishigaku* [A Court in History: Ienaga's Textbook Lawsuit and Historical Studies] (Tokyo: Otsuki Shoten, 1998), 205–214.

38 Ienaga, *"Misshitsu" kentei*, 57–60.

39 See, for example, Sheldon H. Harris, *Factories of Death: Japanese Biological Warfare, 1932–45, and The American Cover-up* (London & New York: Routledge, 1994), 49.

40 Ienaga, *Zoku "misshitsu" kentei*, 42–46.

41 Ienaga, *Zoku "misshitsu" kentei*, 25–31.

42 Ienaga, *"Misshitsu" kentei*, 25–33.

43 Ienaga, *"Misshitsu" kentei*, 14–16.

44 The achievements of the Working Groups during these years also resulted in volumes such as Toyama Shigeki, ed., *Kyokasho kentei no shiso to rekishi kyoiku* [The Ideology of Textbook Screening and History Education] (Tokyo: Ayumi

Shuppan, 1983); and Toyama Shigeki, ed., *Kyokasho saiban: Nihonshi no soten* [The Textbook Lawsuit: The Disputes in Japanese History] (Tokyo: Ayumi Shuppan, 1983).

45 The words of Yasuda Hiroshi in "Zadankai: Kyokasho saiban shien undo no sanjuni-nen" [A Round-Table Talk: The Thirty-Two Years of Movement to Support Textbook Lawsuits], in *Rekishi no hotei*, ed. APIHS, 203.

46 APIHS, *Rekishi no hotei*, 204.

47 "Daisanji-sosho no soten: Nankin daigyakusatsu no shomei" [The Points of Contention in the Third Lawsuit: The Proof of the Nanjing Massacre], in *Kyokasho saiban nyusu: Shukusatsuban 3*, ed. NLSTS (Tokyo: NLSTS, 1985), 286–287. The original was published in *Kyokasho Saiban Nyusu* 195 (April 20, 1984): 4–5.

48 APIHS, *Rekishi no hotei*, 206.

49 "Akuma no hoshoku o kokumin ga sabaku" [People make judgments on the Devil's Gluttony], in *Kyokasho saiban nyusu: Shukusatsuban 3*, ed. NLSTS, 266–267. The original was published in *Kyokasho Saiban Nyusu* 192 (January 20, 1984): 4–5.

50 Morimura had become interested in conducting research on the unit, after accidentally contacting a former member of the Unit 731 in the course of data collection for his novel.

51 Morimura Seiichi, *Akuma no hoshoku: "Kantongun saikin butai" kyofu no zenbo* [The Devil's Gluttony: The Complete Picture of "Japan's Kwantung Army's Bio-Warfare Unit"] (Tokyo: Kobunsha, 1981); Morimura Seiichi, *Akuma no hoshoku: "Kantongun saikin butai" nazo no sengoshi* [The Devil's Gluttony: The Mysterious Postwar History of "Japan's Kwantung Army's Bio-Warfare Unit"] (Tokyo: Kobunsha, 1982); and Morimura Seiichi, *Akuma no hoshoku: Dai san-bu* [The Devil's Gluttony: Part III] (Tokyo: Kadokawa Shoten, 1983). Morimura also published several books on the topic in the early 1980s.

52 APIHS, *Rekishi no hotei*, 206.

53 APIHS, *Rekishi no hotei*, 209–210.

54 In the process of editing the volume, the editors realized that the textbook authors were predominantly male, and mostly university professors. They then made the decision to include the voices of teachers and parents in the volume. Nishikawa Masao, "Atogaki" [An Epilogue], in *Kyokasho mondai towa nanika*, ed. Shakaika Kyokasho Shippitsusha Kondankai, 400.

55 The detail of the MOE's requests had (and has) been reported in *Kyokasho Repoto*, an annual publication by the Publishing Industry Worker's Union; however, the reports usually did not (and still do not) specify the exact names of textbooks (and authors), since to do so would have invited retribution from the MOE against the publisher(s) who disclosed the information.

56 NLSTS, ed., *Ienaga kyokasho saiban no subete: Sanjuni-nen no unodo to korekara* [All the Facts about the Movement Supporting Ienaga's Textbook Lawsuits: The Thirty-Two Years of the Movement and the Future] (Tokyo: Minshusha, 1998), 305.

57 "Ienaga daisanji sosho ni hirogaru kanshin: Kyoiku kenkyu zenkoku shukai" [A Growing Interest in Ienaga's Third Lawsuit: The National Education Research Meeting], in *Kyokasho saiban nyusu: Shukusatsuban 3*, ed. NLSTS, 273. The original was published in *Kyokasho Saiban Nyusu* 193 (February 20, 1984): 3.

58 Kobayashi Takehiko's letter to the NLSTS, as cited in "Jimukyoku eno tegami-kara" [The Letters Sent to the NLSTS Office], in *Kyokasho saiban nyusu: Shukusatsuban 3*, ed. NLSTS, 282. The original was published in *Kyokasho Saiban Nyusu* 194 (March 20, 1984): 8.

5 What Is Historical Fact? Dispute Over Historical Research And Education In Court

1 Barry Smart, "The Politics of Truth and the Problem of Hegemony," in *Foucault: A Critical Reader*, ed. David Couzens Hoy (Oxford: Basil Blackwell, 1986), 161.

2 For further discussion, see Chapter 2. For the term "historical science," also see Georg G. Iggers, *Historiography in the Twentieth Century: From Scientific Objectivity to the Postmodern Challenge* (Hanover: Wesleyan University Press, 1997), 17.

3 This was, to some extent, a strategic move on the part of Ienaga and his legal team.

4 Kyokasho Kentei Sosho o Shiensuru Zenkokurenrakukai (National League for Support of the School Textbook Screening Suit, hereafter NLSTS), ed., *Shucho no oshu: Ienaga kyokasho saiban daisanji sosho chisaihen 1* [The Exchange of Claims: Ienaga Textbook Lawsuit, Third Suit, District Court, Volume 1] (Tokyo: Rongu Shuppan, 1994), 307.

5 NLSTS, *Shucho no oshu*, 307.

6 NLSTS, *Shucho no oshu*, 307.

7 It also indicates the MOE's views on education.

8 "*Gojushichi-nendo shakaika kyokasho kentei kekka no omona jirei*" [Major Examples of Results of the 1982 Fiscal Year Textbook Screening], as cited in Yuge Toru, *Rekishigaku nyumon* [Introduction to Historical Studies] (Tokyo: Tokyo Daigaku Shuppankai, 1986), 57–58.

9 See Chapter 2 for further discussion of the point.

10 Tokinoya had been a textbook examiner for the MOE for twelve years (since 1973). He was a member of a right-wing historians' group (led by Hiraizumi Kiyoshi, a historian and strong advocate for *kokoku shikan*, the emperor-centered view of history) at the University of Tokyo, earned a doctorate in 1979, and at the time of his testimony was a professor at a private university.

11 Ienaga Saburo, *Zoku "misshitsu" kentei no kiroku* [The Record of Textbook Screening Behind "Closed Doors," Second Volume] (Tokyo: NLSTS, 1991), 25.

12 Ienaga, *Zoku "misshitsu" kentei*, 25–31.

13 NLSTS, ed., *Kentei no keika: Ienaga kyokasho saiban daisanji sosho chisaihen 2* [The Process of Textbook Screening: Ienaga Textbook Lawsuit, Third Suit, District Court, Volume 2] (Tokyo: Rongu Shuppan, 1994), 221.

14 NLSTS, *Kentei no keika*, 252.

15 Tokinoya became angry during the questioning, perhaps because the lawyer questioned him in the present tense, asking, for example, "Do you know. .." instead of "Did you know. .. ?" which Tokinoya perhaps perceived as ridicule.

16 NLSTS, *Kentei no keika*, 252.

17 Ienaga Saburo, *"Misshitsu" kentei no kiroku* [The Record of Textbook Screening Behind "Closed Doors"] (Tokyo: NLSTS, 1983), 60–65.

18 NLSTS, *Kentei no keika*, 259–60.

19 Ienaga, *Zoku "misshitsu" kentei*, 38–39.

20 NLSTS, *Kentei no keika*, 267.

21 NLSTS, *Kentei no keika*, 267.

22 Ienaga, *Zoku "misshitsu" kentei*, 42–46.

23 NLSTS, *Kentei no keika*, 223.

24 NLSTS, *Kentei no keika*, 224.

25 NLSTS, *Kentei no keika*, 270.

26 NLSTS, *Kentei no keika*, 272.

27 The phrase, "by the Japanese forces," in Japanese is "Nihongun no tameni," which also contains nuances such as "because of the Japanese forces" and "for the Japanese forces."

28 Ienaga, *Zoku "misshitsu" kentei*, 51–54.

29 NLSTS, *Kentei no keika*, 253.
30 NLSTS, *Kentei no keika*, 254.
31 NLSTS, *Kentei no keika*, 255.
32 NLSTS, ed., *Chosen jinmin no teiko/somo-tai: Ienaga kyokasho saiban daisanji sosho chisaihen 3* [The Resistance of Korean People and Troop Somo: Ienaga Textbook Lawsuit, Third Suit, District Court, Volume 3] (Tokyo: Rongu Shuppan, 1992), 18.
33 NLSTS, *Chosen jinmin no teiko*, 3.
34 NLSTS, *Chosen jinmin no teiko*, 35.
35 NLSTS, *Chosen jinmin no teiko*, 36.
36 NLSTS, *Chosen jinmin no teiko*, 36.
37 NLSTS, *Chosen jinmin no teiko*, 36–37.
38 NLSTS, *Chosen jinmin no teiko*, 51.
39 As observed by a member of the public in the gallery. See Moritani Kimitoshi, "Rekishigaku niokeru 19-seiki to 20-seiki: Kyokasho saiban daisanji sosho" [The Nineteenth and Twentieth Centuries in Historical Studies: The Third Textbook Lawsuit], in *Chosen jinmin no Teiko*, ed. NLSTS, 430.
40 NLSTS, *Chosen jinmin no teiko*, 56–57.
41 NLSTS, *Chosen jinmin no teiko*, 63.
42 NLSTS, *Chosen jinmin no teiko*, 68.
43 Moritani, "Rekishigaku niokeru 19-seiki," 431.
44 NLSTS, *Chosen jinmin no teiko*, 68.
45 NLSTS, *Chosen jinmin no teiko*, 69.
46 NLSTS, *Chosen jinmin no teiko*, 69.
47 NLSTS, *Chosen jinmin no teiko*, 69–70.
48 The words of Henri Houssaye at the 1900 Paris World Exposition; he opened the first session of Section 1—general and diplomatic history—of the First International Congress of Historians. As quoted in Peter Novic, *That Noble Dream: The "Objectivity Question" and the American Historical Profession* (Cambridge: Cambridge University Press, 1988), 37–38.
49 The three issues were seen as related. Until recently, in Japan, the atrocities Japan committed in the battles leading to the capture of Nanjing in 1937 had been discussed under the title "Nanjing Massacre" (*Nankin Gyakusatsu*). Specific attention to the rapes (indicated by the use of terms such as "the rape of Nanjing") seems to be a phenomenon of the 1990s. In this sense, Ienaga's history textbook and his lawsuit were ahead of their time in terms of the inclusion of the issue of rape. No feminists testified for Ienaga on the issue of rape during wartime, or during the Nanjing Massacre.
50 See Chapter 5 for a discussion of Honda's work, and Chapter 6 for a discussion of Fujiwara's involvement in the research on the Nanjing Massacre.
51 Kojima was a graduate of the University of Tokyo. He had been an independent scholar in war history since he left a news agency in 1964.
52 For more details, see Fujita Yasuyuki, "'Shinryaku' 'nankin daigyakusatsu' 'nihongun no zangyaku koi (gokan)' '731 butai' heiwa kyoiku no arikata o meguru soshojo no kobo nitsuite: Honkan o yomutameno sanko toshite" [On the Legal Offense and Defense Over "Aggression," "the Nanjing Massacre," "the Japanese Atrocity [Rape]," "Unit 731," and Approaches to Peace Education: A Guide to Readers of the Volume], in *Nankin Daigyakusatsu/731 Butai: Ienaga Kyokasho-saiban daisanji-sosho chisaihen 4*, ed., NLSTS (Tokyo: Rongu Shuppan, 1991), (1)–(39).
53 NLSTS, ed., *Nankin daigyakusatsu/731 butai: Ienaga kyokasho-saiban daisanji-sosho chisaihen 4* [The Nanjing Massacre and Unit 731: Ienaga Textbook Lawsuit, the Third Suit, District Court, Volume 4] (Tokyo: Rongu Shuppan, 1991), 5.
54 NLSTS, *Nankin daigyakusatsu/731 butai*, 6.
55 NLSTS, *Nankin daigyakusatsu/731 butai*, 6. Emphasis added.

56 NLSTS, *Nankin daigyakusatsu/731 butai*, 7.
57 NLSTS, *Nankin daigyakusatsu/731 butai*, 9–13.
58 NLSTS, *Nankin daigyakusatsu/731 butai*, 19.
59 NLSTS, *Nankin daigyakusatsu/731 butai*, 22.
60 The journal is a publication of *Rekishigaku Kenkyukai* (The Historical Society of Japan). The issue in question features "oral history," and the round-table discussion to which Honda was invited appears as an article entitled "Nyuginia kochi kara Nankin e: Honda Katsuichi-shi o kakonde" [From the Highland of New Guinea to Nanjing: An Interview with Katsuichi Honda], *Rekishigaku Kenkyu* 568 (1987): 51–72.
61 NLSTS, *Nankin daigyakusatsu/731 butai*, 22. Nakamura's article, cited here, is Nakamura Masanori, "Oraru hisutori to rekishigaku" [Oral History and the Study of History], *Rekishigaku Kenkyu* 568 (1987): 2–6.
62 NLSTS, *Nankin daigyakusatsu/731 butai*, 22.
63 NLSTS, *Nankin daigyakusatsu/731 butai*, 23.
64 NLSTS, *Nankin daigyakusatsu/731 butai*, 23–24.
65 NLSTS, *Nankin daigyakusatsu/731 butai*, 28.
66 Azuma Koichiro, "Nankin daigyakusatsu o abaku: Honda Fujiwara shogen" [Bringing to Light the Great Nanjing Massacre: The Testimonies of Honda and Fujiwara], in *Nankin daigyakusatsu/731 butai*, ed. NLSTS, I.
67 NLSTS, *Nankin daigyakusatsu/731 butai*, 119.
68 NLSTS, *Nankin daigyakusatsu/731 butai*, 123–124.
69 Of course, this could be the case if researchers were to take his approach. But by limiting his sources to those he regards as "reliable," his approach limits the scope of historical research and the range and kinds of historical knowledge available.
70 NLSTS, *Nankin daigyakusatsu/731 butai*, 131.
71 NLSTS, *Nankin daigyakusatsu/731 butai*, 131.
72 Later in the cross-examination of Kojima, Ienaga's legal team produced passages from Hata Ikuhiko's work as evidence, citing a report containing the same passages with identification of the regiment.
73 NLSTS, *Nankin daigyakusatsu/731 butai*, 133.
74 NLSTS, *Nankin daigyakusatsu/731 butai*, 137.
75 NLSTS, *Nankin daigyakusatsu/731 butai*, 139.
76 "Nicchu Senso" refers to the part of the Asia-Pacific War that was fought in China. For various Japanese terms for the war that ended in 1945, and for the issues involved in it, see Chapter 5.
77 NLSTS, *Nankin daigyakusatsu/731 butai*, 140.
78 Hosoya Chihiro, ed., *Tokyo saiban o tou* [An Examination of the Tokyo War Tribunal] (Tokyo: Kodansha, 1984), 102–103.
79 NLSTS, *Nankin daigyakusatsu/731 butai*, 141.
80 NLSTS, *Nankin daigyakusatsu/731 butai*, 141.
81 NLSTS, *Nankin daigyakusatsu/731 butai*, 148.
82 In fact, when Ienaga's legal team questioned him about the treatment of Chinese POWs, Kojima betrayed his ignorance of research done by others. Ienaga's legal team pointed out that the name of a regiment that wrote the detailed combat report, which Kojima referred to in the state's examination, was mentioned in a regional newspaper article in 1963. Ienaga's legal team produced Hata Ikuhiko's work on the subject, which cited a combat report with the same contents. Hata Ikuhiko, *Nankin jiken: "Gyakusatsu" no kozo* [The Nanjing Incident: The Structure of "Massacre"] (Tokyo: Chuokoronsha, 1986), 158. Hata was a graduate of the University of Tokyo, had worked for the Ministry of Finance, and was a university professor at the time. Hata briefly studied at Harvard University as well as Columbia University and was once a visiting scholar at Princeton

University. In Ienaga's third lawsuit, he testified for the state on the dispute over Unit 731.

83 NLSTS, *Nankin daigyakusatsu/731 butai*, 150.
84 NLSTS, *Nankin daigyakusatsu/731 butai*, 160.
85 NLSTS, *Nankin daigyakusatsu/731 butai*, 161.
86 NLSTS, *Nankin daigyakusatsu/731 butai*, 161.
87 Jon Simons, *Foucault and the Political* (London: Routledge, 1995), 92.

6 Court decisions on Ienaga Saburo's lawsuits and critical trends in history textbooks, 1980s–1997

1 Ienaga Saburo and Tokashima Nobuyoshi, *Kyokasho saiban wa tsuzuku* [Building on the Textbook Lawsuits] (Tokyo: Iwanamishoten: 1998), 30.
2 Ienaga Kyokasho Sosho Bengodan, ed., *Ienaga kyokasho saiban: Sanjuni-nen niwataru bengodan katsudo no sokatsu* [The Ienaga Textbook Lawsuits: A Summary of the Legal Team's Actions over Thirty-Two Years] (Tokyo: Nihon Hyoronsha, 1998), 101.
3 Ienaga Saburo, "Saibansho wa kokomade darakushitaka" [Did the Court Go Bad to This Extent?], in *Kyokasho saiban nyusu: Shikusatsuban 5*, ed. Kyokasho Kentei o Shiensuru Zenkokurenrakukai [National League for Support of the School Textbook Screening Suit, hereafter NLSTS] (Tokyo: NLSTS, 1998), 173. Original published *Kyokasho Saiban Nyusu* Special Issue (March 30, 1993): 1.
4 David E. Sanger, "A Stickler for History, Even if It's Not Very Pretty," *The New York Times*, May 27, 1993.
5 "Yamanashi Nichinichi Shinbun: Settokuryokunai kyokasho hanketsu" [Yamanashi Daily News: Textbook Ruling Not Persuasive], in *Kyokasho saiban nyusu: Shukusatsuban 5*, ed. NLSTS (Tokyo: NLSTS, 1998), 193. The original was an editorial of *Yamanashi Nichinichi Shinbun*, republished in *Kyokasho Saiban Nyusu* 301 (May 20, 1993): 6.
6 How to count the points was more or less a technical matter. Some points, such as the massacre and rape of Nanjing, were disputed together at the point of filing the lawsuit, but through the courtroom debates they became more or less separate issues.
7 For the 1993 Tokyo High Court decision, see *Kokka to kyoiku, kunigawa shucho, hanketsu: Ienaga kyokasho saiban daisanji-sosho, kosaihen 6* [The State and Education, the State's Arguments, and the Court Decision: The Trial of Ienaga's Third Textbook Lawsuit at the High Court, Volume 6], ed. NLSTS (Tokyo: Minshusha, 1996), 264–325.
8 Ienaga Saburo, *Jokokushin de tetteitekini arasou* [To Fight to the Hilt in the Appeal Court], in *Kyokasho saiban nyusu: Shukusatsuban 5*, ed. NLSTS, 193. The original was published in *Kyokasho Saiban Nyusu* 307 (November 20, 1993): 1.
9 See Ienaga and Takashima, *Kyokasho saiban wa tsuzuku*, 9.
10 Chapter 7 further discusses the political changes of 1993 and Hosokawa's statements.
11 Honda Koei, "Hosokawa hatsugen to kyokasho sosho" [Hosokawa's Statement and the Textbook Lawsuits], in *Kyokasho saiban nyusu: Shukusatsuban 5*, ed. NLSTS, 224. The original was published in *Kyokasho Saiban Nyusu* 305 (September 20, 1993): 8.
12 Tawara Yoshifumi, 1998, "Nankin daigyakusatsu jiken to rekishikyokasho mondi" [History Textbook Controversy and the Nanjing Massacre], in *Nankin jiken o domiruka; Ni-Chu-Bei kenkyusha niyoru kensho*, ed. Akira Fujiwara (Tokyo: Aoki Shoten, 1998), 116–131.

13 The 1984 edition of *Chugakko shakaika: Rekishi bunya* [Junior High Social Studies: The Area of History], as cited in Tokutake Toshio, *Kyokasho no sengo-shi* (Tokyo: Shinnihon Shuppansha, 1995), 207.

14 Ienaga Saburo, *Zoku "misshitsu" kentei no kiroku* [The Record of Textbook Screening behind "Closed Doors": The Second Volume] (Tokyo: NLSTS, 1991), 51–54.

15 Kodama Kota et al., *Chugaku shakai: Rekishiteki bunya* [Junior High Social Studies: The Area of History] (Tokyo: Nihon Shoseki, 1987), 267.

16 *Sekaishi B* [World History B], a textbook published by Hitotsubashi Shuppan, as cited by Tawara, "Nankin daigyakusatsu jiken," 127.

17 The recent textbooks still have some flaws. For example, Christopher Barnard finds problematic the language used to describe the Nanjing Massacre in the textbooks used in 1995. See Christopher Barnard, "Isolating Knowledge of the Unpleasant: The Rape of Nanking in Japanese High School Textbooks," *British Journal of Sociology of Education* 22, no. 4 (2001): 520–529.

18 The Supreme Court decided to hear the case in a "small court" (*shohotei*), consisting of several justices, rather than "grand court" (*daihotei*), consisting of all the justices. This meant that it would not change the previous decisions regarding the question of the constitutionality of the state's textbook screening.

19 Ienaga Saburo, *Saigo no kotobenron* [The Last Oral Pleadings], in *Kyokasho saiban nyusu: Shukusatsuban 5*, ed. NLSTS, 547. The original published in *Kyokasho Saiban Nyusu* 352 (August 20, 1997): 3.

20 Minobe influenced Ienaga greatly when he was young.

21 Ienaga Saburo, *Saigo no doryoku o katamuke saibankan no kokoro o yusubutte* [Make all Possible Efforts and Convince the Minds of the Justices], in *Kyokasho saiban nyusu: Shukusatsuban 5*, ed. NLSTS, 536. The original was published in *Kyokasho Saiban Nyusu* 350 (June 20, 1997): 4.

22 The game of legal truth does not necessarily coincide with the game of historical truth. In struggles for and against a given hegemony, multiple games of truths are played.

23 For further discussion on the Japanese nationalist movements to revise history, especially those developed by Fujioka Nobukatsu, see Chapter 7; and Yoshiko Nozaki, "Feminism, Nationalism, and the Japanese Textbook Controversy Over the Issue of 'Comfort Women,'" in *Feminism and Antiracism: International Struggles for Justice*, ed. France Winddance Twine and Kathleen Blee (New York: New York University Press, 2001), 170–189.

24 For a complete analysis of the decision as a whole, see NLSTS, ed., *Kentei ni iho ari! Ienaga kyokasho saiban saikosai hanketsu* [Textbook Screening is Found Illegal! The Supreme Court Decision on the Ienaga Textbook Lawsuit] (Tokyo: Aoki Shoten, 1997).

25 I examine here some of the important points of these decisions.

26 NLSTS, *Kokka to kyoiku, kunigawa shucho, hanketsu*, 305–310.

27 NLSTS, *Kentei ni iho ari!*, 96.

28 NLSTS, *Kokka to kyoiku, kunigawa shucho, hanketsu*, 316–318.

29 NLSTS, *Kentei ni iho ari!*, 114–116, 120–124.

30 NLSTS, *Kokka to kyoiku, kunigawa shucho, hanketsu*, 319–320.

31 NLSTS, *Kentei ni iho ari!*, 100–102, 108–109.

32 NLSTS, *Kokka to kyoiku, kunigawa shucho, hanketsu*, 312–314.

33 NLSTS, *Kentei ni iho ari!*, 97–98.

34 NLSTS, *Kentei ni iho ari!*, 106.

35 NLSTS, *Kokka to kyoiku, kunigawa shucho, hanketsu*, 321–322.

36 NLSTS, *Kentei ni iho ari!*, 102–104.

37 NLSTS, *Kentei ni iho ari!*, 108.

38 NLSTS, *Kentei ni iho ari!*, 126.

39 NLSTS, *Kentei ni iho ari!*, 114–116.

40 For an interesting exchange between Ienaga and Takashima on these issues, see Ienaga and Takashima, *Kyokasho saiban wa tsuzuku*, 54–63.
41 Ienaga Saburo, *Sanjuni-nen o furikaette* [Reflection on Thirty-Two Years], in *Kyokasho saiban nyusu: Shukusatsuban 5*, ed. NLSTS, 602. The original was published in *Kyokasho Saiban Nyusu* 361 (June 20, 1998): 4.

7 Nationalism, democracy, and the textbook market

1 Wartime rape has a history of impunity, and to consider it as war crime is a recent development. See, for example, Dorothy Q. Thomas and Regan E. Ralph, "Rape in War: Challenging the Tradition of Impunity," *SAIS Review of International Affairs* 14, no. 1 (1994), 82–99.
2 The issue surfaced as a part of the U.S.–Japan diplomatic conversations also. In the fall of 1990 LDP representatives visited the United States and held meetings with Dick Cheney, Robert S. Macnamara, and others, in which one of the major topics of their discussion was "Japan's international contribution," i.e., sending Japan's Self Defense Force (SDF) overseas. They regarded "education" as the major obstacle against the oversea deployment of the SDF. See "Jiminto kokubo sanbukai hobei hokokusho: Jieitai kaigakihahei o aotta amerika no tainichi atsuryoku" [A Report Written by the Three Liberal Democratic Party's National Defense Committees that Visited the United States: The American Pressure to Send the Self Defense Forces Overseas], *Bunka Hyoron* 360 (1991): 62–83.
3 Joan Wallach Scott, *Gender and the Politics of History* (New York: Columbia University Press, 1988).
4 Tom Bender, "Textbook Controversies and the Limit of American History" (paper presented at the Department of History Symposium "History Textbooks and the Profession: Comparing National Controversies in a Globalizing Age," University of Chicago, IL, May 2007).
5 See, for example, Kimijima Kazuhiko, *Kyokasho no shiso: Nihon to kankoku no kingendaishi* [Perspectives in Textbooks: The Modern History of Japan and Korea] (Tokyo: Suzusawa Shoten, 1996); and Tawara Yoshifumi, *Kyokasho kogeki no shinso: "Ianfu" mondai to "jiyushugishikan" no sajutsu* [The Truth of Textbook Attacks: The Swindling Technique of the "Comfort Women" Issue and "Liberal View of History"] (Tokyo: Gakushu no Tomosha, 1997).
6 Nagano Tsuneo, "'Shinpen nihonshi' jiken nitsuite" [On the Event of the *New History Textbook*], in *Kyokasho ronso o koete*, ed. Kakinuma Masayoshi and Nagano Tsuneo (Tokyo: Hihyosha, 1998), 133–146. See also "'Shinpen nihonshi' naze gokakuka" [Why *Shinpen Nihonshi* Passed], *Kyokasho Repoto* 31 (1987): 12–13.
7 "'Shinpen nihonshi' naze."
8 "'Shinpen nihonshi' naze."
9 Kimijima, *Kyokasho no shiso.*
10 See Uesugi Satoshi, "'Tsukurukai' tono tatakai 2005-nen: Seika to kadai, soshite korekara" [The Battle against the JSHTR in 2005: Achievements and Remaining Tasks from Now On], *Senso Sekinin Kenkyu* 50 (2005): 59.
11 Ishikawa Masumi, *Sengo seijishi* [History of Postwar Japanese Politics] (Tokyo: Iwanami Shoten, 1995).
12 A few were indeed published during the war. See Takasaki Ryuji, ed., *Hyakusatsu ga kataru "ianjyo" otoko no honne: Ajia-zeniki ni "inanjyo" ga atta* [The "Comfort Facility" and Men's Confessions that One Hundred Books Tell: There were "Comfort Facilities" All over Asia] (Tokyo: Nashinokisha, 1994).
13 Nakasone Yasuhiro, "Nijusansai de sanzen'nin no soshikikan" [The General Commander of Three Thousand Men at the Age of Twenty-Three], in *Owarinaki Kaigun*, ed. Matsuura Takanori (Tokyo: Bunkahoso Kaihatsu Senta, 1978), 98.

14 Indeed, in recent years, Nakasone has defensively explained that what he had actually set up was a "recreation center," where men played Japanese board games. See, for example, Norimitsu Onishi, "Japan's Textbooks Reflect Revised History," *The New York Times*, April 1, 2007.

15 See Yoshiko Nozaki, "Feminism, Nationalism, and the Japanese Textbook Controversy," in *Feminism & Antiracism: International Struggles for Justice*, ed. France Winddance Twine and Kathleen M. Blee (New York: New York University Press, 2001), 170–189.

16 As many critics have pointed out, the phrase "military sexual slavery" would be more accurate than the phrase "comfort women"; however, I employ the latter term in this chapter (hereafter, without quotes) because it is the one that has been most often used. For further discussion of the emergence of the issue in Japan as well as internationally, see, for example, Laura Hein, "Savage Irony: The Imaginative Power of the Military Comfort Women in the 1990s," *Gender and History* 11, no. 2 (1999): 336–372.

17 "Jugun ianfu chosakekka nikansuru kanbochokan danwa" [Chief Cabinet Secretary's Unwritten Statement on the Results of the Investigation into War Comfort Women], *Asahi Shinbun*, August 5, 1993. Kono stated this in the form of danwa (a form of official statement without a written document), which was reported in newspapers.

18 Ohama Tetsuya et al., *Chugakusei no shakaika rekishi: Nihon no ayumi to sekai* [Social Studies History for Junior High Students: Japan's Progress and the World] (Tokyo: Nihonbunkyo Shuppan, 1997), 252.

19 "Hosokawa shusho kishakaiken no yoshi" [An Outline of a Press Conference of Prime Minister Hosokawa], *Asahi Shinbun*, August 11, 1993.

20 "Shusho no shoshin hyomei enzetsu" [The Prime Minister's Address on his Positions], *Asahi Shinbun*, August 23, 1993.

21 The committee reached its conclusion and disbanded itself in February 1995.

22 Wada Haruki, Ishizaka Koichi, and the Sengo Gojunen Kokkai Ketsugi o Motomerukai, ed., *Nihon wa shokuminchi shihai o do kangaetekitaka* [How Japan has Reflected on its Colonialism] (Tokyo: Nashinokisha, 1996).

23 Wada et al., *Nihon wa shokuminchi*. See also Steven T. Benfell, "Why Can't Japan Apologize? Institutions and War Memory since 1945," *Harvard Asia Quarterly* VI, no. 2 (2002).

24 See also Nozaki, "Feminism, Nationalism," 170–189.

25 See, for example, Gavan McCormack, "The Japanese Movement to 'Correct' History," in *Censoring History: Citizenship and Memory in Japan, Germany, and the United States*, ed. Laura Hein and Mark Selden (Armonk: M. E. Sharp, 2000), 53–73.

26 The group also circulated an English brochure. Japanese Society for History Textbook Reform (JSHTR, hereafter), *The Restoration of a National History: Why was the Japanese Society for History Textbook Reform Established, and What Are its Goals?* (Tokyo: JSHTR, 1998).

27 Tawara Yoshifumi, *"Ianfu" mondai to kyokasho kogeki: Dokyumento* [The Issue of "Comfort Women" and the Attack on Textbooks: A Document] (Tokyo: Kobunken, 1997), 27.

28 See, for example, Tawara Yoshifumi, "Kenpo ihan shinryaku senso kotei no 'abunai kyokasho' no jittai" [The Reality of an Ideologically "Dangerous Textbook" that Affirms Aggressive War and that Breaches the Constitution], *Senso Sekinin Kenkyu* 30 (2000): 28-49.

29 For further discussion on the comparison of the old and new editions of these textbooks, see Tawara, "Kenpo ihan shinryaku," 35-37 and 43-49. The titles of texts were not disclosed during the time of the screening process; however, usually, the information (not the actual titles) about the content is made available

for the public though groups and critics (such as Tawara Yoshifumi) closely connected to the Publishers' Workers' Union.

30 The draft text was eventually published as Sasayama Haruo et al., *Mirai o mitsumete* [Looking Hard at the Future] (Tokyo: Kyoikushuppan, 2002). This text, in its 1996 edition, contained a good number of discussions on unresolved issues of the war from critical, peace-and-justice perspectives; the 2002 text dropped many of these discussions. Another text that dropped a good number of descriptions on critical issues of the war was one published by Osaka Shoseki.

31 Two texts were drafts for those eventually published by Shimizushoin and by Teikokushoin. Their 1996 editions did refer to the comfort women issue, but not as extensively as Sasayama Haruo et al., *Mirai o mitsumete*.

32 The text eventually was published as Kodama Kota et al., *Watashitachi no chugaku shakai: Rekishiteki bunya* [Our Junior High Social Studies: The History Area] (Tokyo: Nihon Shoseki, 2002). The published text, indeed, contains two excellent columns related to the issues of the war: "Rekishi o kangaeru: Maboroshino daitoa kyoeiken" [Thinking about History: The Illusion of the Great East-Asian Co-Prosperity Bloc] and "Nihon no sengoshori" [Japan's Confronting Postwar Issues]. The former section contains a description of the comfort women during the war; the latter discusses the lawsuits brought by former comfort women to the Japanese court, with a photo of Kim Haksoon.

33 The text was a draft for Kodama Kota et al., *Watashitachi no chugakushakai.*

34 Those drafts submitted by Tokyo Shoseki and Osaka Shoseki.

35 The text was a draft for Sasayama Haruo et al., *Mirai o mitsumete.* For Unit 731, see Sheldon H. Harris, *Factories of Death: Japanese Biological Warfare, 1932–45, and the American Cover-Up* (London: Routledge, 1994).

36 The texts submitted by Tokyo Shoseki and Osaka Shoseki.

37 Even the new (2006) edition of *Watashitachi no chugaku shakai*, now published by Nihon Shoseki Shinsha (an offshoot of Nihon Shoseki), dropped the phrase "comfort women" in its descriptions of the issues of comfort women (though the term still appears in the photo illustration showing the newspaper report a lawsuit brought by the former comfort women). The ways in which the textbook authors and publishers are currently fighting back against the right-wing nationalist pressure requires close examination, which is beyond the scope of this volume.

38 See, for example, Tawara, "Kenpo ihan shinryaku." The term "Jugun" means "serving in the war" or "accompanying the military"; *jugun kangofu* for "war nurse"; *jugun kisha for* "war correspondent." The right-wing nationalists made the comfort women issue controversial in part by attacking the use of the term *jugun inanfu*, a term that had not existed during the war but was frequently used in the early 1990s. The nationalists argued that the textbooks taught students a lie by using a term that had not existed during the war. Some even argued that *jugun inanfu* had not existed because no such term had existed. Fur further discussion, see Yoshiko Nozaki, "The 'Comfort Women' Controversy: History and Testimony," *Japan Focus* 348 (2005), available at <http://japanfocus.org/products/topdf/2063> .

39 Tawara Yoshifumi, *Abunai kyokasho: "Senso ga dekirukuni" o mezasu "tsukurukai" no jittai* [Ideologically Dangerous Textbooks: The Reality of the "JSHTR," Which Wants to Have a "Country that Can Fight a War"] (Tokyo: Gakushu no Tomosha, 2001).

40 A draft civics textbook, whose content was as problematic as the history text, was also submitted at the same time (and later authorized by the MOE). This volume only discusses the history text.

41 See, for example, Uesugi Satoshi, "Uyoku no seijiundo ga tsuini kyokasho o tsukutta" [Finally, Right-Wing Politics Developed and Published School Textbooks], in *Iranai*

"kaminokuni" rekishi komin kyokasho, ed. Uesugi Satoshi, Kimijima Kazuhiko, Koshida Takashi, and Takashima Nobuyuki (Tokyo: Akashi Shoten, 2001).

42 See, for example, Tawara, "Kenpo ihan shinryaku."

43 The MOE became the Ministry of Education, Culture, Sports, Science, and Technology in 2001 due to ministerial reorganization. Since then, in its short form, it has been called *Monbukagakusho,* the Ministry of Education and Science (hereafter MOES).

44 For analysis of the text's description of modern Japanese history, see, "Facts Sheet Concerning *New History Textbook*" posted at the web site of *Critical Asian Studies* <http://csf.colorado.edu/bcas/campaign/textbk3.htm> . Also see John. K. Nelson, "Tempest in a Textbook: A Report on the New Middle-School History Textbook in Japan," *Critical Asian Studies* 34, no. 1 (2002): 129–148.

45 The extent to which the Internet helped enhance community activism against the nationalist text varied in Japan as well as in Korea. See Isa Ducke, "Activism and the Internet: Japan's 2001 History Textbook Affair," in *Japanese Cybercultures,* ed. Nanette Gottlieb and Mark McLelland (London: Routledge, 2003), 205–221. For some specific web sites, see Yoshiko Nozaki, "Japanese Politics and the History Textbook Controversy, 1982–2001," *International Journal of Educational Research* 37, nos. 6 and 7 (2002): 603–622.

46 The mayor's note was published in *Asahi Shinbun,* and cited in Fujii Kazuo "'Tsukurukai' kyokasho saitaku no hoshin ga kogisatto de yuragu tochigiken shimotsuga" [Shimotsuga, Tochigi-Pref, Shaken by Protests Against its Decision to Adopt the Textbook Written by the JSHTR], *Shukan Kinyobi* 372 (2001): 45.

47 Uesugi Satoshi, "'Tsukurukai' no haiboku wa heiwa jinken ishiki no shori" [The Defeat of the JSHTR is the Victory of Consciousness for Peace and Human Rights], *Senso Sekinin Kenkyu* 33 (2001): 44–47.

48 "2002 nendoyo kyokasho no saitakukekka: Mujun kaiketsu no itoguchisura izenmienai kyokasho-saitaku" [The Result of 2002 Textbook Adoption: The Textbook Adoption and We Cannot See the Clue for Solving its Contradictions], *Kyokasho Repoto* 46 (2002): 66. The market share slightly increased in the following years to 0.047 percent. In addition, some private schools bought the texts as supplemental readings.

49 Generally a 10 percent market share is the break-even line for the textbook publishing business in Japan.

50 The JSHTR's membership was more than 10,000 in 2001; it declined to 7,840 in September 2004. See Tawara Yoshifumi, "'Tsukurukai' kyokasho no mondaiten to 2005-nen no tatakai" [The JSHTR Textbook, its Problems, and the Battle against it in 2005], *Senso Sekinin Kenkyu* 48 (2005): 9. For further discussion on Japan's right-wing civic groups, see, for example, Kenneth J. Ruoff, *People's Emperor: Democracy and the Japanese Monarchy, 1945–1995* (Cambridge: Harvard University Asia Center, 2001); and Franziska Seraphim, *War Memory and Social Politics in Japan, 1945–2005,* (Cambridge: Harvard University Asia Center, 2006).

51 A comment on Koizumi made by Tanaka Makiko, politician and Tanaka Kakuei's daughter, who became the Minister of Foreign Affairs in Koizumi cabinet, but was soon ousted, because of internal strife in the LDP.

52 The reasons for the defeat were manifold. See Uesugi, "'Tsukurukai' tono tatakai," 60–62.

53 Nihon Shoseki, whose textbook has included a number of wartime issues from critical, peace-and-justice perspectives, went bankrupt from a loss of market share in 2002 (from 13.7 percent to 5.9 percent), and its new company (Nihon Shoseki Shinsha) is at risk of another bankruptcy because of its losses in 2006 (to 3.1 percent). Uesugi, "'Tsukurukai' tono tatakai," 58–59 and 65.

54 Laura Hein and Mark Selden, "The Lessons of War, Global Power, and Social Change," in *Censoring History*, ed. Hein and Selden, 4.
55 See also Yoshiko Nozaki and Hiromitsu Inokuchi, "Japanese Education, Nationalism, and Ienaga Saburo's Textbook Lawsuits," in *Censoring History*, ed. Hein and Selden, 96–126; and P. Midford, "The Logic of Reassurance and Japan's Grand Strategy," *Security Studies* 11, no. 3 (2002): 1–43.
56 Michel Foucault, "Governmentality," in *The Foucault Effect: Studies in Governmentality with Two Lectures by and an Interview with Michel Foucault*, ed. G. Burchell, C. Gordon, and P. Miller (Chicago: University of Chicago Press, 1991), 95–96.
57 Michel Foucault, "Preface to the History of Sexuality, Volume II," in *Foucault Reader*, ed. P. Rabinow (New York: Pantheon Books, 1984), 338.
58 The school districts, teachers, parents, and students (or citizens) perhaps need to have strategies not only to fight against a text (and its ideology) but also to struggle for the inclusion of critical, peace-and-justice perspectives in all textbooks and in the processes occurring after the adoption—namely, teaching and learning in schools. It is beyond the scope of this volume to examine the ways history has been taught in Japanese classrooms. For a historical case study on this topic, see Yoshiko Nozaki, "Japanese Critical Teaching about the Asia-Pacific War, 1960s and 1970s" (paper presented at the Spring Fellows' Retreat, National Academy of Education, Brown University, Providence, RI, March 2003). For a study of the contemporary classroom, see Peter Cave, "Teaching the History of Empire in Japan and England," *International Journal of Educational Research* 37, nos. 6 and 7 (2002): 623–641.

8 Epilogue

1 Immanuel Wallerstein, "The Construction of Peoplehood: Racism, Nationalism, Ethnicity," in *Race, Nation, Class: Ambiguous Identities*, ed. Etienne Balibar and Immanuel Wallerstein (London: Verso, 1991), 78.
2 George Orwell, *Nineteen Eighty-Four* (New York: Signet Classic, 1950), 32. Orwell's picture of total Party control of the nation's past did not and does not exactly match the Japanese case.
3 Patrick Wright, *On Living in an Old Country: The National Past in Contemporary Britain* (London: Verso, 1985), 24–26.
4 Needless to say, the war situation continues, to date, in some places in Asia, including the situation that divides South and North Korea.
5 See Wada Haruki and Ishizaka Koichi, "Hajimeni" [Introduction], in *Nihon wa shokuminchi-shihai o do kangaete kitaka*, ed. Wada Haruki, Ishizaka Koichi, and Sengo Gojyu-nen Kokkai Ketsugi o Motomeru-kai (Tokyo: Nashinokisha, 1996), 1–5.
6 One good example of such an examination is Yoshida Yutaka, *Nihonjin no sensokan: Sengo-shi no nakano henyo* [Japanese Views on the War: Changes in Postwar History] (Tokyo: Iwanami Shoten, 1995).
7 Michel Foucault, "Space, Knowledge, and Power," in *The Foucault Reader*, ed. Paul Rabinow (New York: Pantheon, 1984), 245.
8 Yoshida, *Nihonjin no sensokan*, 160–161.
9 Indeed, his court challenges for the most part preceded the lawsuits brought against the Japanese state (and some Japanese companies) by the Asian victims of the war.
10 While the current view on war responsibility among the Japanese is more complex than one that simply replaces the old emperor-centered view with a new critical one, the last fifty years have clearly brought about a shift to a more critical perspective. See Yoshida, *Nihonjin no sensokan*.

11 See, for example, Michael W. Apple and Linda K. Christian-Smith, ed., *The Politics of the Textbook* (New York: Routledge, 1991).

12 Recent debates over national curriculum and frequent curriculum controversy in many nations indicate that the significance (and intensity) involving the question is on the rise.

13 Raymond Williams, *Resources of Hope: Culture, Democracy, Socialism* (London: Verso, 1989), 36–38.

14 Todd Gitlin, *The Twilight of Common Dreams: Why America is Wracked by Culture Wars* (New York: Metropolitan Books, 1995), 23.

15 John Fiske, "Black Bodies of Knowledge: Notes on an Effective History," *Cultural Critique* 33 (1996): 209.

16 In particular, recent feminist discussions on this topic are critically important. See, for example, Sandra Harding, *Whose Science? Whose Knowledge? Thinking from Women's Lives* (New York: Cornell University Press, 1991).

17 For further discussion of this point, see Yoshiko Nozaki, "Riding Tensions Critically: Ideology, Power/Knowledge, and Curriculum Making," in *Ideology, Curriculum, and the New Sociology of Education: Revisiting the Work of Michael Apple*, ed. Lois Weis, Cameron McCarthy, and Greg Dimitriadis (New York: Routledge, 2006).

18 Michel Foucault, *Discipline and Punish: The Birth of the Prison*, trans. Alan Sheridan, (New York: Pantheon Books, 1979), 27. For further discussion, see Jon Simons, *Foucault and the Political* (London: Routledge, 1995); also see Nozaki, "Riding Tensions Critically," 73–75.

Index

Fujiwara Akira 89, 109, 110
Fukuda Takeo 74
Fundamental Law of Education
(*Kyoiku Kihon Ho*): early postwar
years 1945–65 10, 19; historical facts
106; politics over education 30–32, 34,
35, 37, 38, 42, 47; right-wing nationalist
history textbook projects 148
Fusosha 144, 146, 149
Fuzanbo 4, 5

G

gakute trials 31
"games of truth" (Foucault): historical
facts 94, 120; ordinary people's war
responsibility 70; significance of
lawsuits xiv, xv, xvii, xviii, 152, 155,
156; third lawsuit 85, 87, 88
Gendai Nihon no Naritachi (The
Formation of Contemporary Japan) 15
Gendai Sekai no Naritachi (The
Formation of Contemporary World)
15
gender 137
General Guide (1947)
Goldhagen, Daniel xiv
Gramsci, Antonio 72, 93
Great Tokyo Air Raid 66
Group to Defend Textbooks
(Kyokasho o Mamorukai) 41
gyokusai xvi, 55, 56

H

Hara Shobo 138, 139
Hashimoto Ryutaro 142, 143, 144
Hata Ikuhiko 100
Hata Tsutomu 142
Hatoyama administration 19, 29
hegemony 94, 152, 156
High School Teachers Union in Kobe 91
Hinomaru 129, 142
Hirai Jiro 106, 107
Hirohito, Emperor: counter-memories
of the Asia-Pacific War 51, 58, 66–
68, 71; early postwar years 1945–65
1, 7, 9, 15–16, 23; right-wing
nationalist history textbook projects
136, 138; significance of lawsuits 153
Hiroshima xiv, 23, 51
historians 43–45, 88, 89
historical facts 94–121; dispute over
Battle of Okinawa 102–3; dispute

over Korean resistance 98–99;
dispute over Nanjing Massacre and
rape 99–100; dispute over Unit 731
100–102; Honda Katsuichi's cross-
examination 112–15; Honda
Katsuichi's testimony and oral
history approach 110–12; Kojima
Noboru's cross-examination 117–21;
Kojima Noboru's testimony 115–17;
overview xv, xvi, 94–95; state's failed
defense of its view of history 107–9;
state's view on history and history
textbooks 95–97; third lawsuit 85;
Yuge Toru's testimony 103–7
historical research 28, 94–97, 101–2,
104, 107, 120–21, 129
historical truth: games of truth xiv, xv;
history textbook controversy in
1980s 88, 93; ordinary people's war
responsibility 70, 71; overview 94;
significance of lawsuits xvi, xvii, 152,
155
history: court decisions and trends
from 1980s to 1997 133; early
postwar years 1945–65 3, 11–13, 21,
22; historical facts 95–97, 103–9, 110,
120; overview xiii, xiv, xv, xvi; third
lawsuit 86
"history as logos" 104, 105
history revision movement 134
history textbooks: counter-memories of
the Asia-Pacific War (Emperor
Hirohito's war responsibility 67;
Okinawa in textbooks and lawsuits
60–63; ordinary people's war
responsibility 68, 69, 71; overview 50,
51; textbook content of other wartime
issues 65–66; textbook reference to
Japanese aggression and Nanjing
Massacre 63–65); court decisions and
trends from 1980s to 1997 122–35
(first and second lawsuits 123–25;
Korean resistance and Battle of
Okinawa 132–33; late 1980s and early
1990s 127–30; Nanjing Massacre, rape
and Unit 731 131–32; overview
122–23; Supreme Court response
133–35; third lawsuit and court
decisions 125–27); early postwar years
1945–65 1–25 (1947 Constitution and
Fundamental Law of Education 10;
attack on textbooks 18–20; blacking-
out textbooks 3–4; content of non-
governmental history textbooks

Lightning Source UK Ltd.
Milton Keynes UK
UKOW051340070313

207232UK00003B/88/P

9 780415 546447